THE ERIE CANAL
SINGS

THE ERIE CANAL

SINGS

• A Musical History of New York's Grand Waterway •

BILL HULLFISH *with Dave Ruch*

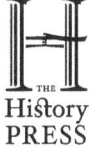

THE
History
PRESS

Published by The History Press
Charleston, SC
www.historypress.com

Copyright © 2019 by William Hullfish
All rights reserved

Front cover, top: Mural, *The Victorian Village on the Erie Canal*, by Brockport artist Helen Smagorinsky.

First published 2019

Manufactured in the United States

ISBN 9781467142090

Library of Congress Control Number: 2019935354

Contents

CONTENTS

FOREWORD

Some years ago, Bill Hullfish published *The Canaller's Songbook*, an accessible, user-friendly collection of canal songs that anyone, a teacher especially, could turn to for any occasion that required a musical take of the Erie Canal. I must have recommended it to teachers dozens of times when I was doing programs on the Erie and Champlain Canals in eastern New York State (as I have for over forty-five years). I always wished, though, for more depth, for a deep inquiry into what the songs could really tell us about the American canal era and those who created it. It's been a quest of my own for ages.

Boy, have I gotten my wish! From a scholar and lifelong canaller who has dug as deeply into canal music history as the old-timers dug canals into the face of America comes *The Erie Canal Sings: A Musical History of New York's Grand Waterway* by Bill Hullfish with Dave Ruch. I believe that it is a book only Bill Hullfish could have written. From his historian's grasp of the scope of the canal era, to his painstaking deconstruction of individual songs (Which canal is this song really about? Is that a reference to a real tavern somewhere?), to his love of performing the material and making it live, to his joy in trekking the old canals himself, this is a labor of love and of a lifetime.

For the true canal buff, I think that—no matter how many good canal histories you've read (and there are plenty)—you will find a new perspective in these pages. The book is about the songs, yes. But in Hullfish's close readings of the texts, hundreds of details of canal life and work emerge. In giving every detail its due, he gives us far more than the simple meaning of the songs. He gives us, piece by piece, a deep insight into canallers' lives and the distinctive subculture created by the nature of their trade. This book is more than a book about canal songs. It is a painstaking, rousing look at a way of life that shaped—and was shaped by—the ferment that was life in nineteenth-century America.

—George Ward
Rexford, New York
mulesong@aol.com

PREFACE

The ballad writers have, again, furnished much valuable material. Their words are but the expression of popular ideas in the reflex of public opinion, clothed in musical form. The old folk songs remain to us now a vast storehouse of historical evidence of manner and customs, of the thoughts and beliefs of bygone times.
—*Fletcher Bassett,* Legends and Superstitions of the Sea and Sailors

The cultural heritage of the canal era is told through the songs. The canal ballads were the words of canallers "clothed in musical form." The ballads serve as "a vast storehouse of historical evidence of manner and custom, of thoughts and beliefs" of the canal era—the heritage. Ballads are storytelling songs that entertain, educate, preserve culture and instill moral values. American screenwriter and journalist Stephen Schiff said that "at the heart of good history is good storytelling." Telling stories of the canal era through song involves hearing history from those who lived it. Schiff goes on to say, "[A]n historian's richest insights generally come when he asks himself what it would have been like to have been there, to have confronted the personalities, conditions and conundrums of which history is made."[1] The songs, or "musical diaries," of the canallers permit us to be there and hear the individual voices of the participants in one of the most exciting eras of transportation in American history.

Although songs were sung on all of the canals, the songs of the Erie Canal became the models for many of the songs heard on other canals.

"The E-ri-e Is A-Risin'" became "The D&H Is A-Risin'" and "The C&O Is A-Risin'" and on and on. The eventual connection of a vast network of canals led to a sharing of songs, and like the spread of many occupational songs, singers merely changed the names to fit the new location: The songs of the lumberjack changed the location from the Penobscot to the Saranac to the Saginaw. The canallers did the same: "A long, long trip on the Erie, boys, we're bound for Buffalo" became "A long, long trip on the Main Line, boys, we're bound for the O-hi-o." Generic canal songs (songs that did not mention a particular location), such as "A Life on the Raging Canal," made their appearance first on the Erie Canal but soon found their way to other canals, where they fit right in without changing a word.[2] Thus, although the Erie Canal is the main focus of this book, songs from many other canals are used in discussing topics that are common to a wide network of interconnected canals.

In order to make the "musical diaries" more readable, especially for those who do not read music notation, examples are given using the lyrics of the songs. This is not a songbook, but stories of the canal era told through song. Part I begins with an introduction to work songs and songs about work, the occupational songs sung on the canals, and introduces the historical background to which the songs connect. It includes examples of how canal songs act as personal "musical diaries" that reveal historical information and descriptions of the canallers' lives, including their feelings and pride in their occupation.

Part II is about America's best-known canal song, "Low Bridge, Everybody Down," or "Fifteen Years on the Erie Canal." Although this is the most-sung canal song, little is known about the song or its composer, and the information available is rife with mistakes and outright misinformation. This section contains the latest research on the origins of America's favorite canal song.

Part III addresses the songs composed to celebrate the canal and life on the canal. This section presents everyday life on the canal through the canallers' eyes. Subjects include the canallers' boats, draft animals, crew members' jobs, recreation, the "raging canal" songs, fears, superstitions and the sources of canal songs in the popular music of the day.

Part IV is about the nostalgia surrounding the demise of the canal era and songs that express the feelings of those reminiscing about the loss of one of the most important eras of transportation in American history. This part examines canal songs on the New York stage, songs from the New York stage adapted to the canal, the evolution of a canal song, the making of a new canal song, the "musical diaries" of an individual canal captain and the canal songs that continue to be sung after most canals closed.

My connection to canals started long before I began collecting canal songs. I was born just as the last fully functioning towpath canal in North America, the Lehigh Canal, closed. My own interest and curiosity about canals came early in my life. It seems I have always lived along canals. Growing up, in Lawrence Township, New Jersey, the Delaware and Raritan Canal provided fishing, canoeing, hiking and bicycling recreation for much of my childhood. My brother and I had a favorite canoe trip where we entered a stream next to the canal and paddled downstream about five miles until it circled back under the canal. Then we carried the canoe up to the canal and paddled back on the canal to where we originally started.

The Delaware Canal, on the Pennsylvania side of the Delaware River, provided much of the same. As a boy, I frequently canoed on the Delaware River and stopped where the Lehigh Canal comes into the Delaware at Easton, Pennsylvania, just opposite the Morris Canal at Phillipsburg, New Jersey. Years later, I met James Lee in his home at the first inclined plane on the Morris Canal. It was here that Jim introduced me to the workings of the inclined planes and played me songs from the Morris Canal.

On up the Delaware River, I floated under the fascinating, cable-hung, John Roebling aqueduct that crossed over the Delaware at Lackawaxen, Pennsylvania. Many years later, I bicycled with my own children from the Hudson River, across the route of the Delaware and Hudson Canal and over that very aqueduct, which still stands today.

In college, near Lebanon, Pennsylvania, I explored the Union Canal and its tunnel, as well as sections of the Pennsylvania Main Line Canal. Recently, performing at the top of the Allegheny Portage Railroad at Gallitzin, Pennsylvania, brought me back to the Main Line Canal for Canal Jam 2015 and 2017.

After joining the U.S. Air Force, I was assigned to Headquarters Command in Washington, D.C., and spent many weekends walking along the Chesapeake and Ohio Canal. Years later, I cycled the entire C&O Canal from Cumberland, Maryland, to Washington, D.C. A temporary duty assignment to Latin America even provided me with a chance to view operations on the Panama Canal. Upon leaving the Air Force, my first teaching position was at the University of Mary Washington in Fredericksburg, Virginia, along the Rappahannock River and what remained of the Rappahannock Canal.

For the last fifty-plus years, I have lived in Brockport, New York, on the Erie Canal. In my folk music classes at The College at Brockport, I began

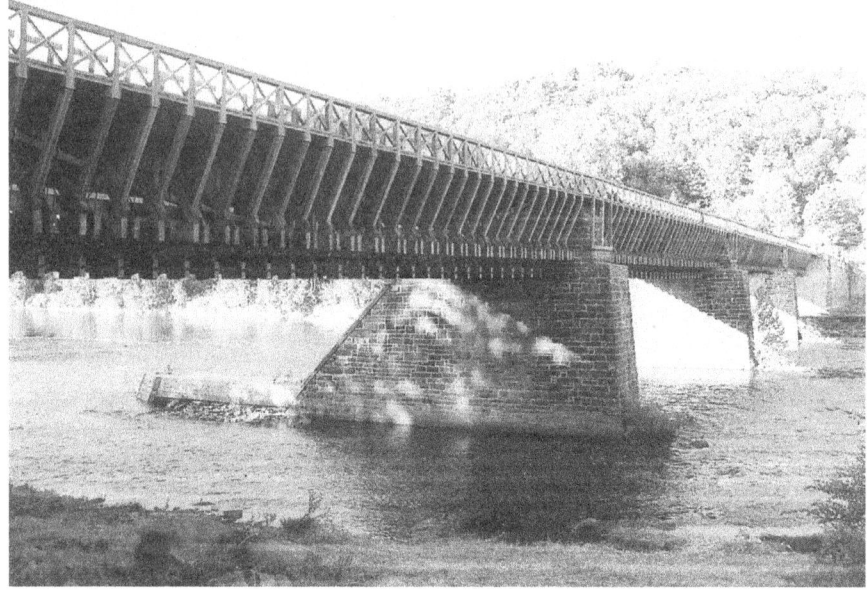

Roebling Aqueduct over the Delaware River on the Delaware and Hudson Canal. *National Park Service.*

gathering, along with help from my students and fellow musicians, songs from the western New York area. Among these songs were a smattering of Erie Canal songs collected from local informants, books and old newspapers. In almost no time, we collected enough Erie Canal songs for the Golden Eagle String Band, a band formed from students in my class, to record an album for Folkways Records. The National Endowment for the Arts awarded the Golden Eagle String Band a grant to tour the Erie Canal on an old wooden touring yacht called *Tigress*, and in the summer of 1981, we set sail from Rochester Harbor down Lake Ontario to Oswego, New York. For the next two weeks, we traveled the Oswego and Erie Canals, playing concerts from Oswego to Lockport. Not only did we learn a great deal about the canals on this trip, but we also made many contacts with informants who sang us canal songs. In Fulton, New York, on the Oswego Canal, a gentleman by the name of Lyman King came out of the audience and sang a number of canal songs for us. We still use his version of "Black Rock Pork" and the little tag he sang, "That's it!"

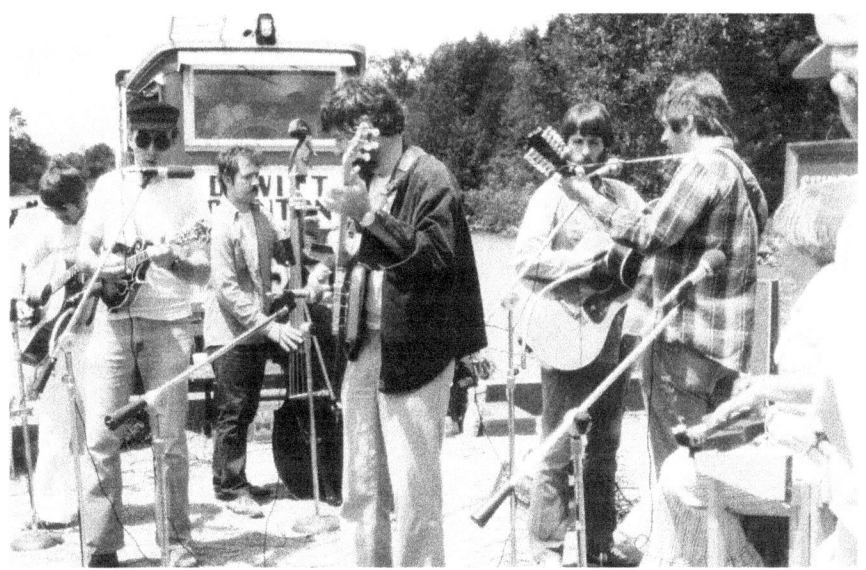

The Golden Eagle String Band. *Photograph by the author.*

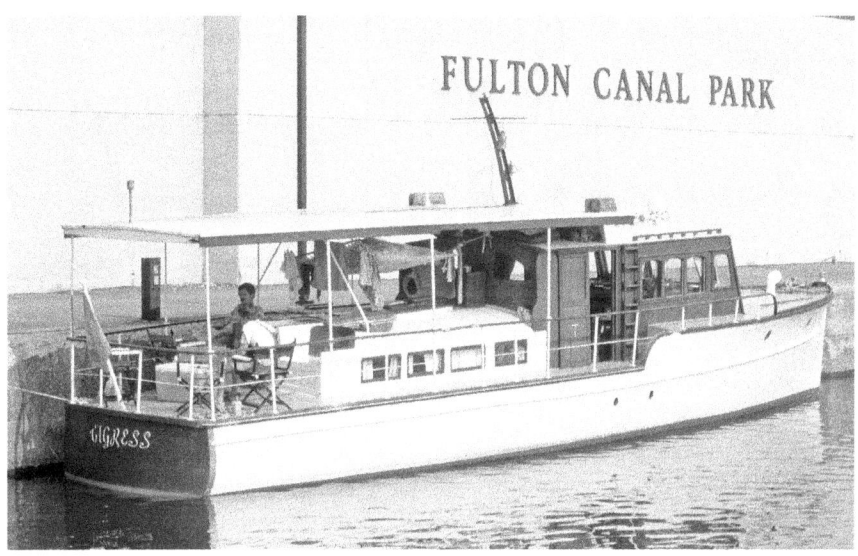

The *Tigress. Photograph by the author.*

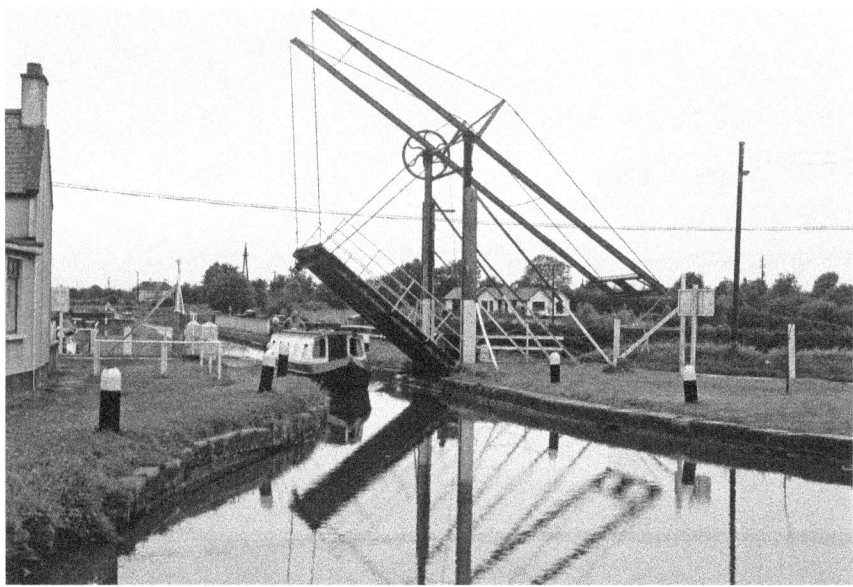

Barrow Canal, Ireland. *Photograph by the author.*

Eventually, I bicycled across the Erie Canal from Buffalo to Albany and, over the years, played at almost every canal festival along its route. After transcribing all of Captain Pearl R. Nye's songs from the Library of Congress and Ohio State University collections, I retraced Nye's steps on the Ohio and Erie Canal. But I still yearned to know more about canals and experience life as a canaller.

In order to get the real feeling of a canaller, I searched out canals the size of the original Erie Canal and selected Ireland's Grand Canal, which runs from Dublin on the east to the Shannon River on the west. We even explored the Barrow Canal down to Athy. Then it was on to England and Wales to explore more canals and live onboard a canalboat, operate the locks and run along in any weather.

Way back in the 1970s, I was surprised to find fourteen canal songs for an album. Now, almost sixty canal songs later, I am still finding canal songs. Fortunately, there were a few collectors back at the beginning of the twentieth century who thought it was important enough to preserve these songs. My job has been to locate as many of these sources as possible and bring them together, and I am indebted to these early collectors.

—William Hullfish, Brockport, New York

ACKNOWLEDGEMENTS

First, I need to acknowledge at least three editors who helped develop this book and bring it to print. Dr. Travis Stimeling, music professor and editor for the West Virginia University Press Sounding Appalachia series, worked for three months through continual rewrites to reshape the manuscript, even though he knew a book on the Erie Canal had little chance of being published by West Virginia University Press. Then, of course, there is J. Banks Smithers, editor for The History Press, who worked tirelessly to see this through to print, even when he was doubtful that telling history through song would be accepted by his press, and Abigail Fleming (The History Press), who meticulously edited and produced the final draft.

Second, I thank Dave Ruch, a fellow musician and canal enthusiast, for his outstanding research that contributed to the accuracy and content of the book. His extensive performing schedule prevented Dave from devoting the time to coauthor the book, but his contributions are present on almost every page.

Third, I wish to thank the musicians who are playing with, and who have played with, the Golden Eagle String Band for staying with me (some for forty years) and helping to fulfill my dream of revitalizing the Erie Canal and its songs. Although we perform other music, our focus, since 1978, is on performing and recording canal songs.

And thanks to all of the others who helped bring this book to fruition: Frank E. Sadowski Jr. with Dragon Design Associates, creator of the eriecanal.org website, for his expert advice and permission to use some images; Helen Smagorinsky, folk artist, for her permission to use one of her paintings for the cover; Dr. Thomas Shaffer, Penn State, for encouraging more research on Pennsylvania canal songs and reading the manuscript; George Ward for his musical inspiration, writing the foreword for this book and reading and commenting on the manuscript; my son, Brian, for reading and commenting on the manuscript; and all my students who helped collect canal songs and provide information on informants.

I

IN THE BEGINNING

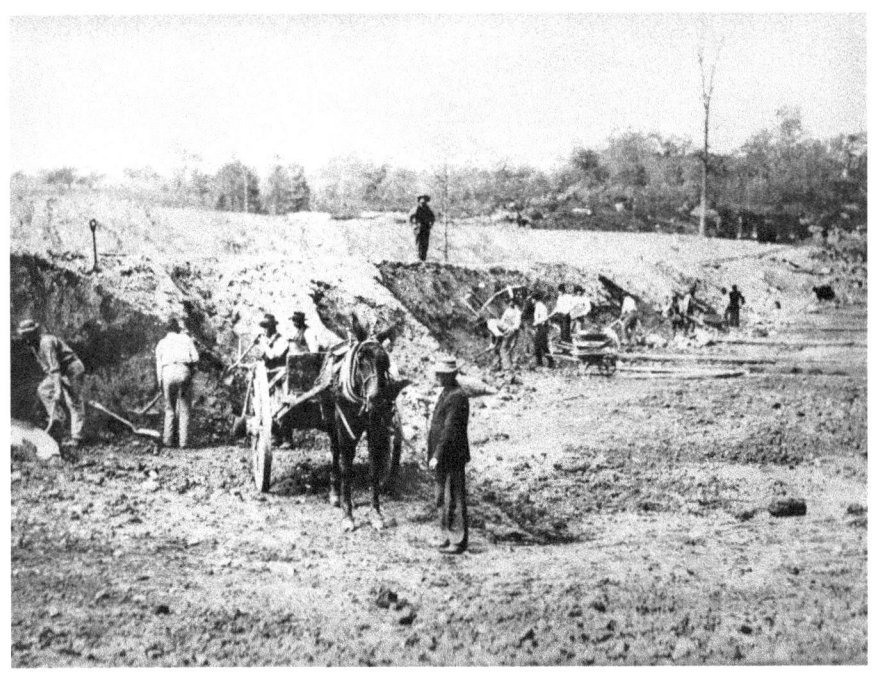

Digging the canal. *Erie Canal Museum, Syracuse, New York, used with permission.*

1

MUSICAL DIARIES

Songs are the statement of a people. You can learn more about people by listening to their songs than any other way, for into the songs go all the hopes and hurts, the angers, fears, the wants and aspirations.
—John Steinbeck

Anthropological evidence suggests that all agrarian societies use work songs and that work songs are as old as historical records, but what type of songs did canallers sing? Contemporary writing on work songs includes songs sung while working (work song), as well as songs about work (occupational song), since the two categories are seen as interconnected.[3]

Work songs are needed to coordinate the efforts of a group of laborers, lift spirits, create a sense of unity, break the boredom of repetitive tasks and even assert the singers' values and beliefs. Work songs vary by the type of work being done and therefore vary from one profession to another. The songs of prisoners on a chain gang coordinate labor (chopping wood, hoeing in a field or breaking rocks), show their spirit (my trouble is hard but I keep on going), create unity among the participants (we are all in this together) and announce their values and beliefs (God). The songs also divert the workers' minds from the repetitive task at hand.

O Lord, trouble so hard. *(2)*
Yes, indeed, my trouble is hard. *(2)*
O Lord, trouble so hard. *(2)*
Don't nobody know my troubles but God. *(2)*
Yes, indeed, my trouble is hard. *(2)*[4]

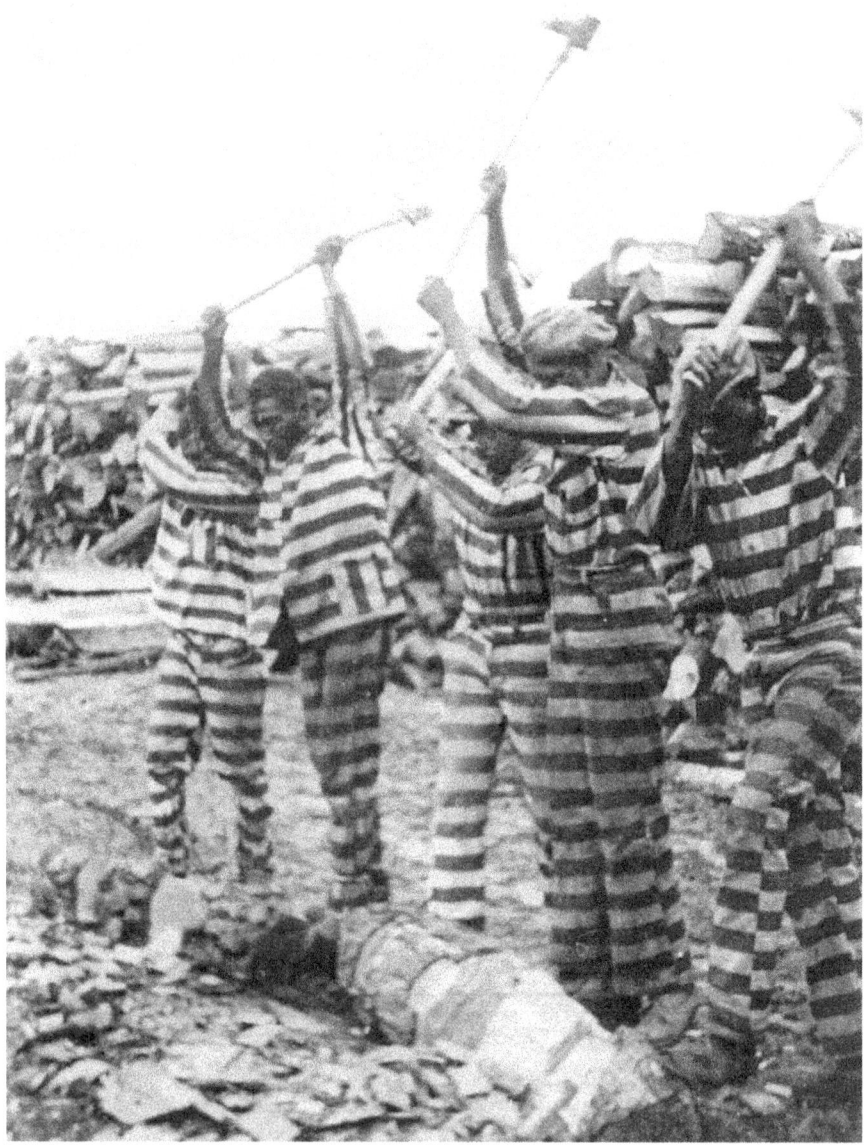

Prisoners chopping wood. *Photograph by Alan Lomax.*

Work songs of the sea are structured to help the crew (which was usually quite large) haul in the anchor, take a reef in a sail or raise the entire mainsail. To haul in the anchor, sailors used a capstan shanty, pushing on wooden bars inserted in a winch. To reef a sail, they required a short haul (or short-drag) shanty, for brief pulling. To raise an entire sail, they needed a long-haul (or long-drag) shanty, with longer periods of rest between pulls. Almost all of the songs used to coordinate work are call-and-response songs in which the leader sang a line and the crew responded while pulling on a specific word, such as "haul."[5]

> Leader: *Haul on the bowline, I'll sing to you of Nancy.*
> Crew: *Haul on the bowline, the bowline* Haul.
> Leader: *Nancy is a New York gal, she's just my cut and fancy,*
> Crew: *Haul on the bowline, the bowline* Haul.[6]

On the canals, occupational songs were the most common form of song. A casual observer might anticipate that the occupational songs of canallers would resemble the songs sung by sailors, especially since the canallers' work consisted of guiding a boat on a body of water. However, the work of the deep-sea sailors was vastly different from work on the canal.

Canallers, by contrast, tied up at docks or to a stake driven into the canal bank and had no need to haul in an anchor. Most canalboats did not have a sail and had no need for short- and long-haul shanties. There were exceptions. The canal schooner is a type of canalboat that plied the waters of the Champlain and Erie Canals and sailed in Lake Champlain and Cayuga Lake.

However, even though these sailing canalboats were used for canal and lake transportation, the typical mule-drawn canalboat had a small crew of no more than five, not including four-legged beasts of burden. There was the captain, who steered the boat; a bowman, who kept watch, handled the ropes and did a variety of chores; a driver, who walked behind the mules or horses along the towpath; and the cook, whose main chore was to prepare meals. The crew worked in six-hour shifts but rarely needed any coordination. Canallers sang occupational songs not to coordinate work but to break the boredom, create a sense of unity with fellow canallers, calm the animals (and themselves) and express their pride in what they did. "Every night you could hear men singing as they drove horse and mule teams along the path."[7] John Lomax wrote that he found in Albany, New York, "a complaint filed in 1835 against singing at night by canallers."[8] An interview with a former driver demonstrates how singing at night was often a requirement:

> *My daddy used to make us ride the mules at night and sing so he knowed we didn't go to sleep and fall overboard.*

You had to sing as you walked down the towpath?
Sing or ride the mules and sing.
Did you get to ride the mules?
Oh, yeah, we'd ride the mules at night. And he was afraid we'd go to sleep and fall off of 'em. You see they was so close to the canal that if you fell off the mule on the inside you went in the canal! And he used to make us sing so he knowed we was still down there.[9]

Those children sang to break the boredom, keep themselves awake, assure their parents and build up their courage as they approached a well-known "haunted" place along the towpath. William Totten, a towpath boy himself, wrote in his poem "Rhyme of the Old Canal" (see appendix A for complete poem): "oft were heard the fierce old yarns / of the panthers in Rome's dread swamp / carrying screaming drivers off / to dismal regions damp."[10] The towpath boy's singing may have served the same purpose as the cowboy's "night herding song" and calmed the animals in the darkness. Totten's poem continues: "Through calm and storm they move along / though bad the night and black / you could hear the song of the driver strong / his tow line never slack."[11]

John Lomax, who was one of the first to recognize that the occupational songs of the American cowboy were worth saving, remarked about the similarity between the occupational songs of the canaller and the cowboy: "Canal-boat mule drivers (the tow-path boys) sang for precisely the same reason that cowboys yodeled and sang when riding around the sleeping herds at night....The singers made music to keep awake and secure entertainment out of their monotonous duties."[12]

For decades, folklorists ignored the songs of the canallers, deeming them too mundane for serious study or possibly missing the fact that these were the "work songs" of the canal. Even noted folksong collector John Lomax, who recorded many of the canal songs from the Ohio and Erie Canal, was more interested in the older Child Ballads of Captain Pearl R. Nye. Of Nye's seventy-two songs recorded by the Library of Congress, only ten (not counting duplicates) were canal songs, despite his letters to Lomax saying that he had many more of that type.[13] Perhaps Lomax recognized that most of the songs were based on popular melodies of the day and did not need to be recorded because notation for the tunes already existed. Only Cloea Thomas, at Ohio State University, made an attempt to record more of Nye's canal repertory.[14]

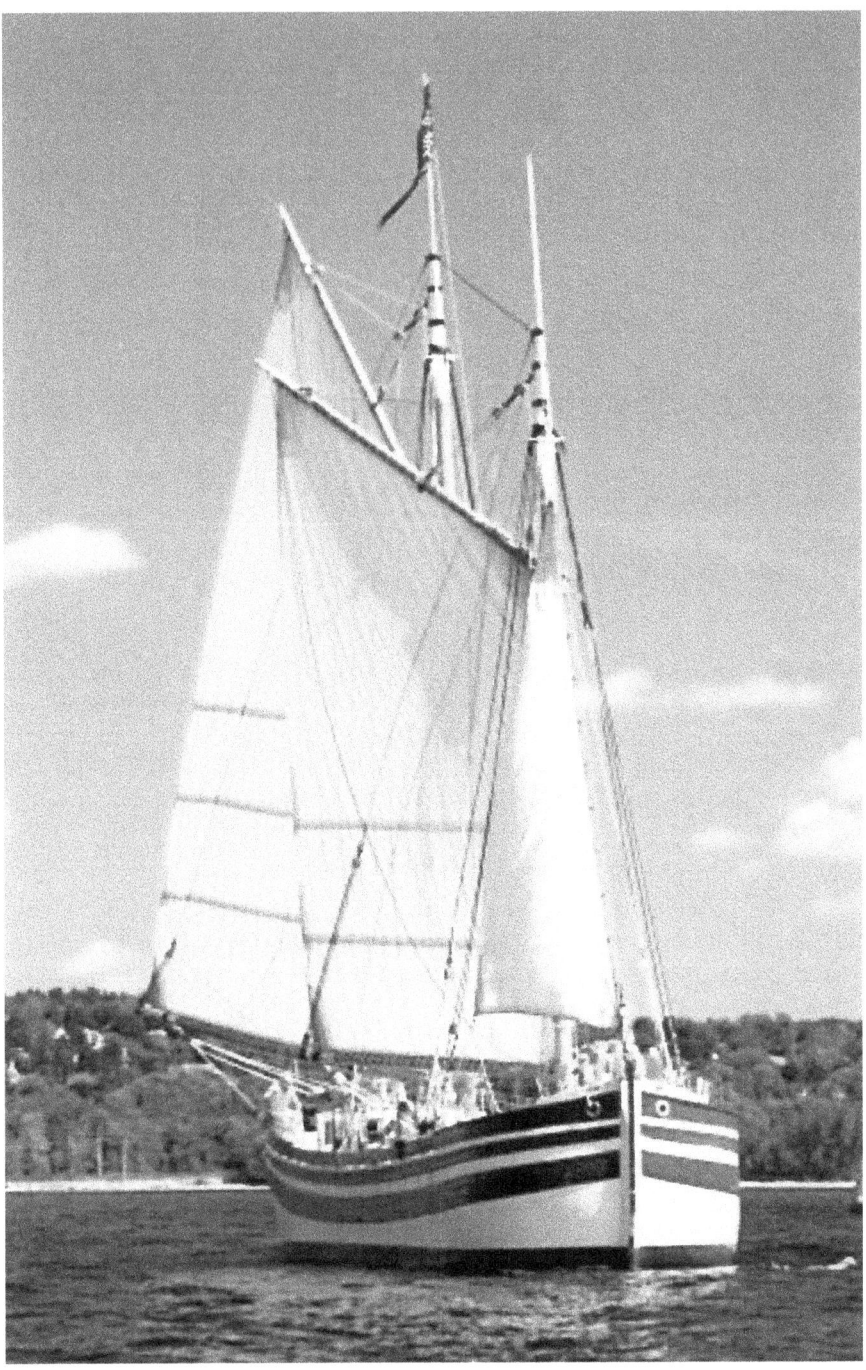

The *Lois McClure* sailing canalboat. *New York State Department of Transportation.*

Canallers, lumberjacks, river rafters, miners, cowboys and many other professions developed their own individual repertory of occupational songs. These individual and communal ballads and songs told of the work the men did, who they were and their pride in their occupation. Most were composed to fit specific occupational situations. In many ways, the songs serve as the "musical diaries" of an occupation.

Not all occupations required coordinated labor. Coal miners, cowboys, lumberjacks, and canallers all worked jobs largely devoid of the need to maintain a group rhythm, so their songs were typically sung "solo" and tell stories about workers on the job, warn against the dangers of the occupation or relate what is required to be a successful worker. Canal songs are unique in that they spread quickly from one canal to another because so many canals were interconnected and the songs were part of a transportation system in constant motion. The canal also attracted professional songwriters, and many of their songs were adopted and adapted to the canal. It is often difficult to pinpoint where a canal song originated, but some give clues as to their location.

"PADDY ON THE CANAL"

The stories of the canal era are told in occupational songs that often carry more information than the casual listener realizes. In cases, such as "Paddy on the Canal," enough internal clues are given to ascertain the location of the canal the singer is on, the work he is doing and the general time frame for the content described in the song. By combining information contained in the personal musical diaries of canallers and what is known about the history of a particular canal, much can be learned from only one canal song.

"Paddy on the Canal" is a typical canal occupational song. The song immediately identifies the worker as Irish, the tools he used, his pay, songs he sang, what it takes to be successful on the job and the satisfaction with his occupation. What is not so obvious is the year Paddy arrived in this country, what canal he worked on and on what project he worked. Knowledge about the history of canals and clues from the lyrics provide the answers to these questions.

Not every canal song was born on the Erie. At least three sources suggest that this song is about the Erie Canal. Harold Thompson said that it gives "the picture of our Irish digging the ditch."[15] Lionel Wyld stated that "Paddy

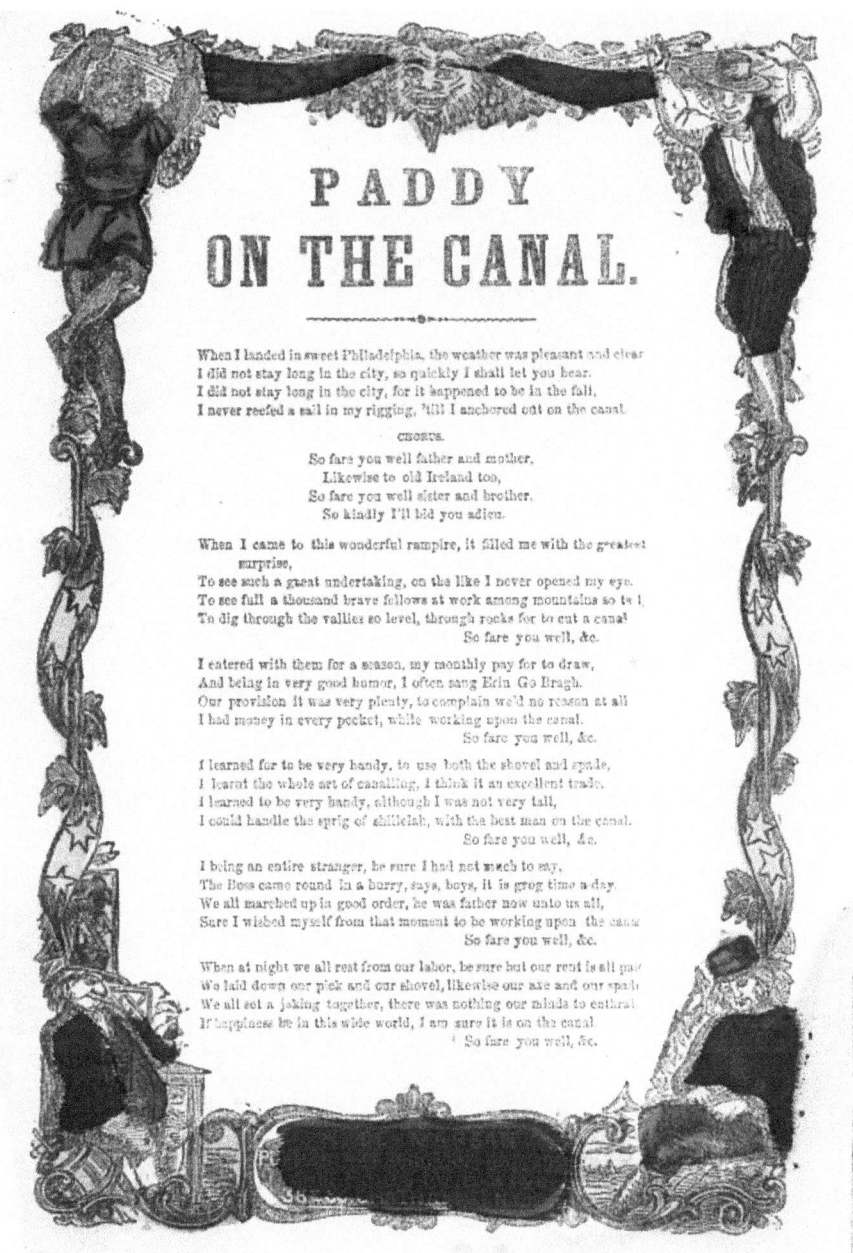

"Paddy on the Canal" broadside. *Buffalo-Erie County Library, reproduced by the author.*

on the Canal" "may be assumed to have referred to Clinton's ditch,"[16] and Gerard Koeppel added that Irish immigrants "adapted their hopeful 'Paddy on the Canal' to the canal country of Western New York."[17] However, given the information in the lyrics, "Paddy on the Canal" may have been adapted to the Erie Canal at some later date, but it did not originate with the Erie Canal. The version provided by Koeppel starts with the second verse—"When I came to this wonderful empire." That would lead many to think of the Empire State, New York. However, that is not the first verse of this song.

"Paddy on the Canal"[18]

1. When I landed in sweet Philadelphia, the weather was warm and was clear,
But I did not stay long in that city, as you shall quickly hear.
I did not stay long in that city, for it happened to be in the fall,
And I ne'er reefed a sail in my riggin', 'til I anchored out on the canal. So,
    Chorus:
Fare-you-well Father and Mother, Likewise to old Ireland, too,
And fare-you-well sister and brother, for kindly I bid you adieu.

Two things give away the ethnicity of the singer: the title of the song and the chorus. The name Paddy, used in the title, was the nickname applied to virtually every male Irishman. The lyrics of the chorus are fairly obvious: "Fare-you-well father and mother, likewise to old Ireland, too."

The song also tells us that Paddy "landed in sweet Philadelphia," and this places him in Pennsylvania. Although he could have traveled anywhere from there, we learn that he arrived in the fall, which was already late in the season to find work on a canal. To find work quickly ("I did not stay long in that city, as you will quickly hear"), he probably looked for work on a Pennsylvania canal then under construction. What canal is that likely to be?

2. When I came to this wonderful empire, it filled me with greatest surprise,
To see such a great undertakin', on the like I never opened my eyes.
To see a full thousand brave fellows, at work among mountains so tall,
A-draggin' a chain through the mountains to strike a line for the canal. So,

Aside from the obvious references to Philadelphia, the fall and "farewell to old Ireland," hidden in the lyrics are clues to the unnamed canal on which our Irish immigrant worked, the year he arrived and the exact construction project on which he worked. Pennsylvania's Main Line Canal, that state's answer to the Erie Canal, was under construction from Philadelphia to Pittsburgh between the years 1826 and 1834. Paddy observes "a full thousand brave fellows, at work among mountains so tall / a-draggin' a chain through the mountains to strike a line for the canal." While the Erie Canal did not cross any mountains, Pennsylvania's Main Line Canal did.

From Philadelphia, a horse-drawn railroad brought travelers and goods to Columbia, on the Susquehanna River. They proceeded along the Susquehanna River and then west by canal, through the Juniata Valley, to Hollidaysburg. Here is where the mountain comes in. The canal had to cross the Allegheny Mountains to reach Johnstown. The first proposal was to construct a tunnel through the mountain. When this proved impractical, a portage railroad was proposed. This dates the action described in the song because work was begun on the Allegheny Portage Railroad in the summer of 1831 using a workforce exactly described in the song—two thousand men. Canals required a workforce of thousands, but most sections of the canal had a much smaller workforce. The section of the Main Line Canal known as "Duffy's Cut" only required a workforce of fifty-seven men. The Allegheny Portage Railroad project required thousands of workers at one site. Since they were in the process of "striking a line through the mountains for the canal," the work on this project was still in its early stage of construction. Paddy was probably looking at a thousand men on the eastern slope of the Allegheny Mountains in the fall of 1831.

Proposals from contractors having been invited, the grading and masonry of the twenty-six miles from the summit of the mountain to Johnstown were contracted for at Ebensburg, the county seat of Cambria County, on May 25, and the work on the eastern slope of the mountain, at Hollidaysburg, commenced on July 26, 1831.[19]

> *3. I learned for to be very handy; To use both the shovel and spade;*
> *I learned the whole art of canalling: I think it an excellent trade.*
> *I learned for to be very handy, Although I was not very tall,*
> *I could handle the "sprig of Shillelah," With the best man on the canal.*

Although this song was published in broadsides and songsters, it was also passed along the canal by oral transmission, and almost immediately, new verses were added. At least one new verse was added between the time the sheet music was published in 1843 and the aforementioned broadside was published. The added verse describing the jobs Paddy learned to do and how handy he became would suggest he worked on the Allegheny Portage Railroad site, which involved all of the jobs listed above. Instead of just digging, these lines suggest that Paddy worked on a project with a great variety of jobs.

> *4. I entered with them for a season, my monthly pay for to draw,*
> *And being of very good humor, I often sang "Erin Go Bragh,"*
> *Our provision it was very plenty, to complain I'd no reason at all,*
> *I had money in every pocket, while working upon the canal, So,*

The lyrics also tell of the worker's Irish heritage by the song he sings. "Erin Go Bragh" is often called "The Irishman's Lament." Paddy is obviously happy with his job on the canal and the money he is being paid, but homesick: "And being of very good humor, I often sang 'Erin Go Bragh.'"

> *5. When at night we'd all rest from our labors, sure but our rent is all paid,*
> *We laid down our pick and our shovel, likewise our axe and our spade,*
> *We all set a-jokin together, there was nothing our mind to enthrall,*
> *If happiness be in this wide world, I'm sure it is on the canal, So,*

The lyrics go on to tell us that this Irish worker is provided with room and board, is paid monthly and used the following tools for his job constructing the canal:

> *We laid down our pick and our shovel, likewise our axe and our spade.*

Workers, with axes, cleared a thirty-six-mile, 120-foot-wide path through virgin timber over the mountain before they could even begin the work of constructing the inclined planes, laying track for the portage railroad and building the tunnels, aqueducts, bridges and buildings.

Paddy probably arrived in Philadelphia in the fall of 1831, obtained a job on the Pennsylvania Main Line Canal and worked on the Allegheny Portage Railroad. Even though the action described in the song may have occurred between 1831 and 1834, the song could have been composed later. However, copies of the song were found by 1843 on canals in other states. The New York version starts with the second verse, "When I came to this wonderful empire," which may have been why collectors associated the song with the Empire State.

"THE GIRL FROM YEWDALL'S MILL"

Another canal occupational song found in libraries in New York and in books about the Erie Canal is "The Girl from Yewdall's Mill." The first verse could lead to the conclusion that this song originated on the Erie Canal:

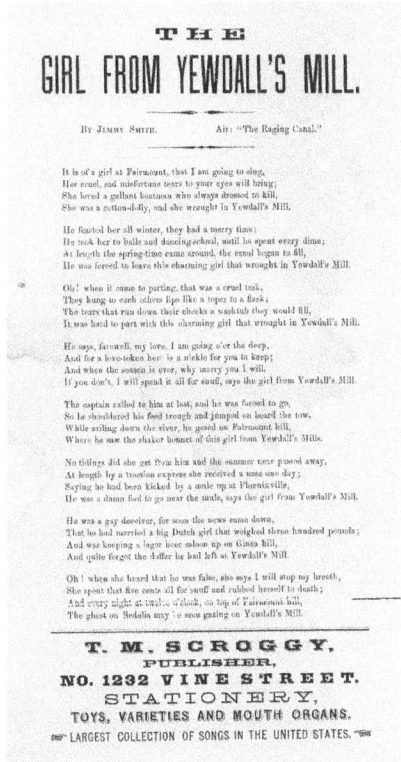

It is of a girl from Fairmount, that I am going to sing,
Her cruel, sad misfortune, tears to your eyes will bring,
She loved a gallant boatman who always dressed to kill,
She was a cotton dolly and she wrought at Yewdall's Mill.

Fairmount, New York, is a town just west of Syracuse on the Erie Canal. The next four verses do not suggest any other canal than the Erie. The fifth verse, however, gives a clue as to the canal in question:

No tidings did she get from him and the summer near passed away,
At length by traction express she received a note one day,
Saying he had been kicked by a mule up in Phoenixville,
"He was a damned fool to go near the mule," said the girl from Yewdall's Mill.

"The Girl from Yewdall's Mill" broadside. *T.M. Scroggy, publisher, 1232 Vine Street, Philadelphia, Pennsylvania, reproduced by the author.*

A search of New York towns does not find a single Phoenixville. The closest Phoenixville does lie on a canal near Philadelphia, Pennsylvania—the Schuylkill Canal. Phoenixville, Pennsylvania is twenty-eight miles northwest of Philadelphia. Another verse mentions "Ginea Hill," which is one of the seven hills surrounding the town of Pottsville, Pennsylvania. Pottsville is only two miles from the source of coal hauled on the Schuylkill Canal—Port Carbon.

He was a gay deceiver, for soon the news came down,
That he'd married a big Dutch girl that weighed three hundred pounds,
And was keeping a lager beer saloon up on Ginea hill,
And quite forgot the doffer he had left at Yewdall's Mill.

A further search finds that Fairmount is a section of Philadelphia, and a mill owned by John Yewdall was located there. The publisher of the broadside, T.M. Scroggy, was located at 443 Vine Street in Philadelphia as early as 1854. Scroggy moved to 1232 Vine Street in 1880 and ceased operation around 1884, which would date this piece from about that period. It uses the tune to "The Raging Canal," which was published in 1844. So, again, a canal song thought by some to have originated on the Erie Canal is actually a Pennsylvania canal song.

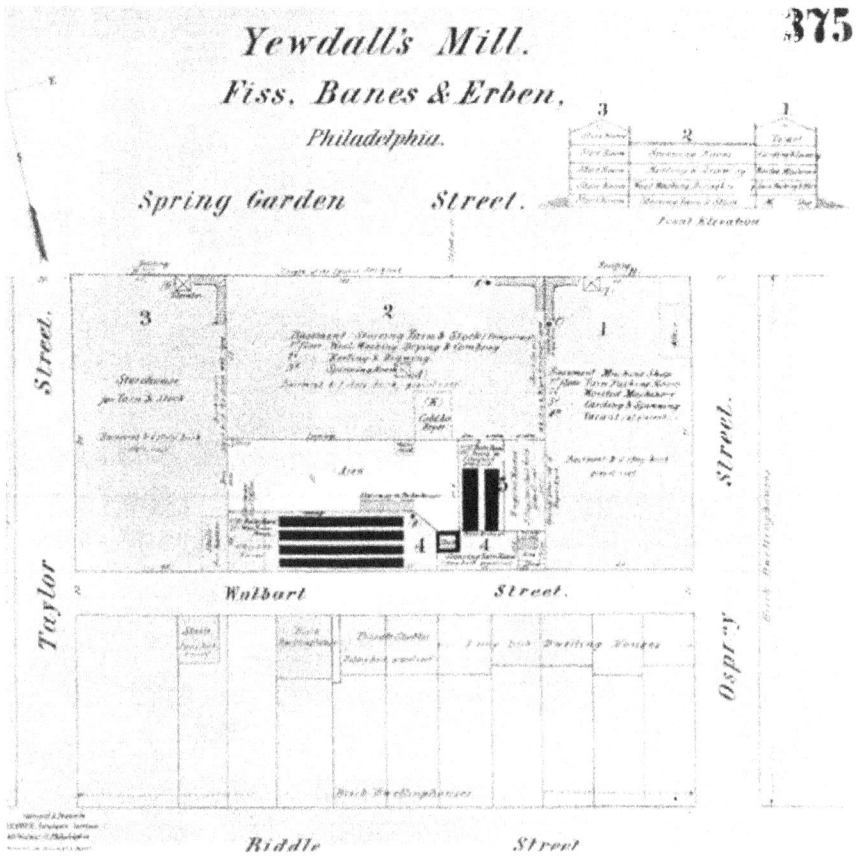

Yewdall's Mill, Ernest Hexamer. *Hexamer General Surveys*, volume 5, plate 375. Industrial Site Surveys. *Free Library of Philadelphia, Philadelphia, Pennsylvania.*

"Comin' 'Round the Mountain"

Another example of a canal occupational song is "Comin' 'Round the Mountain" (also known as "Otho's Song"). The melody for "Comin' 'Round the Mountain" is based on the folksong "Sweet Thing" (later known as "The Crawdad Song"). The origins of the song are given as African American and suggest that it was sung in the levee camps. This all helps to identify the source of the melody, but it does not help in identifying the canal or dating this canal song. A verse in the song may help locate the canal:

> *Ain't got no money but I'll soon have some, Honey,*
> *Ain't got no money but I'll soon have some,*
> *When this boat gets to Washington, Honey, Oh, darlin' mine.*[20]

Although many states with canals have a town or city named Washington, this helps zero in on a particular canal. We are getting a little closer now because the Chesapeake and Ohio Canal connected Cumberland, Maryland, with Washington, D.C., and the canallers would get paid at the end of their run. The addition of the next verse helps confirm this:

> *I'll go up to the office and I'll see G.L., Honey,*
> *I'll go up to the office and I'll see G.L.*
> *I'll get my money just as sure as Hell, Honey, Oh, darlin' mine.*

The name of the paymaster might help name this canal, if he can be identified by his initials. Canallers saw no need to make up fictitious people since they had plenty of canal characters to sing about. Chances are, G.L. is a real person. He is well documented in records pertaining to the C&O Canal and the Baltimore and Ohio Railroad. A letter from the National Archives refers to a meeting with G.L. Nicholson, manager of the C&O Canal, at his office in Georgetown.[21] There also is a newspaper article identifying G.L. Nicholson as "General Manager C&O Canal Co."[22] G.L. did serve as general manager of the C&O Canal for almost fifty years (1889–1938).

Why is a canal connecting Cumberland, Maryland, and Washington, D.C., called the Chesapeake and Ohio Canal? The southern terminus of the canal is Washington, but canalboats, or their cargo, could be transferred to the Potomac River and towed down to the Chesapeake Bay. The northern terminus of the C&O Canal was originally meant to be the Ohio River, but that stage was never completed and the canal ended at Cumberland,

Maryland, 180 miles from Washington, D.C. Is there anything in the song that would identify the location of the canalboat within this 180-mile canal?

And on my way I'll stop at Wardell's, Honey,
And on my way I'll stop at Wardell's,
Gonna get some whiskey sure as hell, Honey, Oh, darlin' mine.

Was Wardell's a town, store or saloon along the C&O? Wardell does not show up as any town along the C&O Canal. Wardell's turns out to have been a bar near Paw Paw, West Virginia, frequented by C&O canallers. The town of Paw Paw (named for paw paw fruit) was incorporated on April 8, 1891.

The first verse of this musical diary might provide a possible location for the action described in the song:

Comin' 'round the mountain and the wind did blow, Honey,
Comin' 'round the mountain and the wind did blow,
Couldn't hear nothin' but the rudder blade roar, Honey, Oh, darlin' mine.

There were mountains along the C&O Canal. The canal followed the Potomac River to avoid the mountains and take advantage of the gaps provided by the river. The C&O was bordered on one side by a number of mountain ranges: Evitts Mountain, Warrior Mountain and Cacapon Mountain. Handling a ninety-foot canalboat can be difficult when strong winds in the gaps catch the bow of the boat, exerting great pressure on the rudder. The steersman has all he can do to hold the boat in the narrow canal. Sometimes it takes the bowsman, working with a snubbing pole, to hold the boat in line. The water pressure against the rudder could cause the roaring sound described in the song.

"Comin' 'Round the Mountain" is one of the occupational songs with enough information to ascertain an approximate date for when the canal song was written. George L. Nicolson worked on the C&O Canal from late in the nineteenth century to the first part of the twentieth century. This means the song was not being sung, at least with the verse about G.L., before 1887. "Comin' 'Round the Mountain" is also referred to as "Otho's Song" and may have come from a C&O canaller and lock tender by the name of Otho Swain (1901–1976). According to C&O Canal records, Otho Swain worked on the canal between 1908 and 1923.[21] If Otho Swain wrote the song while he worked on the canal, it was probably written during the second decade of the twentieth century.

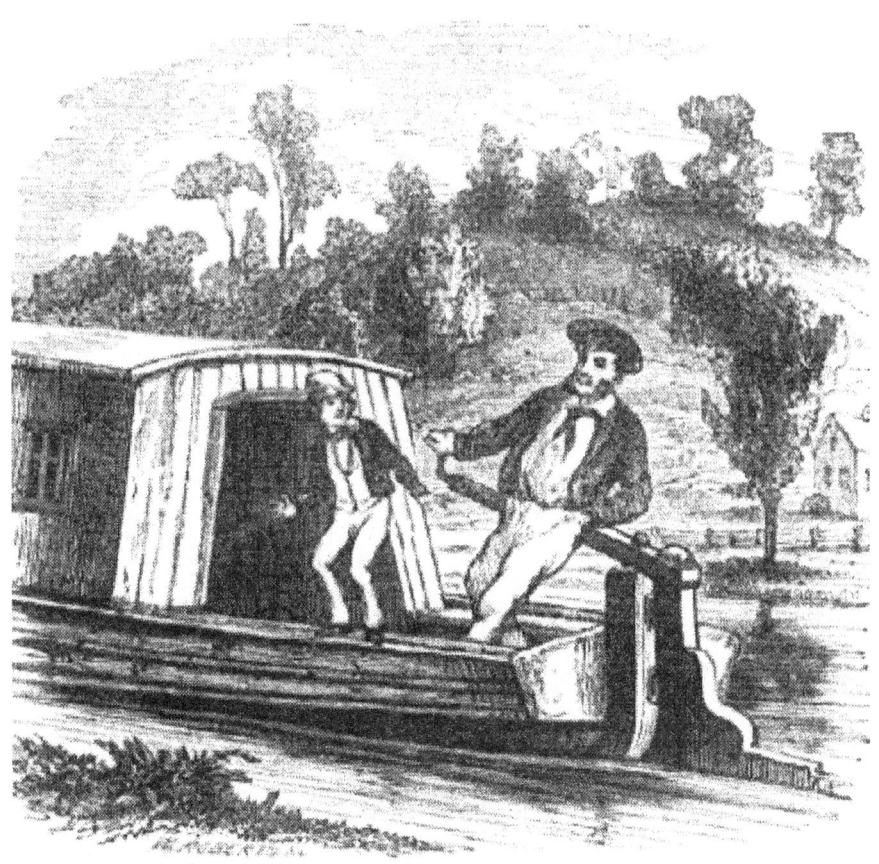

Steersman on canalboat. From *Marco Paul's Voyages and Travels: On the Erie Canal*, New York: Harper & Brothers, 1852, 130. *Reproduced by the author.*

The canaller in this song was headed south toward Washington and most likely carrying coal from Cumberland. The C&O Canal operated from 1831 to 1924 and served primarily to transport coal from the Allegheny Mountains to Washington, D.C. The coal came from mines in western Maryland, West Virginia and southwestern Pennsylvania. The canaller in this song was definitely above Paw Paw, West Virginia, and the Paw Paw Tunnel because he was looking forward to Wardell's bar, which was twenty-two miles south of Cumberland. The Spring Gap, formed by the Potomac River and Evitts Mountain, is only a short distance below Cumberland and could be where the canaller experienced strong winds that made steering difficult and increased the turbulence that caused his rudder blade roar.

To sum up what we know from this occupational canal song, we have a boatman on the C&O Canal traveling from Cumberland, Maryland, to Washington, D.C., most likely with a load of coal. In one of the gaps between Cumberland and the Paw Paw Tunnel, possibly Spring Gap, formed by the mountains and the North Branch of the Potomac River, he encounters a strong wind that makes steering difficult. The canaller is looking forward to visiting Paw Paw, West Virginia, for a drink of whisky at his favorite bar, Wardell's. Since the average trip from Cumberland to Washington took seven days, he was nearing the end of day one and looking forward to getting paid in six days—when he arrived in Washington, D.C.—by the paymaster, George L. Nicholson.

The information obtained from canallers' musical diaries helps us understand the canal era from the people who worked and lived on the canals. The history of the canal era has been written from the historian's perspective, but now, for the first time, the canal era can be told from the songs of the people who lived it.

2

THE CANAL ERA

We're digging a ditch through the mire,
Through the mire, the mud and the muck, by heck!
And the mud is our principle hire,
In our pants, up our sleeves, down our neck, by heck!
—lyrics found on the backing paper of an oil painting in the Adam's Basin Inn,
Adams Basin, New York

The dates for the canal era in America change depending on the perspective of the historian. The canal building era took place between 1790 and 1850. The "golden age of canals," when canal transportation in America was at its peak, was 1840 to 1880. This book, because of its emphasis on song, will consider the canal era from 1817 to 1917, a period that covers the start of construction on the Erie Canal to the time when the Erie Canal ceased to be a towpath canal. The reason for this is that the earliest canal songs collected in the United States are associated with the construction and dedication of the Erie Canal, and the last canal songs (there are a few exceptions in the twentieth and twenty-first centuries) were written as the towpath era on the Erie ended. Canals in the United States were being proposed and constructed before the start of the Erie Canal, and they continued to function long after the last mule pulled a canalboat, but the "golden age of canal song" took place between 1817 and 1917.

The vision of using man-made water routes started in America before the Revolutionary War. The war brought an end to the plans for canals for a while, but after the war, canals were once again on the agenda. George Washington hoped to use the Potomac River and a series of canals to reach the Ohio River Valley, the shortest route from tidewater to the Ohio River. The Potowmack Company was formed in 1785, and construction started on five short canals around obstructions in the upper Potomac. However, using the Potomac River proved to be more problematic than originally imagined. Low water on the upper Potomac during the summer and spring floods limited navigation to only a few months a year, and in 1828, the Potowmack Company went out of business and assigned its assets to the C&O Canal Company. Late in the eighteenth century and early in the nineteenth century, other states built short canals and proposed longer projects that stalled. It took the Erie Canal to introduce America to the canal era.

When the Erie Canal opened the country from the Atlantic Ocean to the Midwest, canal building in Pennsylvania, Ohio, Indiana, New Jersey, Maryland and New York began in earnest. Most of these canals were connected. The Monongahela Navigation, consisting of locks and slack-water navigation created by dams, connected West Virginia to the Pennsylvania Main Line Canal. The Main Line Canal connected to Ohio via the Pennsylvania and Ohio Canal, which joined the Ohio and Erie Canal at Toledo, Ohio. Indiana canals connected to the Ohio canals. For a short time, the Main Line Canal also connected to the Erie Canal by way of a northern extension and the Chenango Canal. The Lehigh Canal linked to the Morris Canal in New Jersey, the Delaware Canal in Pennsylvania and the Delaware and Raritan in New Jersey. The Delaware and Hudson Canal came from Honesdale, Pennsylvania, and crossed New York State to the Hudson River. The Hudson River served as a link to New York City, Lake Champlain and the Erie Canal. The Lehigh, Delaware and Hudson, Chesapeake and Ohio and the Schuylkill Canals opened the Pennsylvania coal fields to major markets in Philadelphia, New York, Washington and Baltimore, fueling the Industrial Revolution.

The Erie Canal and the Pennsylvania Main Line Canal served to carry immigrants west and carry freight in both directions, but many of the other canals were built to haul coal in one direction. The first anthracite coal to reach markets in New York City came by way of the Delaware and Hudson Canal from Honesdale, Pennsylvania. The Werts brothers discovered a large pocket of "stone coal" near Honesdale and took the coal to Wall Street to demonstrate its properties to investors who immediately financed the canal. The Lehigh Canal brought coal from Mauch Chunk (now Jim Thorpe) to markets in Philadelphia via the Delaware Canal and New York City via the Morris Canal. The Schuylkill Canal carried coal from Port Carbon (Schuylkill County) to Philadelphia and later to New York City on New Jersey's Delaware and Raritan Canal. The Chesapeake and Ohio Canal carried coal from the northern Maryland coal fields to Washington, D.C. It could also carry coal on down the Potomac River to the Chesapeake Bay and on to Baltimore. The Monongahela Navigation carried coal out of West Virginia to Pittsburgh.

Much of the story of the canal era can be told through song, but a little groundwork must be laid first. The Erie Canal not only created a model for the American canal era but also became a model for canal songs. Some of the earliest canal songs collected are from the Erie Canal, so it behooves us to examine a bit of the background on how this came to pass.

A poet may well have been one of the first to imagine the Erie Canal, bringing to mind the line from *The Green Hero* by Bernard Evslin, "What if imagination is viewed as an uncanny form of insight?"[23] In his poem "The Visions of Columbus," written in 1787, Joel Barlow's imagination provides insight into the internal improvements of the future:

> *He saw, as widely spreads the unchannelled plain,*
> *Where inland realms for ages bloom'd in vain,*
> *Canals, long winding, ope* [open] *a watery flight,*
> *And distant streams, and seas and lakes unite.*
>
> *From fair Albania, tow'rd the falling sun,*
> *Back through the midland lengthening channels run,*
> *Meet the far lakes, the beauteous towns that lave* [wash the shores],
> *And Hudson joined to broad Ohio's wave.*[24]

Thirty years after Barlow wrote these words, construction began, and the Hudson joined "broad Ohio's wave."

The logical place to start is with the canal that inspired the canal era, the Erie Canal. Although the Erie Canal was not the first canal built in the United States, it was the canal project that started the canal era, and its influence is almost incalculable. Bill Shank, former president of the American Canal Society, asserted that the opening of the Erie Canal was "one of the most significant events in American history since the Revolutionary War."[25]

What is not told in song is the long struggle to get to Rome, New York, in 1817 to begin construction of America's most ambitious canal project. Prior to that, years of proposals, surveys and political struggles took place.

The lack of a water route to the west was a real problem for the movement of people and commerce across the Appalachian Mountain chain. In the eighteenth and early nineteenth centuries, with the population and trade largely confined to the Eastern Seaboard of the United States, the resource-rich western frontier was inaccessible to all but the hardiest of travelers. The digging of the Erie Canal might have started in Rome, but the beginning of the Erie Canal project can be traced back to the end of the eighteenth century in western New York, where only small, isolated settlements existed. This was the western frontier.

The year 2017 marked the bicentennial of the start of the Erie Canal construction, when the first shovelful of earth was taken from the ground just outside of Rome, New York, on July 4, 1817. We know that song was a part of the canal from the beginning. "The Digging Song" (quoted earlier) has no date, but the lyrics link it to the digging conditions encountered in the Cayuga Swamp in 1822 where "the mire, the mud and the muck"—along with swarms of insects—almost stopped construction.

It was the financial failure of a western New York flour merchant named Jesse Hawley (1773–1842) that propelled interest in the construction of the Erie Canal. Hawley badly underestimated the difficulties of moving products from western New York to major markets in Albany and New York City. In the fall of 1806, Jesse Hawley declared bankruptcy and fled to western Pennsylvania to escape his creditors.[26] In August 1807, Hawley returned to New York and was sent to debtors' prison.[27] Instead of wasting his time in prison consumed by anger over his misfortune, Hawley proceeded to compose a series of essays that would transform New York State into the Empire State. From his confinement, Hawley predicted the effect a canal connecting the Hudson River and Lake Erie would have on the entire country and foretold the route of the canal, the number of miles of waterway it would open up and the cost of the canal project. Hawley even predicted the effect the future Illinois and Michigan Canal would have in opening transportation from the Great Lakes to the Mississippi River. When completed, this canal would afford a course of navigation from New York by sloop navigation to Albany (160 miles), from Albany to Buffalo by boat navigation (300 miles) and from Buffalo to Chicago by sloop navigation (1,200 miles)—making a distance of 1,660 miles of inland navigation upstream where the cargo has to be shifted but three times. Hawley enumerates some potential transport costs:

> *The probable charges of freight would be—from New York to Albany (the present price on small packages of merchandise up freight is about) five*

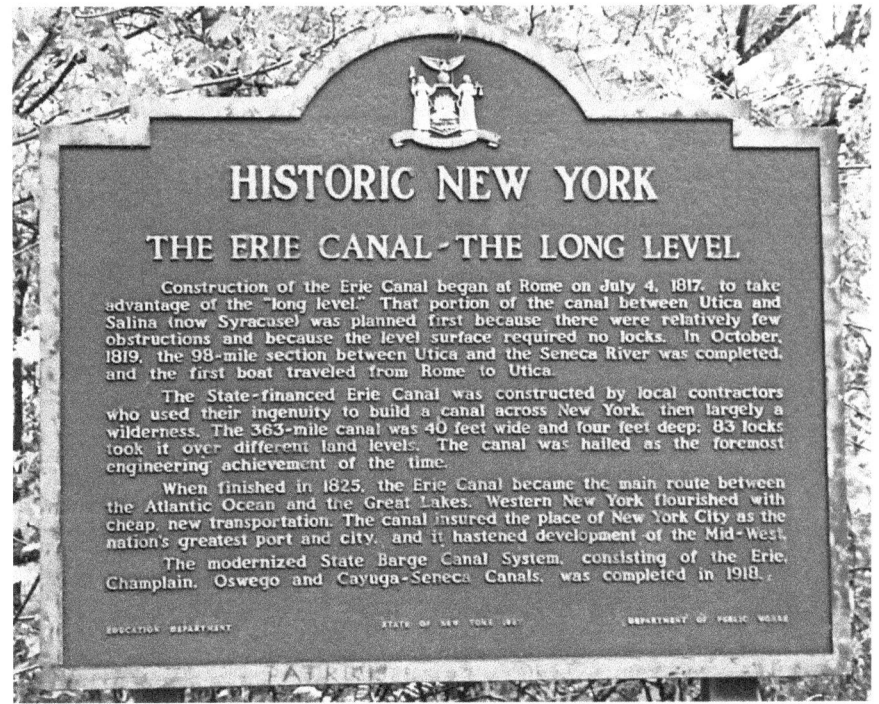

Above: Sign showing the place the digging began for the Erie Canal. *New York State Department of Transportation.*

Right: Jesse Hawley (Hercules). *Miriam and Ira D. Wallach Division of Art, Prints and Photographs: Print Collection, 1825, New York Public Library Digital Collections.*

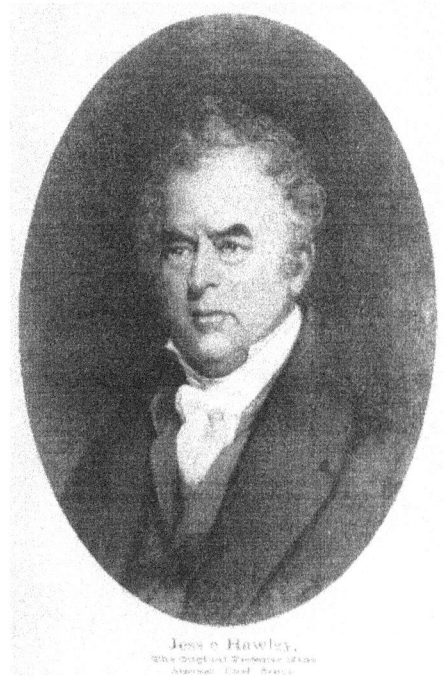

dollars per ton, from thence to Buffalo (full large enough, including no charge for lockage) fifty dollars per ton, from thence to Chicago, say large fifty dollars per ton—is equal to 105 dollars per ton, or five cents per pound nearly. From Chicago harbor it might be continued up its river, by portage, into and down the Illinois, and up the Mississippi; and into, as yet, almost unknown regions.[28]

Hawley's essays, published under the pseudonym Hercules, soon came to the attention of New York State assemblyman Joshua Forman. In 1808, Forman initiated the first legislation calling for surveys to determine the practicality of a four-hundred-mile water route from the Hudson River to the Great Lakes. Foreman even traveled to Washington, D.C., to enlist federal aid for the canal. Thomas Jefferson dismissed the project as "little short of madness."[29] This must have dismayed Jesse Hawley, as his initial essay was based on Thomas Jefferson's remarks that a surplus of federal funds should be used for "the improvement of some great national object, the undertaking of which is to be immediately commenced."[30] Hawley believed that a canal across New York State was just such an improvement. In 1810, U.S. senator DeWitt Clinton was approached by Joshua Forman to lend his support to the canal project. A bill was introduced in the New York State Senate to establish a Canal Commission and survey the proposed route of the canal. After this, and with Clinton's support, the bill approving construction of the canal was passed on April 15, 1817. But that was hardly the last word. The fate of the Erie Canal now hung on a single vote. After the state legislature approved funds for the canal, it still needed the approval of the Council of Revision. The Council of Revision was the unique creation of the New York State Constitution. The Council of Revision had the power to veto any legislation it deemed inappropriate.[31] There were five members on the Council of Revision, and the vote was split. James Kent, the undecided member of the Council, liked the idea of the canal but was not sure the time was right. While Kent was trying to decide, Daniel Tompkins, vice president of the United States, entered the chambers with the intent of influencing a vote against the canal. Tompkins told the members of the council that a war with England may be eminent because only a fragile truce had been established at the close of the War of 1812 and they should not spend their money on a canal but use it to arm the state for war. Following that speech, James Kent stood up and said, "If it is a matter of voting for the canal or war, I vote for the canal."[32] Thus, the construction of the Erie Canal was decided by a single vote.

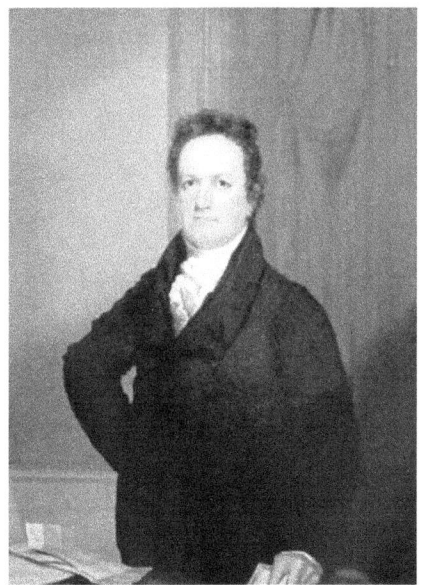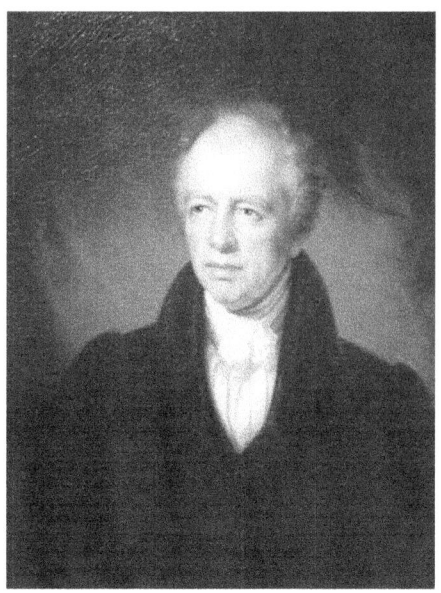

Left: DeWitt Clinton. *Miriam and Ira D. Wallach Division of Art, Prints and Photographs: Print Collection, 1825, New York Public Library Digital Collections.*

Right: James Kent. *Miriam and Ira D. Wallach Division of Art, Prints and Photographs: Print Collection, 1825, New York Public Library Digital Collections.*

But the story is still not over. The canal may well have failed but for the person, or persons, who decided where to dig that first shovelful of earth on that July day in 1817 and what two places to connect. Those two decisions would determine the success or the failure of the Erie Canal. It would seem logical to have one group start digging at the Hudson River and another at Lake Erie and meet in the middle. This, however, may well have resulted in complete failure. On the eastern end, the falls at Cohoes required sixteen locks, and the Niagara escarpment at the other end required blasting through solid rock and building a staircase of five locks at Lockport. The time and expense required to advance the canal only a few miles at either end would have doomed the project before it even got started. Opponents of the canal in the state legislature would have seized upon the expense and the lack of progress and quickly ended funding for the canal.

Jesse Hawley himself may have been the source of the spot chosen to begin the canal; he wrote in his first essay that "from the canal at Rome or Fort Stanwix, down Wood Creek to Oneida Lake, is twenty miles through a tract of very level land."[33] Starting in the middle, at Rome, New York, served three purposes: first, the ease, or comparative ease, of digging where it was flat and required no locks; second, the speed at which one quarter of the canal's length would be finished (a few short years); and third, the diminished chance that construction would be stopped partway through the project because the state would be left with a canal that went nowhere.

Another critical decision was how to proceed from Rome. It was decided that one group would dig east from Rome to Utica. The other group would dig southwest toward what is now Syracuse. The first section of the Erie Canal, from Utica to the Seneca River, was completed in just two years, and the entire length completed within eight years of that first shovelful of earth in Rome, New York. Ronald Shaw's book *Erie Water West* provides a map that shows the completion dates of the following eight sections of the Erie Canal.[34]

Segment	Year of Completion
1. Utica to Seneca River	1819
2. Utica to Little Falls	1821
3. Little Falls to Schenectady	1822
4. Seneca River to Rochester	1822
5. Rochester to Brockport	1823
6. Schenectady to Albany	1823
7. Brockport to Lockport	1824
8. Lockport to Buffalo	1825

In order to survive financially, the canal needed products to transport, even before the entire canal was completed. One of the most profitable products, and the most in demand, was at Salina—salt. Salt had the potential for providing huge revenues for the Erie Canal and the State of New York, and Salina (later absorbed into Syracuse) had enough salt for the whole country. It was salt that helped build the canal, and the decision to loop the canal southwest to Salina was well thought out.

We were loaded up with Star Brand salt,
The captain was loaded, too.
—*Erie Canal song, "Boating on a Bullhead"*

The effect of the canal on Western New York commerce is reflected in the shipment figures for the very product that bankrupted Jesse Hawley. In 1818, five years before the canal reached Rochester, 26,000 barrels of flour were

FIVE HUNDRED.

L A B O R E R ̃,

ARE wanted, for about ten weeks, to to work in the construction of the Canal through the Cayuga Marshes. Good hands shall receive from twelve to thirteen dollars per month, in cash, at the end of every month, week, or day, at their option. They shall be well fed, and lodged in comfortable shanties, with sufficient blankets. They will be subject to some inconvenience, from water and mud; but a portion of the work will be dry; and all experience proves that men may labor on the Marsh without any unusual exposure of health until the middle of July, before which it is intended to have this portion of the Canal completed. Those who are willing to be employed, under this notice, can apply to either of the subscribers at Montezuma.

HOVEY & WETHY,
Canal Contractors.

April 5, 1822.

I certify that Hovey & Wethy are responsible men, and that I have full confidence that they will pay all the hands employed by them according to agreement.

MYRON HOLLEY,
—'60.4w · Canal Commissioner.

An 1822 newspaper advertisement for Cayuga Marshes workers. *Reproduced by the author.*

shipped to New York City. Three years after the completion of the Erie Canal (1828), Rochester transported 200,000 barrels of flour to New York City, and in 1838, 500,000 barrels of flour were shipped to New York City.[35]

Some 80 percent of the state's population lived within twenty-five miles of the canal. Most of the major cities in New York State today are connected to the Erie Canal: New York (connected by the Hudson River), Albany, Schenectady, Utica, Syracuse, Rochester and Buffalo. The work of digging the 363-mile canal began with local labor. Sometimes workers were given a contract for as little as a half mile of canal. The recipient of one such contract was "The father of Newark [New York], Joseph Miller, a shrewd Vermonter, who had the contract for digging one and a quarter mile of the Ditch in the area."[36] With little more than picks, shovels and wheelbarrows, laborers completed the first section of the canal. As the canal progressed, the construction became more difficult. Just west of the Seneca River, diggers encountered the Cayuga Marshes, or Nine-Mile Swamp, and work came to a standstill. An outside workforce was recruited. The diggers' dilemma is described in the following song:

> *We're digging a ditch through the mire,*
> *The mire, the mud and the muck, by Heck!*
> *And the mud is our principle hire,*
> *In our pants, up our sleeves, down our neck, by Heck!*
> *—Erie Canal, "The Digging Song"*[37]

The usual digging tools were useless, and mud scooped out during the day slid back into the ditch at night. As the words to the song relate, "mud is our principle hire." Even worse than the mud were the mosquitoes. A call went out for an outside workforce.

43

As the need for skilled workers to build locks, bridges and aqueducts grew, an even more diverse workforce started to emerge, bringing great change to the culture surrounding the canal. Never before had Western New York experienced the languages, songs and customs brought by new immigrants. Once the canal was constructed, these workers became a part of communities along the canal and contributed their culture and skills. Although the Irish are the most commonly mentioned, German immigrants almost equaled the Irish, and German expressions and canal songs were heard on the middle section of the canal as soon as it opened in 1819. German canallers were called "long-level Dutchman." The name referred to Erie canallers who worked the level sixty-mile stretch from Syracuse to Utica. Around this area, Germans settled in great numbers, accounting for the misused term "Dutchman."[38] The large German presence in New York and Pennsylvania also accounted for one of the only "Dutch" canal songs.

"Der Mule"[39]

Der mule sthoot on der canal boat deck,
Fer de towpath he wouldn't dret,
Un dey tied a halter round his neck,
Un racked him on der het.
Dey curshed and shwore, but he wouldn't go,
Until he felt inclint,
Un do day dundered blow on blow,
He altered not his mint.

This canal song was most likely written by a non-German canaller or canal observer who imitated the speech of new German immigrants. The practice was to be repeated over and over again in minstrel shows that made fun of the speech of African Americans, Italians, Germans and any other new immigrant group. One "Dutch" stage song from *The Little Frauds*, by Harrigan and Hart, goes like this:

"Little Fraud"[40]

He-Oh? vere is dat leetle deicher darling,
Der pootiest littl vaiter-gal of all;
Oh! vere is der pickles by der gaurten,
Der mock oranges hanging by der vail?

How sweet she used to vait on der table,
Mit sarsaparilla vater by her tray;
Und sometimes put bottles by der labes,
Ven efer der boss he vas away.

George Korson does not believe "Der Mule" is a stage piece and calls it a "Dutch-English parody of Felicia Herman's famous poem ["Casabianca"]," first published in the *New Monthly Magazine* in August 1826.[41]

"Casabianca"

The boy stood on the burning deck
Whence all but he had fled;
The flame that lit the battle's wreck
Shone round him o'er the dead.
Yet beautiful and bright he stood,
As born to rule the storm;
A creature of heroic blood,
A proud, though child-like form.[42]

During the period when canals were being constructed in the United States (1790–1850), the number of German and Irish immigrants was almost equal. From 1820 to 1870, over seven and a half million immigrants came to the United States—more than the entire population of the country in 1810. Nearly all of them came from northern and western Europe—about a third from Ireland and almost a third from Germany.[43]

As early as 1818, three thousand Irish were employed on the Erie Canal. There was hardly a canal built anywhere in the United States before the Civil War without Irish labor. By 1826, five thousand Irish were at work on four canal projects.[44]

Although the difference has been exaggerated, most Irish who immigrated to the United States were poor, while the German immigrants had more wealth and more skills. Unlike the Irish, many Germans had enough money to journey to the Midwest in search of farmland and work. The largest settlements of Germans were in New York City, Baltimore, Cincinnati, St. Louis and Milwaukee. However, Germans had a more difficult time because of the language barrier. "For this the Germans themselves were largely to blame, because of their stubborn refusal to learn the English language."[45]

The Irish tended to stay near the East Coast, settling in the urban areas of Boston and New York and in cities along the canals. The Irish immigration to Ohio was a direct result of canal construction. Many Irish immigrants who landed in New York City were recruited to work on the Erie Canal, which was completed in 1825. Upon completion of the Erie Canal, these Irish workers came to northeast Ohio to work and made up the bulk of the labor force on the northern segment of the Ohio and Erie Canal. In fact, the 1850 State of Ohio Census lists 22 percent of the state's immigrants as coming from Ireland.[46] Although the numbers of Germans and Irish were nearly equal, the two groups settled in different areas of the country. The poorer Irish workers tended to stay close to where they worked, bringing Irish music, dances and customs to the area.[47]

The Erie Canal touched off a flurry of canal building. It was not until 1825, with the completion of the Erie Canal, that early canal proponents were vindicated, and states such as Pennsylvania struggled to keep up. The Erie served as the model and ushered in the canal era with great fanfare, proving that America could indeed benefit from a system of inland waterways and do it without the federal government.

Canal building and the movement of immigrants and goods by canalboat flourished in the middle of the 1800s with Manifest Destiny and the movement west, leading to a frenzy of canal building. Following the Erie Canal's success, Pennsylvania, faced with the loss of business at its port in Philadelphia to rival ports in Baltimore and New York, began work on a cross-state transportation system in 1826. Maryland was already at work connecting the state to the port at Baltimore.

The canals were usually named for the locations they connected. However, as with the Erie Canal, there were exceptions. The single-named canals Erie, Schuylkill, Chenango, Oswego and Champlain included only one location. The Erie connected the Hudson River to Lake Erie. The Schuylkill connected Port Carbon to Philadelphia. The Chenango connected the Erie Canal and the Susquehanna River, and the Champlain connected Lake Champlain to the Hudson River. Even some of the other canal names were misleading; the Delaware and Hudson Canal connected Honesdale, Pennsylvania, with the Hudson River, and the Chesapeake and Ohio was never finished to the Ohio River and only connected Cumberland, Maryland, to the Potomac River in Washington, D.C. Following the completion of the Erie Canal, canals opened, one by one, in the East and Midwest. The Delaware and Hudson Canal opened in 1828; the Farmington Canal (New Haven, Connecticut, to Farmington, Connecticut) opened in 1828; the Lehigh in

1829; the first section of the Chesapeake and Ohio in 1831; the Ohio and Erie in 1833; the Chenango in 1834; the Pennsylvania Main Line in 1834; and the Hampshire and Hampton Canal (Massachusetts) in 1835. By 1840, fifteen years after the opening of the Erie Canal, over three thousand miles of canals were in use.

The history of the canal era told in the number of miles, locks, aqueducts, bridges, boats and the cost of shipping a product per ton, tell one story, but the songs tell another. The songs are the people's history of the canal as sung from the "musical diaries" of those who lived during the canal era.

II

AMERICA'S CANAL SONG

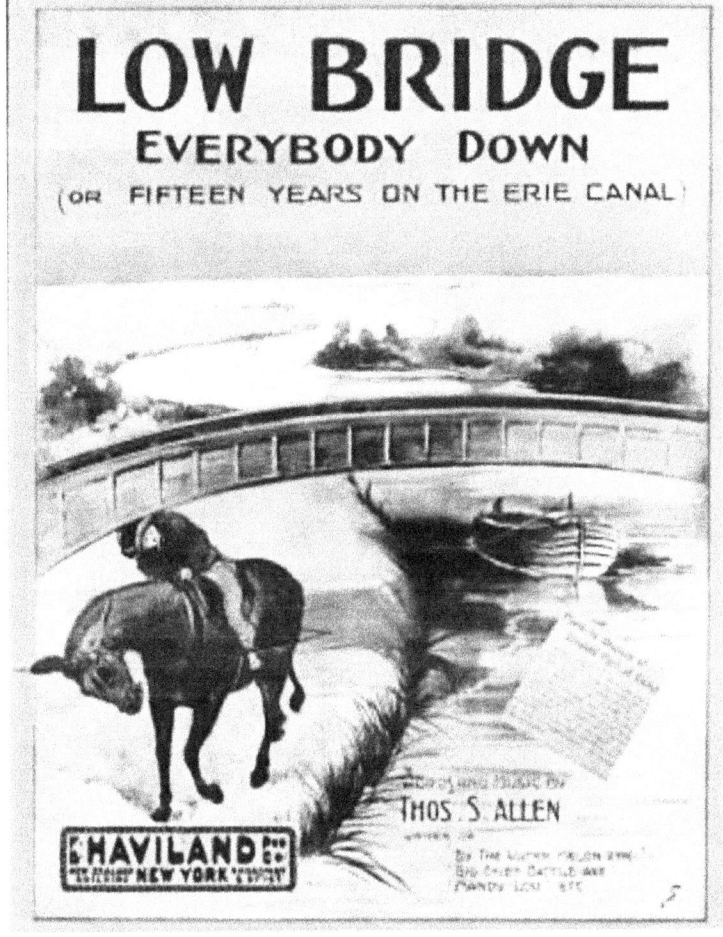

Sheet music cover for "Low Bridge, Everybody Down," or "Fifteen Years on the Erie Canal." *Reproduced by the author.*

3

"Low Bridge, Everybody Down"

Oh, ev'ry band will play it soon, Darned fool words and a darned fool tune,
You'll hear it sung ev'rywhere you go, from Mexico to Buffalo.
—Thomas S. Allen, "Low Bridge, Everybody Down"

This may be the best known of all canal songs. Carl Sandburg asserted that it is America's equivalent of "The Volga Boatman."[48] The song may be remembered today because it was composed in the twentieth century, but that would be taking away from the talent of Thomas Allen, who provided us with a catchy song with "darn fool words and a darn fool tune."

By the time "Low Bridge, Everybody Down" was composed, almost every canal had been replaced or forever changed by the new technology. Motors replaced mules, and railroads replaced most canals. Nostalgia for a bygone era was at its peak, and it was time for William Totten's "Rhyme of the Old Canal," George M. Cohen's "Down by the Erie Canal" and Thomas Allen's "Low Bridge, Everybody Down." "Low Bridge, Everybody Down" is the best-known canal song and, in most cases, the only canal song people know. It is sung by people in places that do not even have canals. It is still being recorded by performing artists in the twenty-first century. Only a few years after it was written, it was assumed to be a folk song and was quoted in Walter Edmonds's book *Rome Haul* (without credits),[49] published in books of folk songs (without credits)[50] and used in a Hollywood film, *The Farmer Takes a Wife* (1935) (without credits).[51]

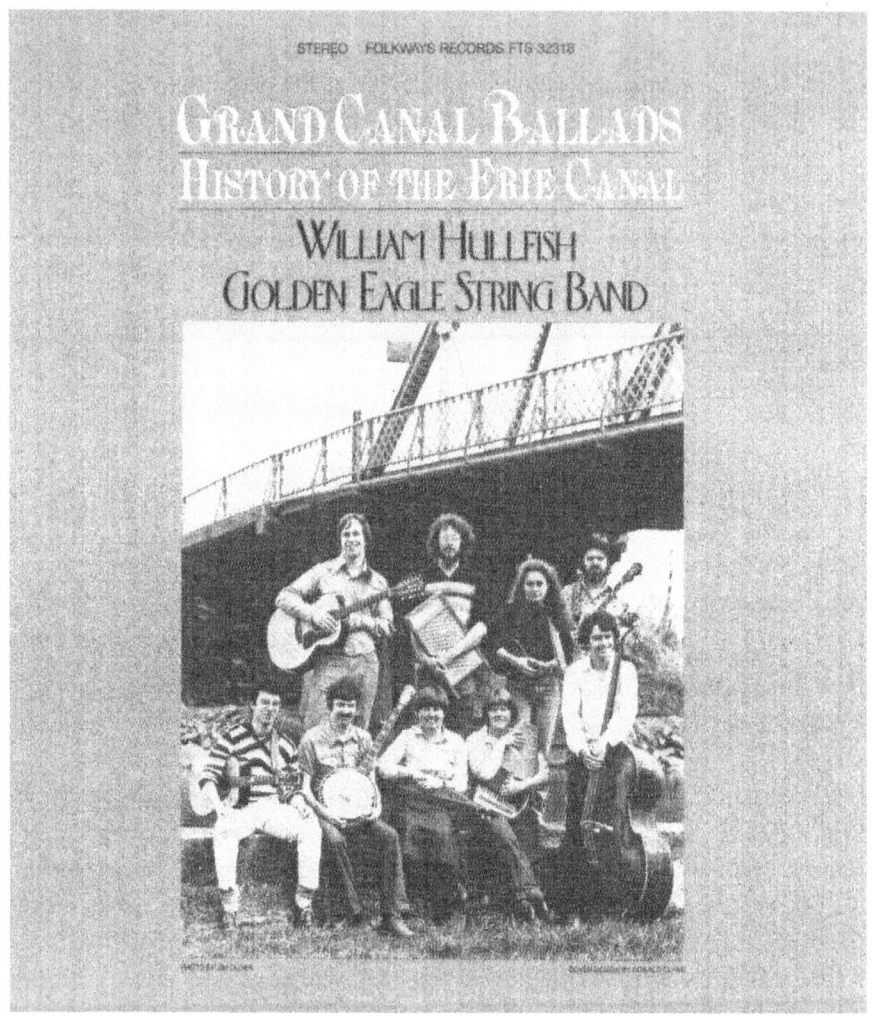

Grand Canal Ballads, Smithsonian/Folkways Records. *Photograph by the author.*

"Low Bridge, Everybody Down" is often a point of contention for musicians who keep these songs alive. Not only is it a song composed by a professional composer and not canallers, but it is sung frequently as the only canal song people know. The Golden Eagle String Band recorded an album of canal songs for Smithsonian/Folkways Records (*Grand Canal Ballads*) and, a few years ago, got a call from the Smithsonian to play a concert of canal songs for a tour the Smithsonian was sponsoring. As the band went over the tunes to play for the program, one of the band members asked, "What

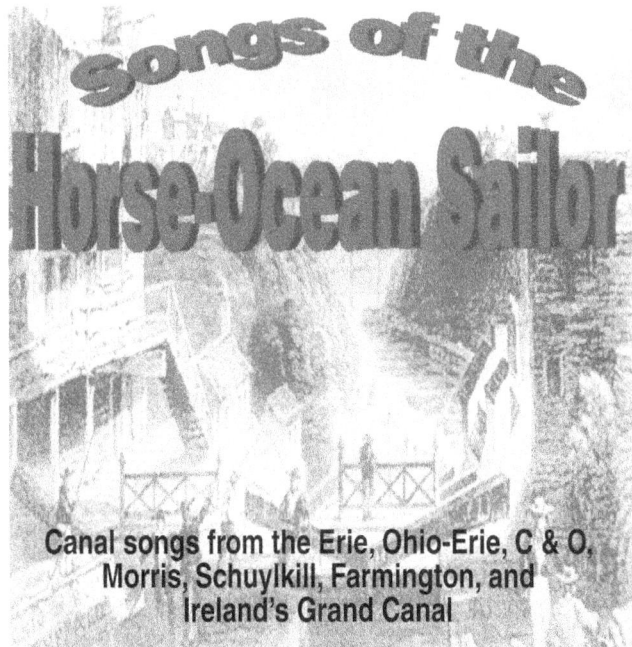

Songs of the Horse-Ocean Sailor CD cover. *Photograph by the author.*

about 'Low Bridge, Everybody Down'?" The consensus was that the song was overdone and the band could omit it from the program. At the concert, the band performed fifteen or sixteen canal songs, and as they were taking their bows, someone from the audience shouted, "Aren't you going to play 'Low Bridge, Everybody Down'?"

The second example also involves the Golden Eagle String Band. They recorded two more canal albums, *The Canaller's Songbook* and *Songs of the Horse-Ocean Sailor.* One album sells very well, and the other one does not. The band members went to the manager of the shop that sells the greatest number of their albums, Lockport Locks and Erie Canal Cruises, to see if she could tell them why one is preferred over the other.

"Customers look at the selection of tunes on the two albums," she said. "If the song they are looking for is there, they buy it. If not, they seldom purchase it." *And what is that one song everyone looks for?* You guessed it—"Low Bridge, Everybody Down."

Folksinger George Ward had a similar experience. When George recorded an album of Erie Canal songs (*Oh! That Low Bridge*), he deliberately left out "Low Bridge, Everybody Down." He started to hear from people who bought his album asking him why he did not include that song. Finally, he went back into the studio and recorded "Low Bridge, Everybody Down" and included it in the new pressing of the album.[52] As a consequence of its popularity, the song requires more careful attention and discussion here.

It is surprising how little is known about the origins of "Low Bridge, Everybody Down." The majority of sources say it was composed in 1905.[53] Other sources say it is a folk song that was circulating in the nineteenth century and the composer of the song is unknown.[54] John and Alan Lomax, in *American Songs and Ballads*, identify the composer as William S. Allen (no relation to Thomas S. Allen).[55] There are those who believe the original song only had two verses and two choruses and that the other verses were added later. All of this competing information and misinformation only raises additional questions.

COPYRIGHTS AND RECORDINGS
OF "LOW BRIDGE, EVERYBODY DOWN"

One of the first questions is, when was "Low Bridge, Everybody Down" written? The majority of existing sources say it was written in 1905 (one says 1906, another 1904), but this date only brings up more questions. If it was written in 1905, why did Allen wait so long to copyright it? Why did it take so long for the sheet music to be published? According to the Library of Congress, Allen's song was not copyrighted until 1912 and 1913. On November 18, 1912 (the exact date the song was first copyrighted), popular singer Billy Murray recorded "Low Bridge, Everybody Down," and a short time later, the Peerless Quartet recorded it. In 1913, Edward Meeker recorded it. Apparently, because of Billy Murray's recording on November 18, 1912, F.B. Haviland Publishing Company was forced to quickly copyright a manuscript copy of the song. It then copyrighted "Low Bridge, Everybody Down" in sheet music form in 1913, two months after it was recorded and eight years after the majority of sources say it was written. The copyright date for the sheet music (1913) is confirmed, and the date Allen wrote the famous canal song is certainly earlier based on the 1912 recording and the copyright of the manuscript copy.

Did Allen compose the song in 1905 and wait seven years to do anything with it? That year, 1905, is when New York State decided to modernize the canal and gradually do away with the need for a towpath, and this is the subject of the song, but there is no indication that Allen wrote the song at this time. In 1928, Allen's publisher, F.B. Haviland, sued Doubleday-Page

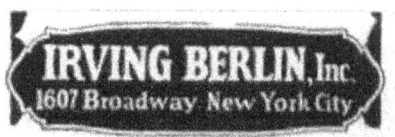
Notice of F.B. Haviland lawsuit against Doubleday, Page & Co. *Reproduced by the author.*

Publishers for using "Low Bridge, Everybody Down" without permission. Doubleday-Page claimed that the song was "in circulation long before Mr. Haviland copyrighted it." Haviland lost the lawsuit after witnesses claimed to have heard the song before 1912 (more on that subject in chapter 5).

Certainly, "Low Bridge, Everybody Down" is different in content and subject from most of Allen's output, which consists of vaudeville songs ("Good-bye, Mister Greenback"), ragtime piano pieces ("Cabaret Rag"), marches ("Step Lively"), gallops ("Whip and Spur"), two-steps ("Hoop-E-Kack"), waltzes ("Wonderland") and character pieces ("Chee Wee—A Chinese Novelty'). Yet no one can suggest any folk song that Allen may have used as a source, and further efforts to uncover such a song have been in vain.

CHANGES IN THE LYRICS TO "LOW BRIDGE, EVERYBODY DOWN"

Despite the fact that "Low Bridge, Everybody Down" first appeared in written form, oral transmission of the song resulted in changes in the lyrics. The obvious changes occur in the following three lines of the original lyrics: "Fifteen years on the Erie Canal"; "You can always tell your neighbor, you can always tell your pal, if he's ever navigated on the Erie Canal"; and "Gid-dap there gal, we've passed that lock."

The original wording of the second and fourth lines of the verses is "fifteen *years* on the Erie Canal." In fact, that is the subtitle on the 1913 sheet music cover. By 1926, the lyric was published by Sigmund Spaeth in *Read 'Em and Weep* (the subject of the lawsuit mentioned earlier) as "fifteen *miles* on the Erie Canal." Whether it was the influence of this publication or simply the "folk process," the change in wording to "fifteen *miles* on the Erie Canal" stuck. Is there a reason why the words changed over the years? Many of the changes make sense and can even be justified in terms of the workings of the canal. In the case of "fifteen miles on the Erie Canal," "miles" is not, in and of itself incorrect. Many boats traveled day and night, and the crew shared the driving and other chores in six-hour shifts. At two or two and a half miles per hour, the shifts usually averaged out to about fifteen miles. Obviously, the mileage depended on the number of locks and the length of the wait at each lock, along with other factors. If the six-hour "trick" was along a "long level" (no locks), the mileage would be better than one that involved many locks. If traffic was heavy and the driver had to drop the line many times to allow boats to pass, the mileage would be reduced. Nevertheless, "fifteen miles on the Erie Canal" is now in oral tradition despite the fact that it does change the meaning of the song. With the use of the original word, *years*, Allen was suggesting a canaller's nostalgic look back on a fifteen-year career that was now coming to an end. *Miles*, rather than a sentimental look back, suggests a present, working canaller on a single six-hour shift. Whatever the case, "fifteen miles on the Erie Canal" is not the intended wording, or feeling, of the original composed by Thomas S. Allen in 1912.

You Can Always Tell Your Pal,
If He's *Ever Navigated on the Erie Canal*

Another subtler change of wording can be heard after listening to numerous recordings and performances of "Low Bridge, Everybody Down." There is a change in the following line: "You can always tell your neighbor, you can always tell your pal, if *he's* ever navigated on the Erie Canal." Most of the performances change that line to "You'll always know your neighbor, you'll always know your pal, if *you've* ever navigated on the Erie Canal." It is a small difference indeed, but Allen's original wording suggests the camaraderie shared by canallers. The change of wording is a bit more inclusive, suggesting everyone is your pal. This may be the result of making "he's" into something more gender neutral, but the change came long before this trend. Recordings by Bruce Springsteen, Pete Seeger, Hughes Rudd and a host of others (all available on YouTube) confirm these changes.

Of course, most people do not think about the wording. They simply sing what they have heard or remembered, and that is the way oral transmission works. The change of wording is not wrong per se, but the point is that oral tradition has altered Allen's original lyrics.

Gid-dap There Gal, We've Passed that Lock

Another line in the lyrics that changed somewhere along the line is "Gid-dap there gal, we've passed that lock." There is a change from the original line to "Gid-dap there gal, here comes a lock." The original wording probably refers to mules waiting for the boat to "lock through" and then needing to be restarted. The changed version, "Gid-dap there gal, here comes a lock," implies speeding up when a lock is within sight. This change of wording also works because the locks were bottlenecks where boats sometimes waited in long lines to lock through. If there was a delay at one of the locks for an hour or more, dozens of boats could be in line above and below the lock. Many boats sped up when approaching a lock to avoid being passed or in order to pass a boat. "Get that Boat" is a canal song that speaks to the practice of trying to overtake other boats. According to former canaller Albert Lavender (Holley, New York), "Fights? Well it was hard to keep out of them. Generally, they happened when boats tried to hog the locks and beat the other fellow through."[56] The Ohio and Erie Canal had a song describing just such encounters:

"Get That Boat"[57]

Get that boat, we must get past and slip her,
Get that boat, get that boat, I say,
Take her antlers and give them to the skipper,
Pass that boat, pass that boat, I say,
She is pretty fast but faster we can go,
Crowd them in, if they won't lay over, Joe,
Get that boat, the whole crew is with you,
Get that boat, get that boat, I say.

The twenty-four-mile section between the Hudson River and Schenectady was a notorious bottleneck. During the Erie Canal's early years, passengers usually boarded a stagecoach in Albany and met the canal at Schenectady. By 1831, America had its first chartered railroad (Mohawk and Hudson) specifically designed to carry passengers and freight around this twenty-seven-lock bottleneck.[58]

Negotiating a Triple Lock

A personal experience with lines at locks may help explain the above change of wording. While canalling in England and Wales, our boat came to a triple lock. As on the old Erie, this was a single set of locks serving traffic in both directions. The protocol was to alternate a boat from the top and then a boat from the bottom. In the line at the bottom of the chain of three locks was one other boat. After waiting for the boat in front to lock through and a boat from above to complete the process, it was finally our time to enter the lower lock. Two members of the crew worked to snub the boat to a stop, secure the bow and stern, push on the balance beams to close the lock chamber, crank open the paddle gates to fill the lock chamber, hold the boat steady with ropes to keep it from bouncing around in the lock chamber from the turbulent water rushing in, wait for the water levels in the lower and upper locks to obtain the same level, crank the paddle gates closed, untie the boat and open the front gates to let the boat into the next lock chamber. This is all repeated three times. The wait for the other two boats and locking through three locks took about thirty minutes. As our boat finally rose to the top of the third lock, a line of about sixteen boats came into view. At ten minutes a boat to lock through, alternating with a boat below, this might mean waiting for most of a day. It is no wonder that canallers trying to earn a living cried out "Get up there mule, here comes a lock." This is the reason that as many canals as possible built double sets of locks to accommodate boats going in opposite directions. By late in the 1830s, traffic was so heavy on America's canals that the addition of another set of locks was a necessity.

Another change in "Low Bridge, Everybody Down" is the adoption of the first chorus as the *only* chorus. The reason that many researchers, who have seen the original sheet music, believe it only had two verses and two choruses is because the printed copy of the music only displays two verses and two choruses directly under the music. On the inside of the back page of the sheet music are the other three verses and three choruses. Thomas

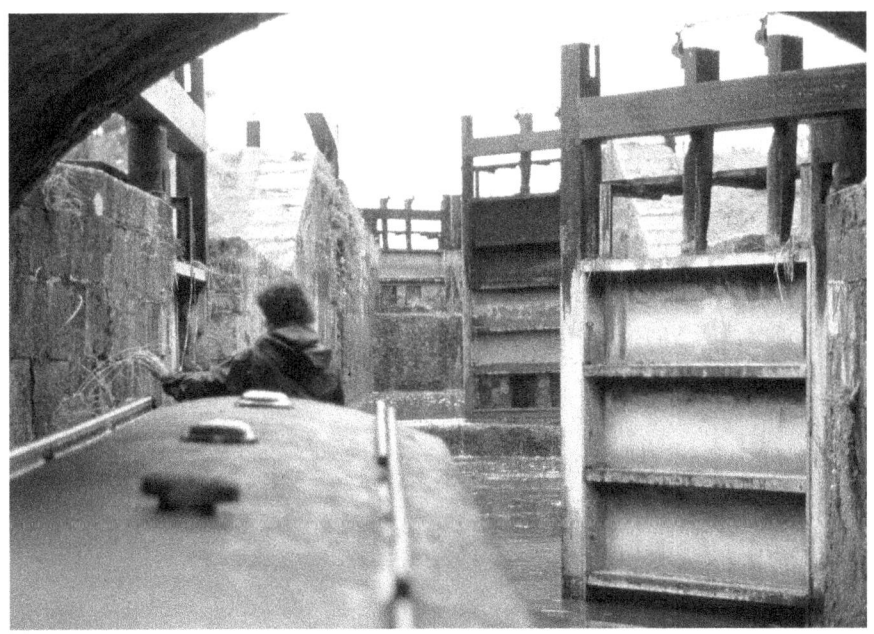

Entering a triple lock. *Photograph by the author.*

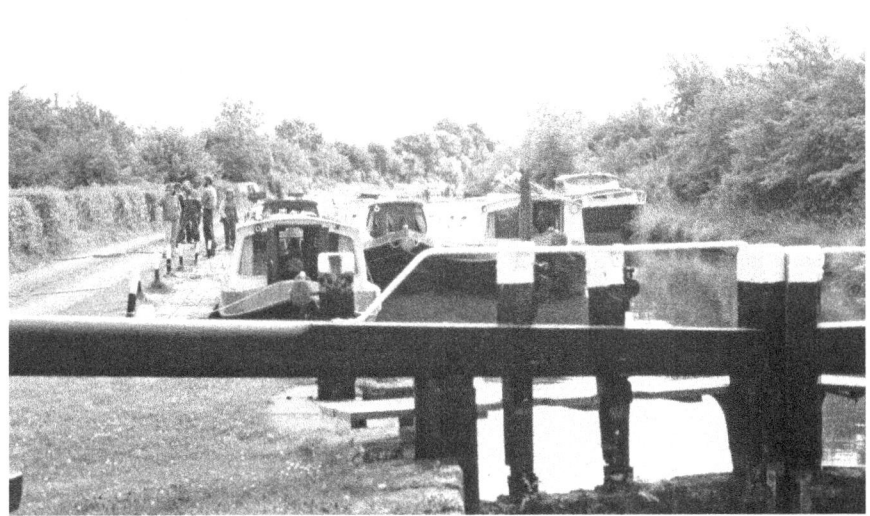

Boats lined up waiting to enter lock. *Photograph by the author.*

Allen wrote five verses and five choruses. This was unusual even for Allen; most popular songs had a series of verses but only one chorus. On the first day the song was copyrighted, Billy Murray's recording had already reduced it to one chorus, a trend that continues today. The reason why the earliest version had one chorus probably had to do with the limited length allowed by the recording. Later, it probably had more to do with the fact that most songs only have one chorus. It makes singing along on the chorus much easier if the same words keep coming back.

The reason Edward Meeker was able to record all the verses and choruses of "Low Bridge, Everybody Down" on a cylinder recording is because Edison's new Blue Amberol records could play for as long as four minutes and forty-five seconds. A surface layer of "indestructible" plastic celluloid that Edison tinted a trademark blue color gave the cylinders their trademark name. Earlier recordings, including the Billy Murray record, were limited to two minutes.

There is little doubt that Allen intended "Low Bridge, Everybody Down" to be a nostalgic song, an old canaller looking back on his life on the canal and making his last trip. The singer remarks in one verse that he and other canallers "better look 'round for another job"; they only had "one more trip and then we'll go, right straight back to Buffalo." Allen's song looked back on an era in American transportation that had all but vanished. Even the canals that still existed were abandoning towpaths and draft animals in favor of larger boats and motors. With profits dwindling, old-time canallers could not afford new boats, and most, like the canaller in Thomas Allen's song, made one last trip and looked for a new job.

THE MAN BEHIND
THE SONG

Who was the man who wrote such an unusual canal song? Thomas S. Allen was born on December 16, 1876, in Natick, Massachusetts, to parents Daniel and Joanna (Donaher) Allen. Both his mother and father were born in Ireland. His father was a cobbler by trade, and Daniel and Joanna had seven children: Daniel, John, Catherine, James, William, George and Thomas.[59] In 1898, Thomas S. Allen married Jessie Johnson, and they had two children.

Other than his famous canal song, his most-played work today is a circus march called "Whip and Spur." He wrote many of his songs for vaudeville productions and a number of his galops, waltzes, marches, overtures and character pieces were printed in collections used to accompany silent films of the day. Many of these pieces were published in *The Jacobs Folios*, advertised as "Modern Movie Music" and the "Photo-Play Pianist's Library." There were folios for galops; rags; dance waltzes; six-eight marches; characteristic and descriptive pieces; Oriental, Indian and Spanish music; tone poems; and reveries and incidental music.

Silent films were not silent. This term was applied to them retroactively after the age of "talkies" began. The Jacobs Folios and others like them allowed pianists, organists and orchestras, providing music for silent films, to choose appropriate pieces to use in the cue sheets describing the type of scene in the film.[60] If you were a moviegoer during the first three decades of the twentieth century, you would have listened to music composed by Thomas S. Allen. Allen's "Cabaret Capers" was used in the soundtrack for

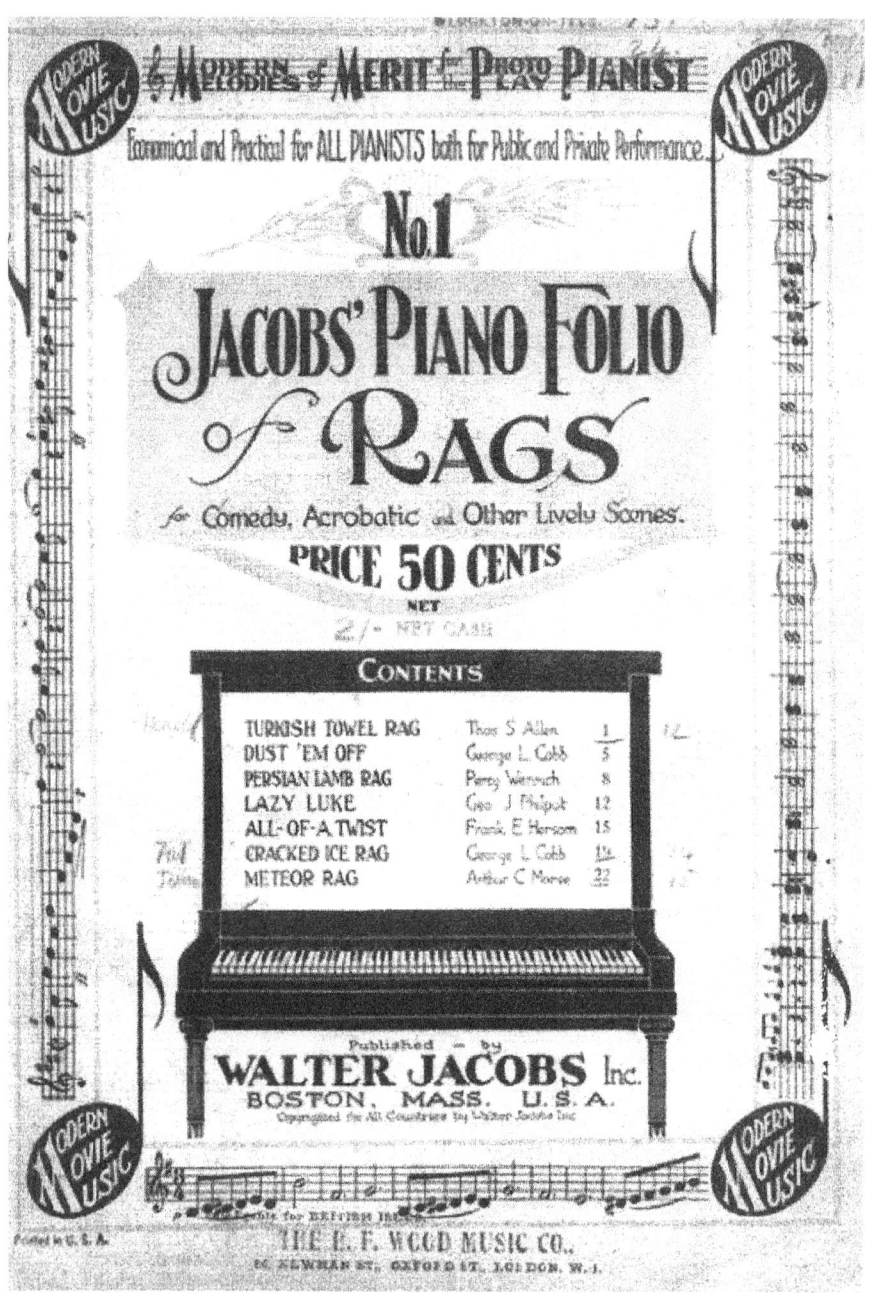

Jacobs' Modern Movie Music Piano Folio No. 1 containing Thomas Allen's "Turkish Towel Rag." *Silent Film Sound and Music Archive.*

the silent movie *Wings*, a pictured about World War I starring Clara Bow and Gary Cooper and directed by William Wellman.[61] *Wings* won the Best Picture Award in the first Academy Award ceremonies in 1929. Thomas Allen's "Dance of the Lunatics" was recorded in a project for the Silent Film Sound and Music Archive, established in 2014 to build "a robust archive of music for silent cinema and related film archive of music for silent cinema and related film technologies for research and performance. The archive includes sheet music for silent film, instruction manuals for film accompanists, and a bibliography of resources on silent film sound and music."[62]

The Silent Film Sound and Music Archive also published sheet music copies of Allen's "Saddle Back," "Under the Spell," "The Marconigram," "'Round the Ring," "Youth and You," "The Periscope," "Fighting Strength," "The Naval Parade," "Pavana," "Winnebago," "Whip and Spur," "The Plunger," "On Desert Sands," "Cabaret Capers," "Step Lively," "Got 'Em," "Salaret" and "The Dixie Rube."

What do we know about Thomas S. Allen, aside from a list of some of his compositions, that might shed a little more light on his famous canal song? Thomas Allen was a performer. At an early age, he began lessons on the violin and became a fine player and conductor. He made his debut with the Knowlton and Allen Dance Orchestra (named for his brothers) in Natick, Massachusetts, at an early age. The orchestra featured Thomas's brothers, Daniel, John, James, William and George. By the age of twenty-two, Thomas was a member of various dance, theater and opera orchestras in Boston.[63]

Around 1894, Walter Jacobs, who had already published some of his own works, was persuaded by violinist Thomas Allen to purchase ten of his songs. This group of songs formed the basis of the Walter Jacobs Publishing Company. Jacobs soon expanded his enterprise to a suite of studios and was selling a booklet called *Jacobs' Banjo Studies*. The Jacobs Music Co. in Boston began publishing the *Jacobs' Band Journal*, including a new Allen work in nearly every issue. Allen's compositions appeared in programs all over the United States, from Honolulu, Hawaii; Bakersfield, California; Ogden, Utah; Pendleton, Oregon; El Paso, Texas; Ottawa, Kansas; Franklin, Indiana; Wilmington, Delaware; Harrisburg, Pennsylvania; Allentown, Pennsylvania; Washington, D.C.; Wilmington and Charlotte, North Carolina. The *Jacobs' Band Journal*'s circulation went beyond the United States, and Allen's music was known in Canada, England, Australia and New Zealand.[64]

Jacobs published a number of similar journals for piano and for orchestra. Those journals also regularly contained compositions by Thomas S. Allen. The *Grand Orchestra Folio*, twenty-three different standard orchestral instruments, included arrangements of some current ragtime favorites and marches. One of the standouts that gave Jacobs Music Co. more visibility was an arrangement of Thomas S. Allen's hit song "Any Rags?," which was originally published in 1902 by another Boston publisher, George M. Krey.

So how did one of Allen's compositions become no. 1 on the *Billboard* charts[65] for eight weeks? It was common practice for Jacobs to publish arrangements of Allen's songs and piano pieces for orchestra, band, banjo and guitar. He also took ragtime piano pieces and piano solos, added lyrics and published them as songs. The big break came in 1903, when Arthur Collins, a popular singer, recorded Allen's "Any Rags?" This brought fame to the Jacobs Publishing Company and Thomas Allen. "Any Rags?" was no. 1 on the *Billboard* charts for eight weeks.[66]

Although some of Allen's compositions are undated, they seem to range from 1897 to 1918. His most prolific period is from 1912, when he published fourteen songs, to 1914 (eighteen songs), the same period of time he resided in Rochester, New York. In 1913, the year he published "Low Bridge, Everybody Down," Allen published eighteen other songs. He seems to have stuck mostly to songs, marches, schottisches, overtures and character pieces. Even though this was the ragtime era, Allen wrote few ragtime pieces. One of Allen's rags, "Turkish Towel Rag," was available on piano roll, and Allen regularly used ragtime rhythms in the accompaniment of many of his songs. Allen's compositions were available in a variety of forms, including individual sheet music copies, collections of sheet music, recordings and piano rolls.

Thomas Allen wrote for a number of publishers after his initial start with Jacobs Music. Most were from Boston, including Bates and Bendix, Jos. M. Daly, O'Neil and Story, G.W. Setchell, B.F. Wood, George M. Krey and Thomas S. Allen Music. Later, Allen published a few pieces with New York publishers, Jerome Remick and F.B. Haviland, for whom he wrote "Low Bridge, Everybody Down," and Lew Berk Music Company, Rochester, New York. Walter Jacobs eventually bought out the Bates and Bendix catalogue, and he and Joseph M. Daly remained Allen's primary publishers right up to the composer's death in 1919.

Thomas S. Allen sold a large amount of music. No publisher would continue to publish the number of compositions (over one hundred) that Allen continued to turn out for two decades if they were not selling. An indication of the popularity of Allen's music is the number of recordings made by banjo players, singers, male quartets, concert bands and orchestras. A partial list of recordings of Allen's music is printed in the *Discography of American Historical Recordings*.[67] From the earliest recording of

"Any Rags?" by Arthur Collins (October 26, 1903), to the Mack Allen recording of "Low Bridge, Everybody Down" on January 21, 1929, there are over forty recordings. Allen's pieces were recorded by the most famous concert bands of the day, among them John Philip Sousa, Arthur Pryor and The Conway Band.

Thomas S. Allen is given credit for being an innovator in popular music in the first two decades of the twentieth century. Allen was able to attach the songs he wrote with trends in popular culture. He was the first to produce the popular vocal tunes known as "street hawker songs" that were soon imitated by other songwriters. Larry Hamberlin, author of *Tin Pan Opera: Operatic Novelty Songs in the Ragtime Era*, credits Allen with another major change in the popular music of the day. He claims that with three songs (all three are "street hawker songs") written within seven years of one another, Allen was able to bring together popular music with African American and Italian characteristics and accomplish a major change in popular music at least a year before any other songwriter. "The complex linking of Italian Americans and African-Americans in the popular mind can be traced in three songs by the Boston composer Thomas S. Allen."[68] The three songs that Hamberlin ascribed to this change are "Any Rags?" (1902), "Scissors to Grind" (1904) and "Strawberries: Here Comes the Strawberry Man" (1909). All three songs are about itinerant street vendors: a rag picker, a scissor grinder and a fruit seller.

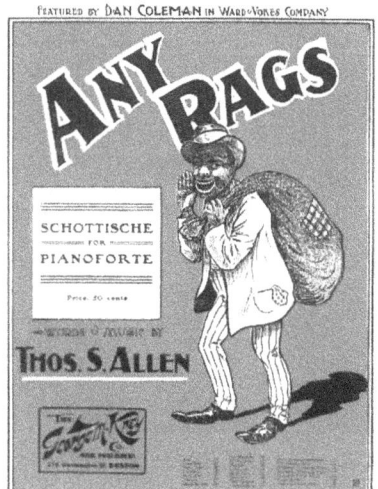

"Any Rags?" sheet music cover. *Author's collection.*

"Any Rags?" is not a ragtime song. It is a popular song about a black street hawker who calls for "rags, bottles and bones." The song is an Afro-American stereotype right from the caricature on the cover to the lyrics that refer to the rag man as a thief. The song does contain some ragtime rhythms in the accompaniment of the chorus, but the verses have a straightforward accompaniment consistent with the popular songs of the day.

"Scissors to Grind" is where the change appears. Instead of a black street hawker, the song is about an Italian street hawker. The lyrical quality of the verse is blended with the ragtime

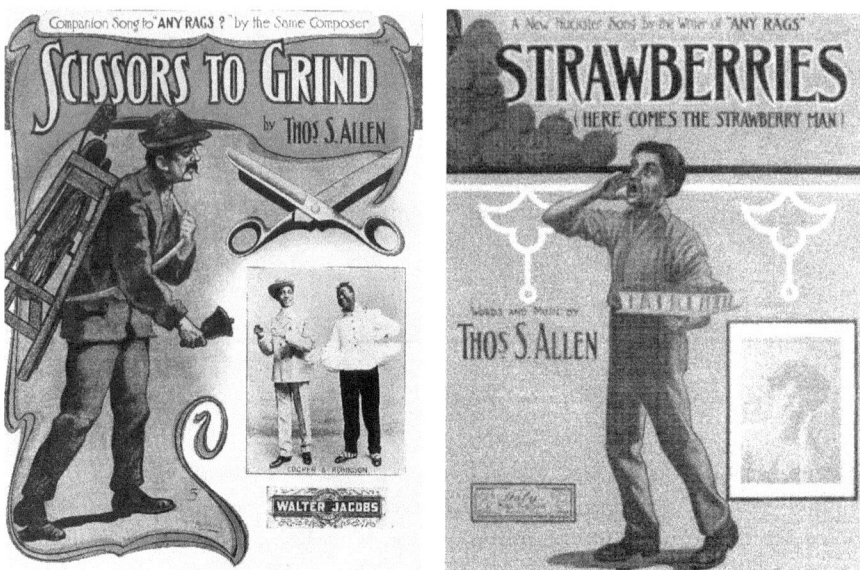

Left: "Scissors to Grind," sheet music cover. *Author's collection.*

Right: "Strawberries," sheet music cover. *Author's collection.*

syncopation of the chorus. The subject of the piece, the music and the image on the cover suggest that Italians are the new immigrants and essentially "black." The cover also pictures an inset of the black song and dance team of George W. Cooper and Bill "Bojangles" Robinson, who performed together from 1902 to 1914. The men were bound by the "two-colored" rule in vaudeville, which restricted blacks to performing in pairs.[69]

"Strawberries" is about an Italian strawberry seller, Michael Tony Angelo, who "came here from sunny Italy." Here, Allen makes an even stronger Italian connection. Michael has a strong voice and wants to be an opera singer. Michael finally realizes his dream and becomes an opera singer, but when he gets on stage, instead of singing the lines from the opera, all he sings is "Strawberries." An actual opera singer of the day, Pietro Mascagni, is mentioned in the song and referred to as Pete Mascagni. The subject and the lyrical, almost Italianate melody, along with the image, combined with ragtime rhythm, again strongly link Italians and African Americans together in the public mind. Hamberlin describes the change from African American to Italian American with the following statement: "Here, one year before the advent of Italian dialect songs, popular songs had already marked the unassimilated immigrant as culturally 'black.'"[70]

66

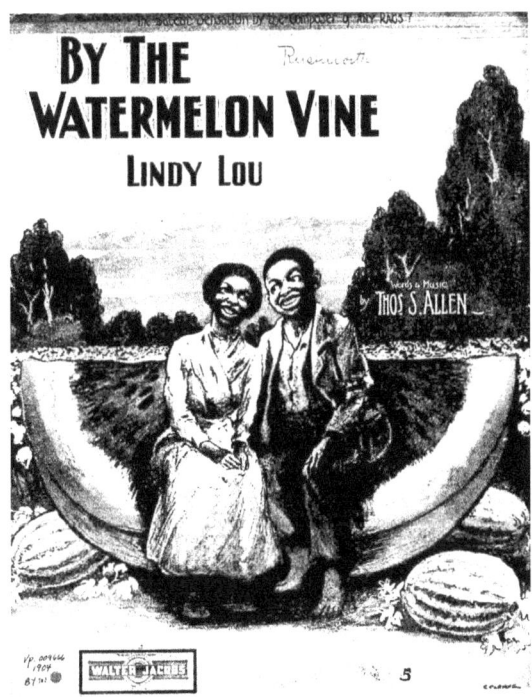

"By the Watermelon Vine," sheet music cover. *Author's collection.*

Hamberlin even carries his thesis from the sheet music to the recorded performance of "Strawberries." "In the recording, Arthur Collins sings in a pseudo-Italian accent with no trace of the Negro dialect used in other recordings."[71] Arthur Collins, the first singer to record a Thomas Allen song, recorded all three of the aforementioned songs. In 1903, he recorded "Any Rags?" "Scissors to Grind" followed soon after in 1904 and "Strawberries" in 1909. Collins also recorded Allen's "My Dusky Rose" in 1906.

Thomas Allen's fame as a songwriter went beyond the field of popular music. During the first drafts of his poem *The Waste Land*, author T.S. Eliot penciled in one of Allen's songs, "By the Watermelon Vine." In the final edit, the first fifty-four lines were dropped, and thus Allen's song was not included in the 1922 version of *Waste Land*. However, it must be noted that a famous author of the day knew Allen's songs and considered including them in his work. "Meet me pretty Lindy By The Watermelon Vine."[72]

So, how did a Boston songwriter end up in Rochester, New York? Allen made an early venture into the business end of music in about 1905 when he became business manager of the Edwin Bates musicians. After returning to playing violin at the Howard Theater in Boston, various biographical sources (*Canadian Musicians—International Military Bands of the World*; a contemporary publisher of a march by Allen; liner notes for an Edison cylinder recording; and Allen's obituary) have Thomas Allen moving to Rochester, New York, in 1911. Actually, according to articles in the November 26, 1910 Rochester newspaper *Democrat and Chronicle*, Allen was already in Rochester leading an orchestra at one of Rochester's prominent hotels, the Eggleston. The Eggleston Hotel, a popular establishment from 1898 to 1925, was located on Main Street.[73] The Rochester newspaper reports that Allen is "late of Boston," strongly suggesting his move to Rochester. A possible reason for his move may have been his 1910 divorce from wife, Jessie.

The 1913 Edward Meeker recording (Edison cylinder no. 1761) reveals even more information about Thomas S. Allen's Rochester connection. Liner notes, similar to those printed on the sleeves of vinyl records or CDs, were printed on a piece of paper and inserted in the tube along with the cylinder recording. Liner notes found in the tube with Edison cylinder no. 1761 have a biographic piece on Thomas S. Allen and a direct quote from Allen about the composition of "Low Bridge, Everybody Down":

> *When a boy in school, a picture of the Erie Canal in a geography, attracted my attention and I exclaimed: "If I ever see the Erie Canal, I'll think I've seen something worth seeing." It was not until a few years ago at Rochester that I ever did see the canal and I heard the expression "Low Bridge." It sounded good for a comic song so I wrote it up. Mr. F.B. Haviland also thought it good, so we inflicted it on the public.*[74]

The only evidence of the year Thomas S. Allen came to Rochester are the newspaper articles from November 1910. If, as he claims in the liner notes, that "it was not until a few years ago at Rochester, that I ever did see the Erie Canal," it would seem that 1912, the year "Low Bridge, Everybody Down" was copyrighted in manuscript, was the year Allen wrote the song.

The liner notes from the Meeker recording give Allen's occupation as leader of the orchestra at the Victoria Theatre in Rochester, New York. The Victoria Theatre was built in 1910 as a vaudeville theater and converted to a motion picture theater in 1912.

There are at least four sources (a biographic dictionary, newspaper articles, liner notes from a recording and an obituary) that place Thomas S. Allen in Rochester, New York. The *Rochester Democrat and Chronicle* articles place Allen in Rochester as early as 1910 and still in Rochester, leading an orchestra, in 1916. There is little doubt that Allen composed "Low Bridge, Everybody Down" in Rochester between the years of 1910 and 1912.

Some Other Coon Songs

1563 *Aunt Dinah's Golden Wedding*, Vaudeville
sketch   Empire Vaudeville Co.

1571 *Darktown Eccentricities*, Vaudeville sketch
       Golden and Hughes

1644 *Unlucky Mose*, Vaudeville sketch
       Golden and Hughes

1725 *Flanagan's Irish Jubilee*, Vaudeville sketch
       Steve Porter and Co.

1712 *Darky School Days*, Vaudeville sketch
       Golden and Hughes

1733 *Underneath the Cotton Moon* (MEYER) Coon song
       Billy Murray and Chorus

1591 *Buddy Boy* (WENRICH) Coon duet
       Arthur Collins and Byron G. Harlan

1735 *Georgia Land* (CARROLL) Coon song
       Walter Van Brunt and Chorus

1719 *When the Midnight Choo-Choo Leaves for
Alabam'* (BERLIN) Coon duet
       Collins and Harlan

1576 *Rap, Rap, Rap on Your Minstrel Bones* (VON
TILZER) Comic song   Edward Meeker

IF THIS RECORD APPEARS DIRTY OR SOILED ON THE SURFACE, IT
CAN BE CLEANED SUCCESSFULLY WITH A DAMP CLOTH.

Edison Record No. 1761

COON SONG, BARITONE
ORCHESTRA ACCOMPANIMENT

By EDWARD MEEKER

Low Bridge—Everybody Down

Music and Words by THOMAS S. ALLEN
Published by F. B. HAVILAND PUBLISHING CO., NEW YORK

THOMAS S. ALLEN, leader of the orchestra at the Victoria Theatre, Rochester, has what might be called an international reputation as a song writer, and his songs have become so popular that in one case, that of "Any Rags," it became so great an affliction that the public arose in wrath and suppressed it. Three publishers in Boston have been sorry ever since the song came out, for they had a "crack" at it, but turned it down. The sales of that piece went far over the 200,000 mark.

Another of Mr. Allen's compositions which threw the public into spasms of delight was "By the Watermelon Vine" or "Lindy Lou." Others of his bringing out are "My Heart Beats Alone For You," "My Dusky Rose," "Scissors to Grind," "On Yo' Way," "Wonderland," "Good-bye

Mr. Greenback," and that song which created such a sensation a season or two ago, "Mandy Lou."

Mr. Allen's songs have been decidedly successful, for the reason that the music is simple and especially catchy, so much so that the choruses can be remembered after one or two hearings.

Mr. Allen writes us about "Low Bridge" as follows: "When a boy in school, a picture of the Erie Canal in a Geography, attracted my attention and I exclaimed: 'If I ever see the Erie Canal, I'll think I've seen something worth seeing.' It was not until a few years ago at Rochester, that I ever did see the canal and I heard the expression 'Low Bridge.' It sounded good for a comic song so I wrote it up. Mr. F. B. Haviland also thought it good, so we inflicted it on the public."

Original cylinder slip for Blue Amberol no. 1761, "Low Bridge, Everybody Down," by Edward Meeker. *www.archeophone.com/archives.*

Another factor that points to the year 1912 as the year Allen composed his famous canal song is that before 1911, Allen published almost exclusively with Boston publishers. After his move to Rochester, he also used little-known Rochester publisher Lew Berk Music and New York publishers Haviland and Remick.

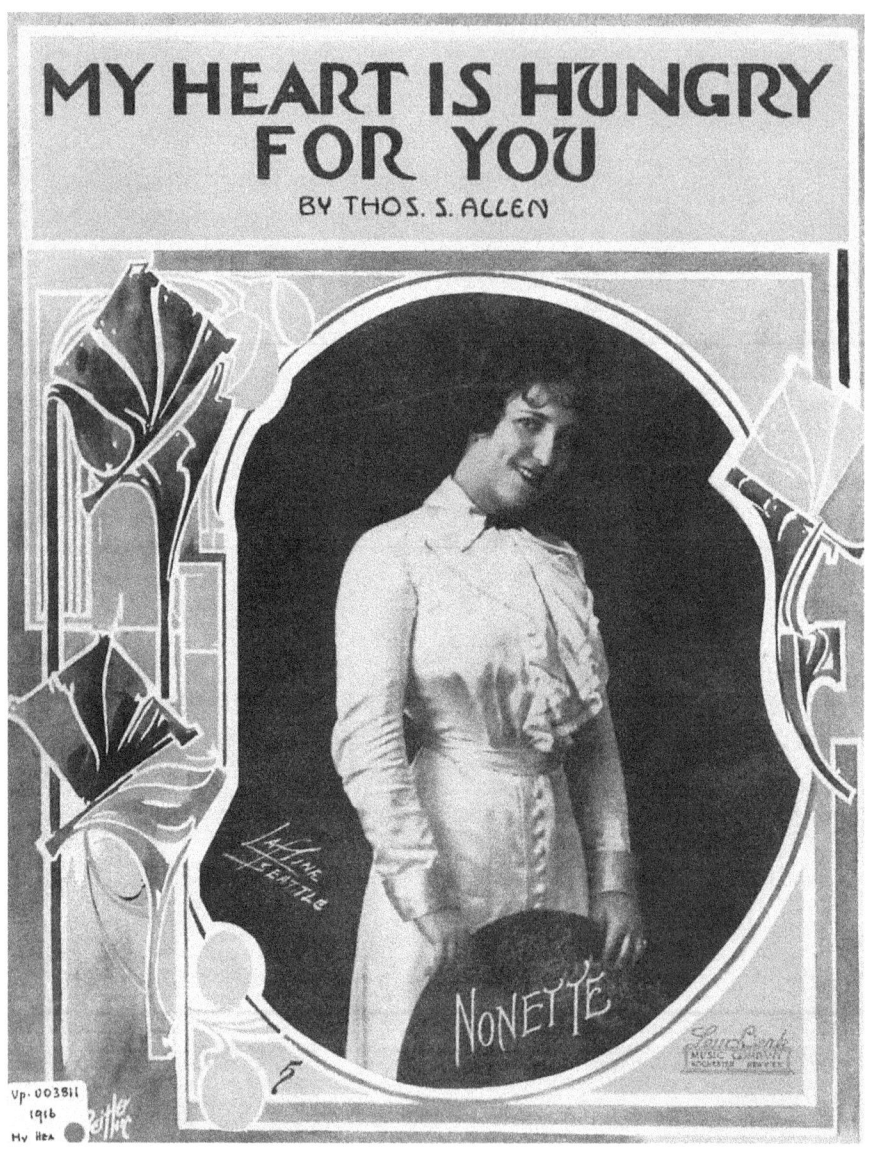

"My Heart Is Hungry for You" sheet music cover. *Author's collection.*

Allen continued to act in various capacities as a booking agent and manager of musical shows and later toured as musical director of the Hastings Burlesque Shows. Allen was still in Rochester in August 1915, when, according to an article in the *Democrat and Chronicle*, he was appointed

CHANGES IN THEATER STAFF.

New Orchestra Leader and New Stage
Manager at Family.

There will be some changes in the
house staff of the Family Theater with
the opening of the vaudeville season
which is announced for next Monday
when the C. B. Keith brand of vaudeville will be shown again. Thomas S.
Allen, a violinist and song writer, wil
take the position of leader of the orche
tra, held by Edward Hdye for two sea
sons. Henry Malone, formerly house
electrician, becomes stage manager, suc-
ceeding John A. Gilbert.

Newspaper clipping from *Rochester (NY)*
Democratic and Chronicle, August 27, 1915,
19. *Public domain.*

director of the Family Theater orchestra. The Family Theater, which began as Cook's Opera House, was built in 1891 as a musical and vaudeville venue. It was purchased by the Fenyvessy family in 1913.[75]

Allen's move to Rochester in 1910 explains some of the mystery behind the canal song "Low Bridge, Everybody Down." As noted earlier, the canal song is different in subject from Allen's other works. He published the canal song with New York publisher F.B. Haviland—"Low Bridge" is the only song Allen published with F.B. Haviland. This may have been a result of living in Rochester, or, possibly, Boston publishers were not interested in a song about a New York State canal. It has always been a mystery how this Tin Pan Alley composer from Boston became so familiar with the Erie Canal. In 1910, the Erie Canal passed right through the center of the city of Rochester, crossing the Genesee River on a long aqueduct. At that time, the canal was undergoing a big change from mule to motor (and steam), and Allen was in the right city at the right time to compose his famous tribute to the canal. As the canal was still open, Allen had contact with canallers who knew the canal and the passing of an era firsthand. Nostalgia for a lost era was running high.

The big change came in 1903 when New York State authorized forming the New York State Barge Canal System to improve the Erie, Oswego, Champlain and Cayuga-Seneca Canals. Construction began in 1905. Because boats now used motors, the towpath was no longer necessary and the path of the canal was altered to take advantage of natural waterways such as the Mohawk, Oswego, Seneca, Genesee and Clyde Rivers and Oneida Lake. The canal would now bypass the center of Rochester and Syracuse. Rochester's aqueduct over the Genesee River would be turned into a road bridge. The reconstruction, started in 1905, was completed in 1918. New Yorkers, and especially the people of Rochester, quickly latched onto a nostalgic song that told the story of a bygone era. The lyrics relate the last trip on the canal for an old canaller and his trusty mule that must look for another job after "just one more

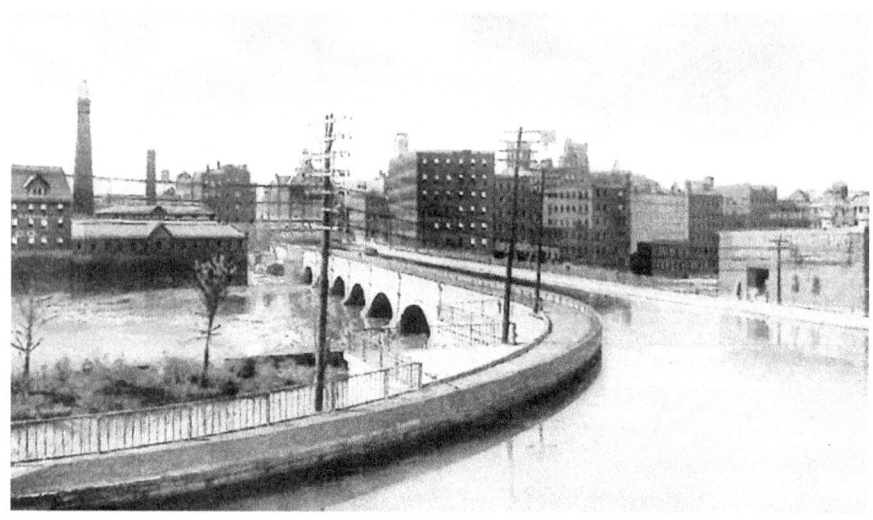

Aqueduct over the Genesee River, Rochester, New York. *Courtesy of Frank E. Sadowski, Jr.*

trip." Thomas Allen was there when one of the last canals in America abandoned the need for a pal like Sal.

So, now that we know who Thomas Allen was and that he did compose "Low Bridge, Everybody Down" around 1912, the big question is, is it original or did he merely use an already existing folk song, as Doubleday, Page and Company asserted in the publisher's 1928 lawsuit?

5

WHO PUT THE "BUFF" IN BUFFALO?

Doubleday-Page Publishers successfully challenged the originality of "Low Bridge, Everybody Down," and F.B. Haviland lost its lawsuit claiming copyright infringement. Haviland's lawyers might have won the lawsuit had they considered the following questions. Did the song appear in newsprint prior to 1912? Was the song in the oral tradition prior to 1912? Does the song contain any musical devices that are specifically associated with Thomas S. Allen?

Many American newspapers of the nineteenth and early twentieth centuries printed song lyrics as regular and occasional columns, often including submissions from readers who had an old favorite song. In fact, at least one of Thomas Allen's songs was found in a newspaper as far away as Oregon.[76] However, a comprehensive online search through historical newspapers prior to 1912 did not turn up a single reference to "Low Bridge, Everybody Down" or any fragment of lyrics from it. If a preexisting canal song mentioned a "mule named Sal," "low bridge everybody down," "15 years (or miles) on the Erie Canal," "16 Years…," or any other major phrases or permutations from Allen's song, it was never printed in an American newspaper. Both authors have spent considerable time over the past several decades studying the oral tradition as it relates to musical activities in nineteenth- and twentieth-century New York State. In our comprehensive and ongoing examinations of interviews, field recordings, folklore archives, published and unpublished folk song collections, graduate student papers and other sources, not a single reference to the song—or any major phrases

Thomas Allen song printed in the *Daily East Oregonian* (Pendleton, Oregon), July 21, 1911. *Public domain.*

contained within it—has been found prior to 1912, including singers who knew many canal songs. In fact, the song does not appear in the oral record at all until the mid-1920s, well after the first run of published recordings.

In 1923, folksong collector and scholar Robert Winslow Gordon was asked by Arthur Sullivant Hoffman to run the folk music column in Hoffman's magazine, *Adventure*.[77] Hoffman and Sinclair Lewis developed the famous Camp-Fire pages in *Adventure*, which featured readers' letters, biographies of the magazine's authors and Gordon's column Old Songs Men Have Sung. In 1924, Gordon was sent the lyrics to one verse and a chorus of "Low Bridge, Everybody Down" from reader Henry A.J. Castor of Albany, New York. Gordon replied, "Your enclosure interests me greatly; I have a number of 1924 issue of *Adventure* canal songs which have come in from various sailors, but none at all like this."[78] The following year, Gordon received a copy of "Low Bridge, Everybody Down" from another reader (this time with three of the original five verses) and said, "Certain things about it make me fairly certain that it originated on the vaudeville stage rather than on the canal, and that it is not very old."[79] F.B. Haviland's lawyers missed a golden opportunity when they failed to use Gordon as a witness.

So, is there a musical device that sets Thomas Allen apart from his fellow composers in the first two decades of the twentieth century? An

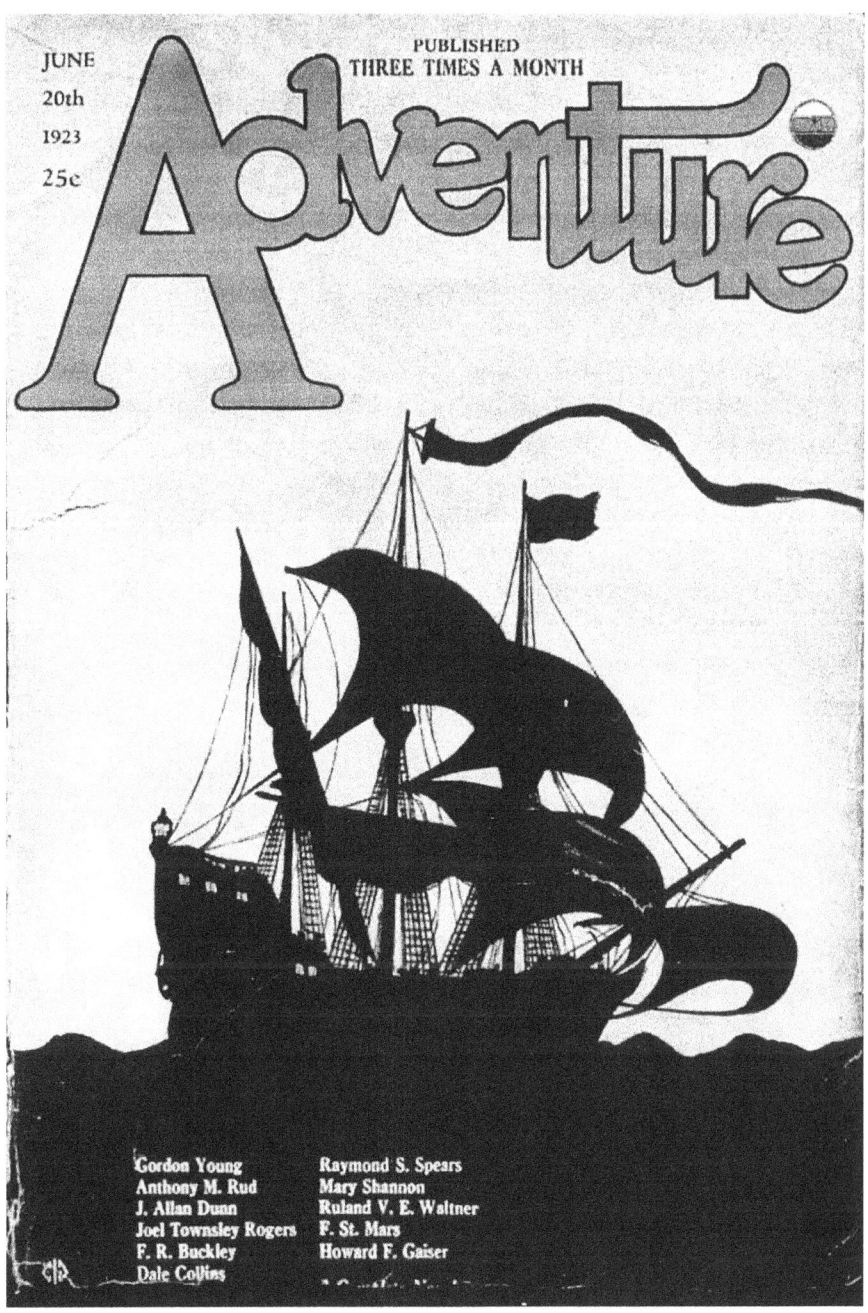

Adventure magazine cover, 1923. *Reproduced by the author.*

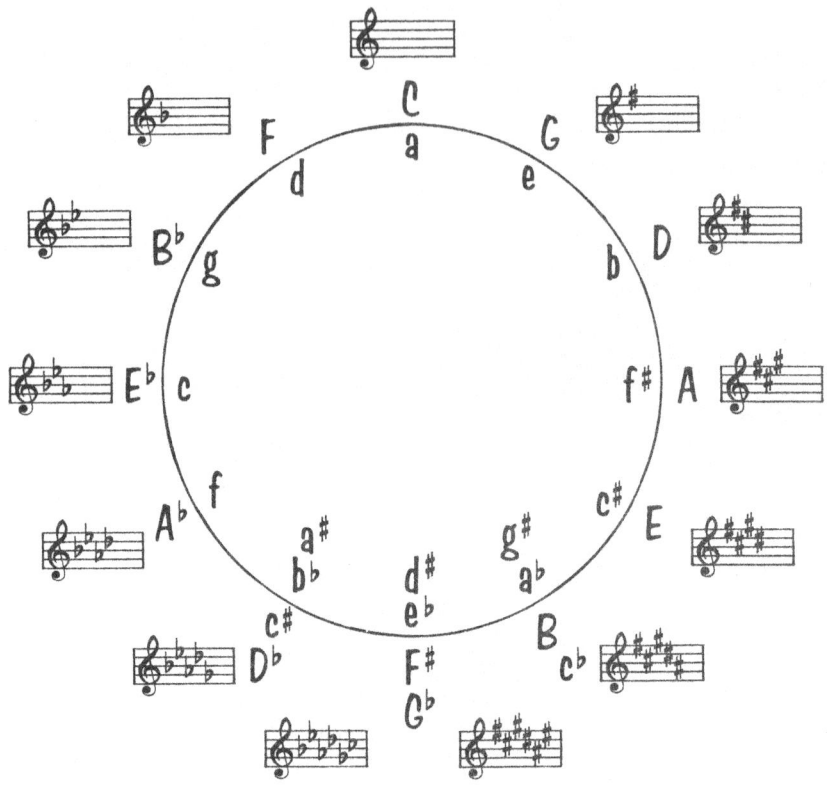

Circle of Fifths. *From William Hullfish,* Listening in Depth, *W.C. Brown, Dubuque, Iowa.*

analysis of "Low Bridge, Everybody Down" reveals that it is composed in the common popular song form with a series of verses followed by a chorus (or refrain)—nothing unusual here. However, what is musically unique about the song is that it uses an uncommon harmonic scheme for popular music during the first decades of the twentieth century. Verses are composed in the minor and choruses in the major.

For every key signature in Western music, two primary musical scales can be derived: the major and the minor scales (see the Circle of Fifths pictured here). The Circle of Fifths will help readers visualize the major and minor keys. The major keys are on the outside of the circle, and the minor keys are shown in lowercase letters on the inside of the circle. Just like a clock, the circle has twelve positions with C major and "a" minor at twelve o'clock. "Low Bridge, Everybody Down" has a key signature of one sharp, indicating either G major or E minor (one o'clock on the Circle of

Fifths). The tune uses both. The verses are in E minor, and the choruses are in G major.

How does that help us establish Thomas S. Allen as the composer of "Low Bridge, Everybody Down"? By looking at some of Allen's songs published before the copyright date of 1912 for "Low Bridge, Everybody Down," we can determine if the practice of composing verses in minor and choruses in major is a characteristic of Allen's style. Three of the songs discussed earlier, "Any Rags?," "Scissors to Grind" and "Strawberries," are a good place to start. Do any of these three songs have verses in minor and choruses in major?

"Any Rags?" has a key signature of one flat (eleven o'clock on the Circle of Fifths), indicating either F major or D minor, and Allen begins his introduction in D minor. There is a one-measure vamp (a repeated figure allowing the singer time to get ready) leading to a verse in D minor. The entire chorus is solidly in F major.

Introduction—D minor
Verse—D minor
Chorus—F major

Not only does "Any Rags?" pass the test of duplicating the harmonic scheme of "Low Bridge, Everybody Down," but in 1903, the year Allen's song "Any Rags?" was no. 1 on the charts for eight weeks, it was the only song in the top ten with a verse in minor and a chorus in major.[80]

What about "Scissors to Grind" (1904)? "Scissors to Grind" makes an easy comparison because it is in the same key as "Low Bridge, Everybody Down" (G major/E minor or one o'clock on the Circle of Fifths), and it passes the test. Just like "Low Bridge, Everybody Down," it has a verse in minor and a chorus in major.

Introduction—E minor
Verse—E minor
Chorus—G major

Does song number three have the same harmonic scheme as "Low Bridge, Everybody Down"? "Strawberries" (1909) is in three flats, which would indicate E-flat major or C minor (nine o'clock on the Circle of Fifths). Allen begins the introduction in C minor and continues through the verse. The chorus provides a little bit of suspense because it begins in C minor.

However, it shifts in the fifth measure to E-flat major, and from that point on E-flat major predominates. The transition from minor to major takes a little longer, but the chorus is definitely in E-flat major. All three songs pass the test.

> *Introduction—C minor*
> *Verse—C minor*
> *Chorus—C minor to E-flat major*

These examples, used earlier to demonstrate Thomas Allen's profound influence on the popular music of the early twentieth century, illuminate a new concept. "Any Rags?," "Scissors to Grind" and "Strawberries" clearly establish Allen's tendency to use verses in minor and choruses in major. Many more of Allen's songs also show this characteristic of writing the verses in minor and the choruses in the relative major. In fact, this is so much a characteristic of Allen's style that even a few marches, dances and rags that do not have the verse-chorus form employ this formula, too. Shifting from minor to major not only provides contrast, but it also provides a psychological lift to the music. Thomas Allen apparently liked the "lift" that it gave to his choruses so much, he employed the technique in many of his other compositions.

Since this practice was little used in the popular songs of the day, it is more evidence that Allen wrote "Low Bridge, Everybody Down" rather than, as has been sometimes suggested, borrowed the song from a previous source. Of the top ten songs on the *Billboard* chart for 1903, only one song had a verse in minor and chorus in major—Thomas Allen's "Any Rags?" All of the others, "In the Good Old Summertime," "Goodbye, Liza Jane," "Come Down, Ma Ev'ning Star," "In the Sweet Bye and Bye," "Hiawatha," "Hurray for Baffin's Bay" and "That's How the Little Girl Got On," have verses and choruses in a major key. ("In the Good Old Summertime" made the list twice under two different artists, and "Uncle Josh on an Automobile" is a comedic dialogue.)

In 1912, of the nine top hits on the *Billboard* chart ("That Haunting Melody," "Ragging the Baby to Sleep," "Come Down, Ma Ev'ning Star," "When You Were Sweet Sixteen," "Ragtime Cowboy Joe," "Everybody's Doing It Now," "Be My Little Baby Bumble Bee," "Waiting for the Robert E. Lee" and "Alexander's Ragtime Band," none has verses in minor. The last two are marches with the march strains and trio all in major. In the decade from 1903 to 1913, there were only three top-ten songs using the minor verse/major chorus formula: "Bedelia," by William Jerome and Jean Schwartz; "Moonlight Bay," by Percy Wenrich and Edward Madden; and Thomas S. Allen's own hit song, "Any Rags?"[81] During the same decade, Thomas Allen wrote dozens of compositions with minor verses and major choruses.

Thomas S. Allen turns out to be quite unique and innovative in the field of popular music in the first two decades of the twentieth century, having developed "street hawker" songs, Italian character songs and a characteristic harmonic scheme between the verse and chorus of his songs. Despite the fact that very little is known about Thomas S. Allen, his music lives on. Currently, "General Mix Up, USA," "Whip and Spur," "Turkish Towel—A Rub Down" and "Homespun Rag" are four of his numbers on YouTube. Allen's marches and galops appear on many contemporary recordings, including a version by the famed Eastman Wind Ensemble under the direction of Frederick Fennell. Allen's music continued to be used in other media. "Any Rags?" appeared in a cartoon starring Betty Boop in 1932. The 1935 movie *The Farmer Takes a Wife* used the song "Low Bridge, Everybody Down." The movie, made in the 1930s, is set in 1850, making the use of Allen's song a bit anachronistic to say the least.

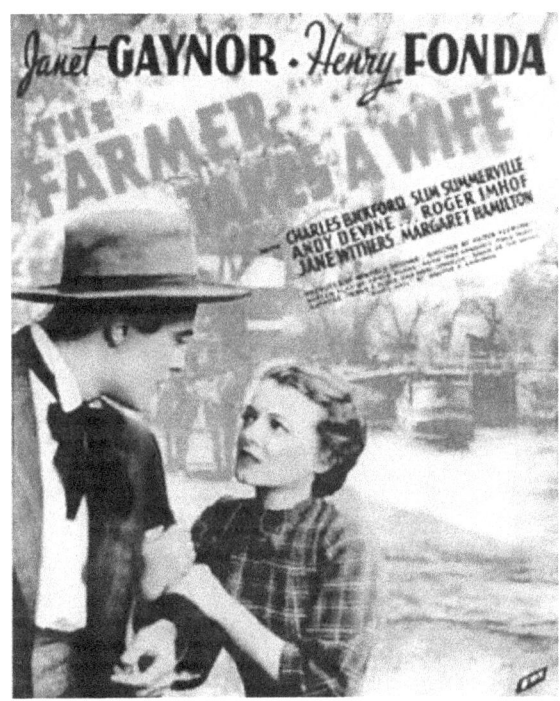

The Farmer Takes a Wife movie poster. *Reproduced by the author.*

Listening to and analyzing Thomas S. Allen's music, along with a few biographical details, go a long way in assessing his contributions and authorship of his most endearing work, "Low Bridge, Everybody Down." It very much casts doubt on Doubleday's assertion that the song was in circulation long before it was published, and it is doubtful that Allen composed the song in the frequently cited year of 1905. It is highly unlikely that the Boston performer/composer wrote a song about the Erie Canal this early in his career, and it is less likely that he waited so long to copyright it. Even compositions his publishers later printed in individual sheet music copies were copyrighted in earlier collections as soon as they were composed. ("Dance of the Skeletons" is a prime example.)

It is more likely that Thomas S. Allen wrote "Low Bridge, Everybody Down" shortly after arriving in Rochester, New York, in 1910 and before the song was recorded in 1912 and published in 1913. The liner notes for the 1913 recording help confirm this. In 1916, Allen published only two songs and, in 1917 and 1918, only one each year. The last composition to be published was "Dance of the Skeletons," by his first publisher, Walter Jacobs. According to concert programs, "Dance of the Skeletons" was published earlier in one of Jacob's collections but not published in individual sheet music form until 1918. Thomas S. Allen went out in style, starting "Dance of the Skeletons" in minor and ending in major.

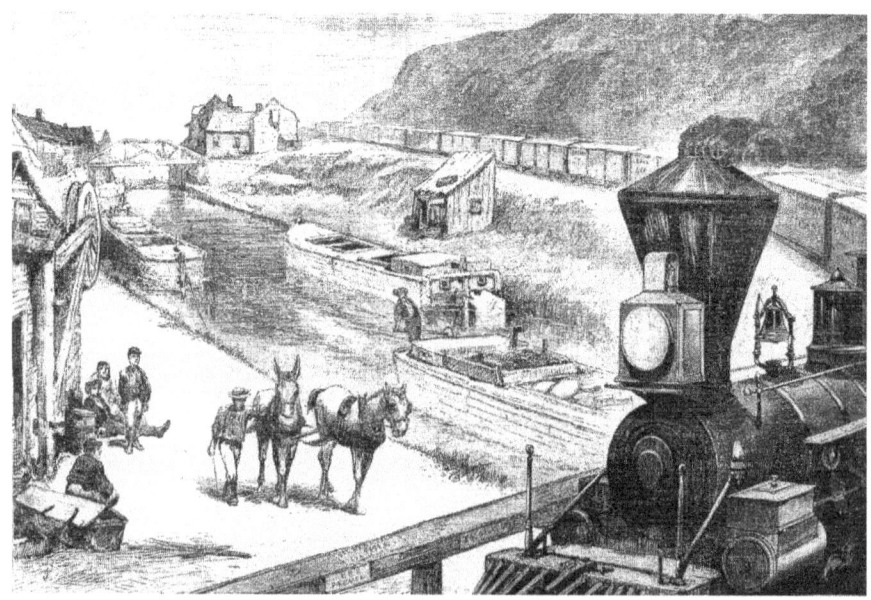

Canal and Railroad, from *Frank Leslie's Illustrated Newspaper*, 1873. *Reproduced by the author.*

In a twist of fate, after leaving Rochester, Allen was on tour with Harry Hastings' Big Show when he collapsed after a matinee in Syracuse, New York, at the Bastable Theater, on April 10, 1919. He was taken to Rochester and operated on the next day. His condition was reported as stomach cancer, but the actual diagnosis was worse. Thomas Allen spent the next six months in hospice care, dying on October 23, 1919, of colorectal cancer. Allen's obituary says that he died at his Boston Back Bay home after a long battle with "stomach cancer" at the age of forty-two.[82]

It is no wonder that over one hundred years after it was written, "Low Bridge, Everybody Down" still contributes to the nostalgia for the canal era. The canal era brought prosperity that would have been impossible without the water routes to move people and commodities to and from the interior of the country. Ironically, the very railroads developed to support the canals ended up leading to their demise. Canals were responsible for bringing in the first locomotives for the portage railroads they established. Railroad technology in America advanced because of what was learned from the railroads established by canal companies. "Low Bridge, Everybody Down" still reminds people of one of the most important eras of transportation in our history.

III

THE LIFE OF A CANALLER

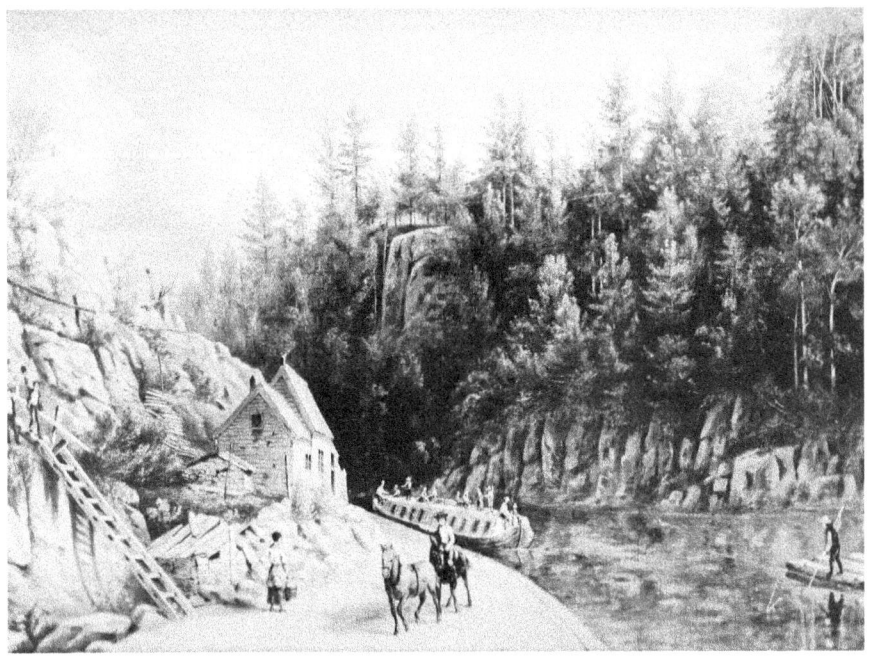

Erie Canal, Little Falls. The New York Public Library, Digital Collections, 1825, the Miriam and Ira D. Wallach Division of Art, Prints and Photographs.

6

CELEBRATION

Let the day be forever remembered with pride,
That beheld the proud Hudson to Erie allied.
—"Meeting of the Waters"

Cannons fired fifty-four rounds in honor of each county in the state of New York. The West Point Band, under the direction of Richard Willis, played "DeWitt Clinton's Grand Canal March" and DeWitt Clinton entered the canal from the Hudson River. This is how the second "opening" of the Erie Canal was celebrated. When the Erie Canal was completed to the Hudson River in 1823, this ceremony announced to the public that it was now possible to travel three hundred miles across New York State by canal, from Albany to Utica to Rome to Syracuse to Rochester and on to the village of Brockport. If this was the second ceremony, when and where was the first?

The first official opening of the Erie Canal was celebrated in October 1819 when Governor Clinton and his entourage made the initial trip on the Erie Canal from Rome to Utica and back. This ceremony announced to the citizens of New York that after only two years, they had a usable section of the canal. News reports may have avoided the fact that the canal bank broke on the first try and left the flotilla high and dry. After some quick repairs, the round trip from Rome to Utica was completed. Ceremonies, designed to announce a newly completed section of the canal, were common and necessary for informing the citizens and the legislature of the progress being made. How many official Erie Canal openings were there?

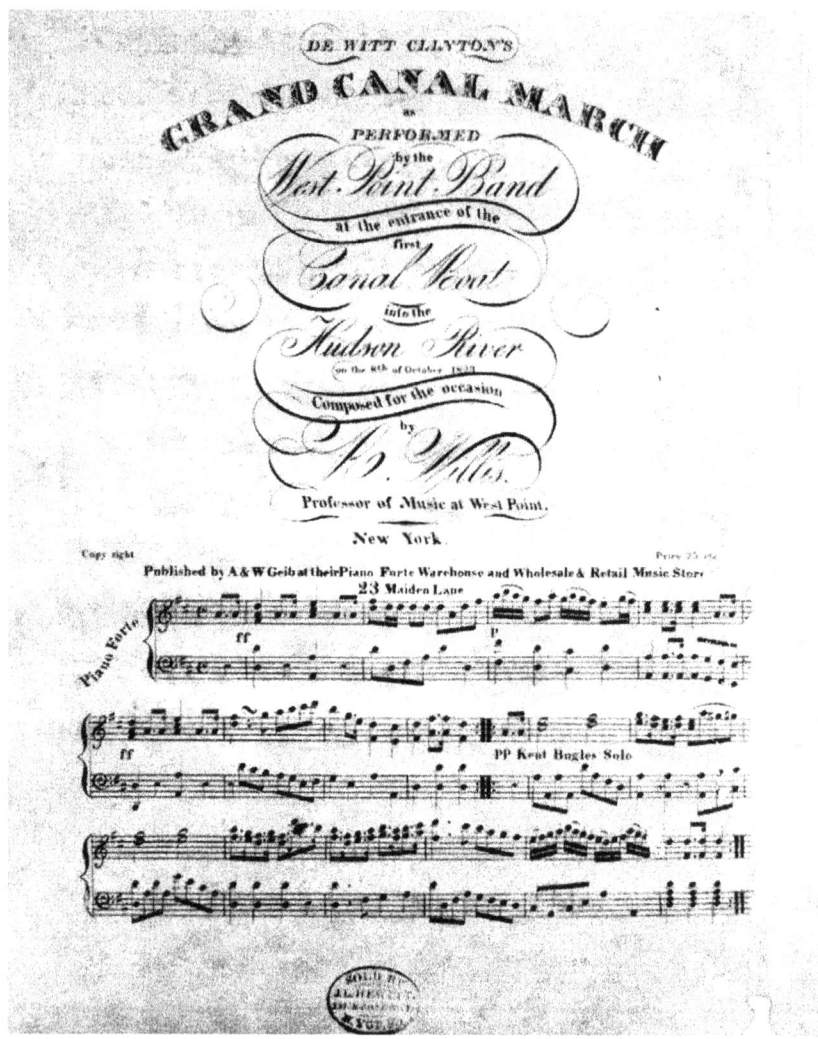

Sheet music for "DeWitt Clinton's Grand Canal March" by Richard Willis. *Lester Levy Sheet Music Collection.*

On October 29, 1825, the third opening ceremony took place. In fact, this turned out to be two ceremonies. Governor Clinton celebrated the opening of the entire canal in Buffalo and again as he entered New York Harbor after traveling from Lake Erie. These ceremonies announced to the whole country the completion of a water route from the Atlantic Ocean to the Great Lakes, and that announcement sparked a flurry of canal construction that launched the canal era.

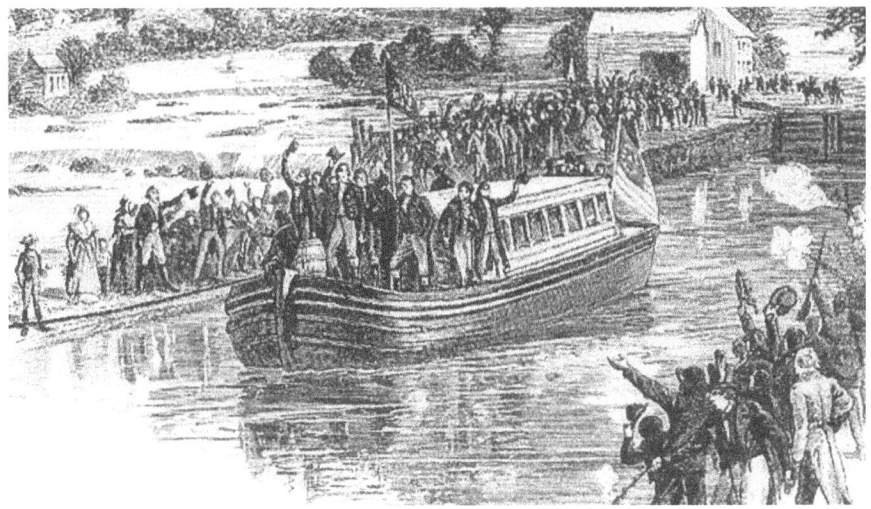

Opening of the Erie Canal—an engraving of a print by Howard Pyle (1853–1911). From "The Evolution of New York," by Thomas A. Janvier, in *Harper's New Monthly Magazine* 87, no. 517 (June 1893). *Courtesy of Frank E. Sadowski, Jr.*

On the morning of October 26, 1825, to the sounds of a choir singing the "Celebration Ode," the first flotilla of canalboats bound for New York Harbor left Buffalo, starting at the signal of a cannon fired at the entrance to the canal from Lake Erie. This shot was echoed, guns having been stationed at regular intervals the whole length of the new waterway, down the Hudson to New York City; precisely one hour and twenty-five minutes after the first gun was fired beside the lake, the last cannon was heard beside the Atlantic Ocean. During the next hour and twenty-five minutes, the answer from the ocean to the inland waters came thundering back to the Great Lakes.

Neither of the dedication songs for the opening of the Erie Canal were sung by canallers, but they are still important in telling the story of the canal era. Both of the dedication songs used tunes borrowed from well-known songs of the day, one American and one European. The American melody, used for the celebration song in Buffalo, was first composed for another important event, the inauguration of our first president. Philadelphia composer Philip Phile wrote a march for the inauguration of George Washington in 1789 ("The President's March"). Joseph Hopkinson added words to the melody in 1798, and it became known as "Hail, Columbia."[83] The "Celebration Ode," sung as the *Seneca Chief*, with DeWitt Clinton aboard, left Buffalo in October 1825, borrowed Philip Phile's melody for a second time.

"Celebration Ode"[84]

Strike the lyre with joyous note, Let the sound through azure float,
The task is o'er, the work complete, And Erie's waves with ocean meet,
Bearing afar their rich bequest, While smiling commerce greets the west.
See where the peaceful waters glide, Thru woodlands wild, as if in pride,
To mark that learning makes her home, Where solitude had set her throne,
Strike the lyre! 'tis envy's knell, Pallid fear within her cell,
Shrinks aghast while truth and fame, On glory's scroll 'grave Clinton's name.

When Clinton and his entourage reached the Hudson, the West Point Band again played "DeWitt Clinton's Grand Canal March." The continuation of the third opening celebration took place in New York Harbor. This, too, was celebrated with a dedication song.

At five o'clock on the morning of November 4th this fresh-water cyclone completed the last stage of its eventful progress "a grand procession, consisting of nearly all the vessels in [the] port [of New York] gaily decked with colors of all nations," went down to the lower bay where Governor Clinton, from the deck of the United States schooner Dolphin, poured a libation of the fresh water brought from Lake Erie into the salt water of the Atlantic Ocean and so typified the joining together of the inland and the outland seas.[85]

In the early nineteenth century, the music popular in the United States was mostly European. Songwriters such as Sir Thomas Bishop ("Home, Sweet Home"), Robert Burns ("Coming Through the Rye," "Auld Lang Syne," "Highland Mary") and Thomas Moore ("Believe Me If All Those Endearing Young Charms," "The Last Rose of Summer," "The Minstrel Boy") dominated American popular music. The dedication song for the celebration in New York Harbor was sung to the well-known nineteenth-century song about the meeting of the Avonbeg and Avonmore Rivers in County Wicklow, Ireland. Irish poet Thomas Moore wrote "The Meeting of the Waters" and set it to the tune "Old Head of Dennis." "The Meeting of the Waters" was popular in America in the 1820s and would have been familiar to American audiences.

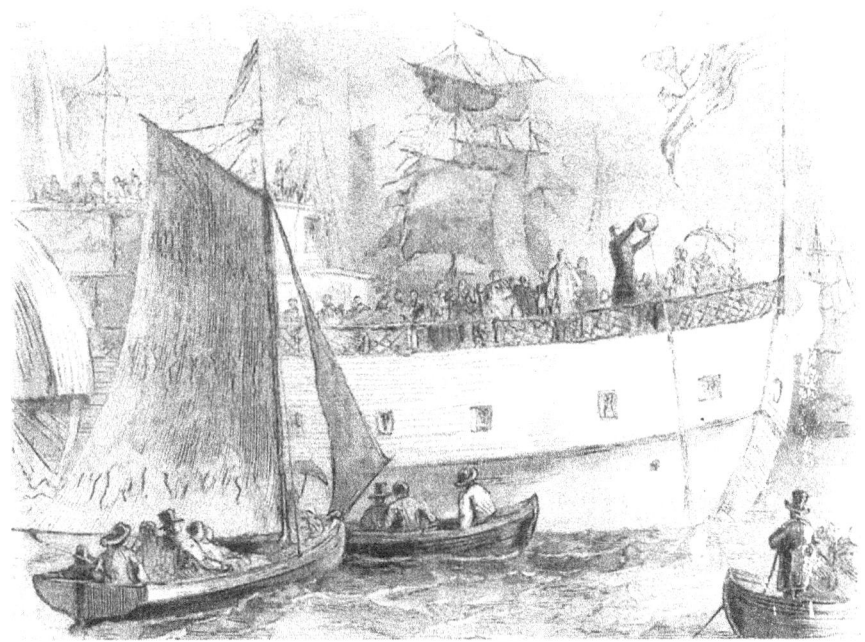

Wedding of the Lakes with the Ocean. From Our Country, *book five, chapter 17, page 1,331; courtesy of Frank E. Sadowski Jr.*

"The Meeting of the Waters"[86]

There is not in this wide world a valley so sweet
As that vale in whose bosom the bright waters meet!
Oh the last rays of feeling and life must depart
Ere the bloom of that valley shall fade from my heart
Ere the bloom of that valley shall fade from my heart.

Moving from a song about a natural meeting of the waters of two rivers to a man-made meeting between an ocean and a lake, Samuel Woodworth fashioned the "Meeting of the Waters of the Hudson and the Erie." The song was sung by a Mr. Keene at the Meeting of the Waters Ceremony in New York Harbor in 1825.

"Meeting of the Waters of the Hudson and the Erie"[87]

Let the day be forever remembered with pride,
That beheld the proud Hudson to Erie allied,

Oh, the last sand of time from his glass shall descend,
E'er a union so fruitful of glory shall end,
E'er a union so fruitful of glory shall end.

Although the wedding of waters was a remarkable achievement, and most celebrations and dedication songs tend toward hyperbole, the third verse of the dedication song "Meeting of the Waters of the Hudson and the Erie" cannot be ignored for its obvious chauvinism:

'Tis that genius has triumphed and science prevailed,
Tho' prejudice flouted and envy assailed,
It is that the vassals of Europe may see,
The progress of mind in a land that is free,
The progress of mind in a land that is free.

Prejudice flouted? Irish workers who were poorly paid, worked in terrible conditions and were discriminated against by Americans who feared immigrants would hardly have agreed with the line "Tho' prejudice flouted." Although Irish workers sang of their joy in obtaining a job and having

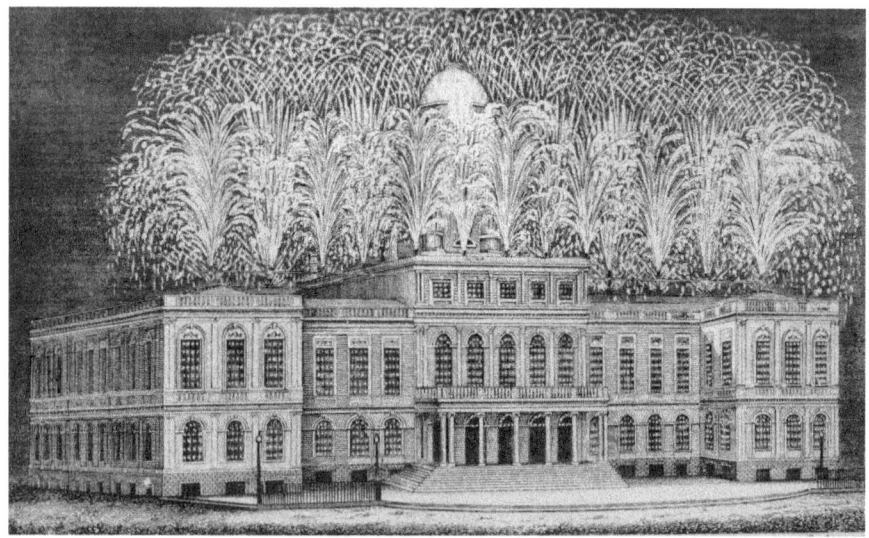

"A view of the magnificent and extraordinary fire works exhibited on the N.Y. City Hall, on the evening of the celebration of the Grand Canal, November 4th, 1825." *Courtesy of* the New York Public Library Digital Collections.

enough food, they turned to sarcasm, or Irish "black humor," to complain about the tendency of their bosses to withhold wages for little or no reason.

A new foreman was Gene McCanna,
By God he was a blaming man
Last week a premature blast went off,
A mile in the air went Big Jim Croft.

When next payday came around
Jim Croft was about a dollar down.
When he asked, "Why?", came the reply,
"You were docked for the time you spent in the sky."[88]

Vassals of Europe? Apparently, Samuel Woodworth, author of the lyrics, was unaware that "the vassals of Europe" were not only the "geniuses" who built canals before we did but also that much of the success of America's canal construction came from information gathered from "the vassals of Europe." As construction began on the Erie Canal, a young, aspiring civil engineer named Canvass White headed to Europe on his own, with no funding from New York State. He took meticulous notes during months of fact-finding along canals in Great Britain.

The "vassals of Europe" supplied a key ingredient for the successful completion of the Erie Canal. Workers, in the early stages of construction on the Erie Canal, were having considerable problems with the aqueducts, culverts and walls. The cement used to fill in the spaces between the rocks and line these structures was unstable, breaking down under pressure. Leaks as well as rot were already developing, requiring constant relining of the canal walls and aqueducts. One of White's important discoveries in Europe was the secret of "hydraulic cement," or cement that hardened under water. The British were using hydraulic cement in their canals, after it was "re-discovered" by civil engineer John Smeaton to construct the Eddystone Lighthouse. Canvass White returned to the United States and began the search for the special type of lime mix necessary for making hydraulic cement. The search was eventually successful in locating just such a deposit of lime, and White obtained a patent for American hydraulic cement. Gerard Koeppel, in his book *Bond of the Union*, states, "Hydraulic cement was the most important discovery in all of the years of Erie construction."[89] There were many other engineering ideas brought back from Europe by Canvass White that helped in canal construction in

America. As it turns out, the "vassals of Europe" had much to contribute to "a land that is free."

When all the dedications were over, it was time for canallers to go to work. Although much of the canal had been in use for many years, the completion of the Erie Canal opened the floodgates of immigrants and commerce.

In eighteen-hundred and forty-three, I sailed across the deep blue sea,
I sailed across the deep blue sea, to work upon the Erie, the E-ri-e,
I'm weary of the E-ri-e, Poor Paddy works on the Erie.

In eighteen-hundred and forty-four, I landed on Columbia's shore,
I landed on Columbia's shore, to work upon the Erie, the E-ri-e,
I'm weary of the E-ri-e, Poor Paddy works on the Erie.
—*Canal song, "Paddy Works on the Erie"*[90]

CANALLERS AT WORK AND PLAY

The Erie Canal inspired more music per mile
than any other link in the Great Lakes waterway.
—*Ivan Walton,* Windjammers

After the canal construction songs ("The Digging Song" and "Paddy on the Canal") and the celebration songs ("Celebration Ode" and "Meeting of the Waters of the Hudson and the Erie"), the story of the canal era continued to be told through the musical diaries of the men and women who plied the inland waterways. The musical diaries of the canallers turned to everyday life on the canal. The Erie Canal was completed and dedicated so late in the season (November 4) that most of the canallers had to wait until 1826 to manage a full season of work on the entire canal. How long did they work on the canal in a typical full season? There is no definitive answer since the length of the season depended upon the weather. Some canal songs give a very general idea of the length of a season:

> *A life on the raging canal, a home on its muddy deep,*
> *Where through summer, spring and fall, the frogs their vigils do keep.*[91]

and

> *Off, Up, with your hats, give three cheers, now three more,*
> *We're afloat, We're afloat, after four months on shore.*[92]

Four months may be typical for the northernmost canals. On the Erie Canal, December, January, February and March would normally be the four months when the canal did not operate. For an exact figure of the operating days for most canals in the North, it is necessary to consult a newspaper. In the first twenty-nine years of operation, the longest period of navigation was in 1828, when boats ran for a period of 269 days. The name of the canal is not given—at this time, every canal was simply called "the raging canal." We may assume because of the New York location of the newspaper that it was a northern canal. The canal ceased to operate for three months and three days and that was a record that stood for at least twenty-one years.

> *The longest period of navigation on the "raging canal" was in 1828, when boats ran for a period of 269 days.*
> —Brooklyn (NY) Daily Eagle, *Saturday, December 8, 1849, 2*

When the canal opened for the new season, it is not surprising that canallers celebrated with "Off, Up, with your hats, give three cheers, now three more." Another canal song greets the opening day with the same enthusiasm:

> *Canal's wide open with the spring,*
> *Canal boat people dance and sing.*
> *Wake up, canal boys, wake, Wake up canal boys, wake,*
> *Pull off your coats and load the boats, get ready to go in the morning.*[93]

With the canal wide open in the spring, the canallers sang about their boats, draft animals, work, recreation, food, fears and the bonds they had with one another. A favorite subject for canal songs was the particular conveyance chosen by the canaller. The canalboat was not only their workplace, but for many their home as well. When the canal closed for the season, canallers often lived on their boats year-round. As canallers came to the end of their working years, their canalboat became their retirement home:

> *A very odd little craft is moored to the berm bank of the canal under the Washington Street bridge. It is about one-third the length of an ordinary canal boat, and is fitted as a house. It has been at or near its present location for nearly nine years, and is the home of Captain Andrew Vincent and his wife.*
> —Democrat and Chronicle (Rochester, NY), *July 2, 1889, 6*

Captain Vincent was not the only canaller who made his "permanent" home on the canal. Sometime in the years after the Ohio and Erie Canal closed in 1913, Captain Nye pulled a canalboat up on the bank, dubbed it "Camp Charming" and made it his home.

What were the types of canalboats the canallers sang about? Just about every type of canalboat finds its way into canal song. "The E-ri-e" mentions two types of boats in one verse, a laker and a scow, as well as their place of origin:

> *"The E-ri-e"*
>
> *Oh, lay me on the horse-bridge.*
> *With my feet up toward the bow,*
> *And let it be a Lockport* Laker,
> *Or a Tonawanda* Scow.[94]

"I'm Afloat on the Raging Canal" is another canal song that mentions the scow:

> *"I'm Afloat on the Raging Canal"*
>
> *I'm afloat! I'm afloat! On the Raging canal*
> *Its wave is my home and my* scow *beats them all.*[95]

The scow was a short canal work boat, square at the bow and stern. It was the cheapest boat to build and often did not have a deck. The scow was generally used to haul coal, sand and gravel.[96] One observer described a scow as "a hole in the water lined with wood."[97] Just tilt the coal cart into a chute and fill her up. In a firsthand account of a trip on New York waterways, William Rideing describes a scow:

> *Ungainly as the regulation canal-boat is, she is a thing of beauty compared*
> *with the scow, which has neither shape nor color nor comfort, and is sworn*
> *at, necessarily or unnecessarily, every time she is passed on the canal.*[98]

A laker was a mule-drawn boat with a rounded bow, completely decked, and usually used for hauling grain. A laker, as the name implies, plied the canals and the lakes. The laker was towed, in a flotilla of other boats, on Lake Champlain and the Great Lakes by a steamer. However, the laker had a flat bottom and was unstable in crosswinds on the lakes.[99] Many of the boats carried their own mules onboard. One other item mentioned in the first line of "The E-ri-e—"Oh, lay me on the horse bridge"—mentions the horse bridge, a small, portable ramp used to load and unload mules. The horse bridge was usually kept on deck, and the crew member in the song is using it for a back rest as he sits on deck with his feet up toward the bow. William Totten, who was a towpath boy driving mules on the Erie Canal, writes about the practice of holding on to the mule's tail as the animal is loaded and unloaded on the horse bridge. The practice of "tailing" a mule was a common way of steadying the mule on the narrow horse bridge:

> He "tailed" the mules from boat to shore,
> And drove till the bridge chains clanked,
> Then, happily, with six hours o'er,
> "Tailed" them in from the bank.

A line in the parody "I'm Afloat on the Raging Canal" sings about "prim painted packets right past us may souse."[100] The alliteration is nice, but this brings up the subject of another type of canalboat—a packet boat.

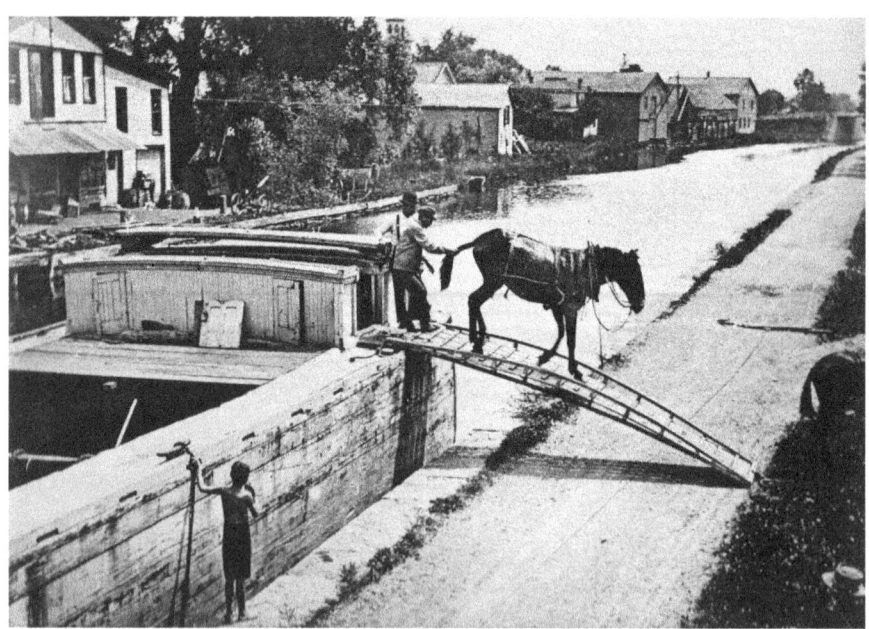

Offloading a mule using a horse bridge. *Courtesy of Frank E. Sadowski Jr.*

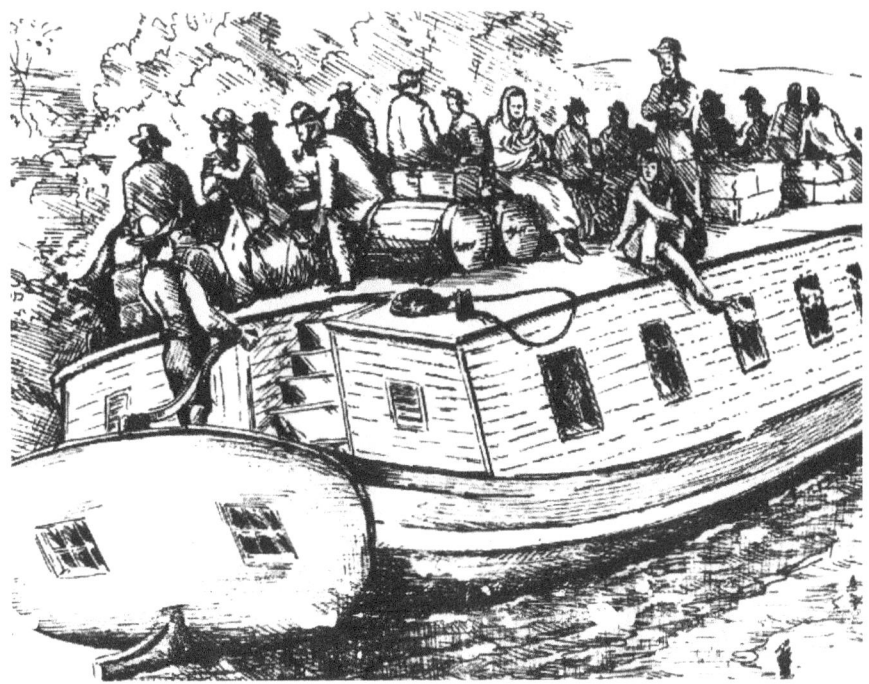

Packet boat. *Courtesy of Frank E. Sadowski Jr.*

Compared to work boats like the scow and laker, they were prim, painted and long and narrow. These boats hauled passengers and, in the beginning, mail. They were pulled by horses because they were faster. Packet boats were given the right-of-way on the canals. That right-of-way extended to passing boats going in the same direction and meeting boats going in the opposite direction. At one time, Brockport, New York, produced more packet boats at Heil Brockway's boatyard than anywhere in the world. The Red Bird Line ran a packet boat that was 100 feet long—too long for any of the original Erie Canal locks. The original locks were only designed for canalboats 69 feet long. The Red Bird Line served as express boats in the two long levels (no locks): Syracuse to Utica and Rochester to Lockport. Between 1836 and 1862, the size of the locks was increased to 110 feet long and 18 feet wide. As the locks were enlarged, the 100-foot packets could travel most of the canal.

"The Gay Old Packet Line," a song from the Ohio and Erie Canal, describes life on a passenger boat.[101] This musical diary tells us that other boats had to yield to the packets ("She had right of way"), that they carried mail ("passengers and mail were hers when she'd sail"), the number of miles the horses pulled ("Relays—each ten miles they rest for a while") and the names of packet boats (*Meteor* and *Queen of Time*).

"The Gay Old Packet Line"

Passengers and mail were hers when she'd sail, Gay Old Packet Line,
Her schedule she kept, had plenty of pep, Gay Old Packet Line,
For she had the right-of-way, yes, let come what may,
She was in grace, feeling fine,
The best, like the Meteor, this canal navigator,
Her beauty, Queen of Time.

"The Gay Old Packet Line" references another canal song, "A Life on the Raging Canal," in its lyrics ("Like frogs in a squall" and "on the dull shore I repine"). "A Life on the Raging Canal" is about a canaller who longs for the speed of a packet boat ("Oh, give me the packet line").

Like a fish on the hook I pine,
On this dull, unchanging shore,
Oh, give me the packet line,
And the muddy canal's dull roar.[102]

The construction of some canalboats contributed to injuries and deaths at low bridges. The bullhead boat was infamous for its high decking ("decked up to the cabin's top") and the narrow distance between the deck of the boat and the underside of canal bridges. "Boating on a Bullhead" tells the story of one unlucky young driver who failed to recognize the dangers of the high-decked boat:

"Boating on a Bullhead"[103]

1. I was sleepin' in a line barn, and eatin' beans and hay,
While the boss was kickin' my stern around, ev'ry night and ev'ry day
So I hired out canalling as a horny hand of toil.
Drivin' mule that kept a-bawlin' on the towpath's smelly soil.

The lyrics mention working in a line barn ("I was sleepin' in a line barn"). The line barns were usually associated with shipping companies

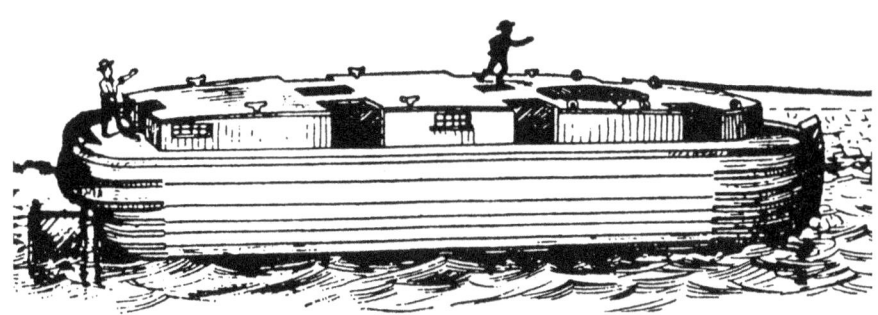

Bullhead boat (from a woodcut in *Rochester and Its Early Days*, 1914). Type of Rochester built bullhead boat, "The Omvard." *Reproduced by the author.*

that supplied fresh animals about every ten to twelve miles along the canal. Some of them rented out teams to individual boats. A canal captain in Rochester reported paying fifty cents a mile to hire his team.

> *The boats were usually contracted for towing by owners of stables, and he had at times paid 50 cents per mile for towing. The price of freight on merchandise from Albany to Rochester was $20 a ton. Captain Vincent said that wheat had been carried to Buffalo the present season for 2.5 cents per bushel and 4 cents was considered high. At these prices boatman could save nothing.*
> —Democrat and Chronicle *(Rochester, NY), July 2, 1889, 6*

While the captain complained about costs, the driver complained about sore feet, corns, blisters and treading behind the mules "on the towpath's smelly soil." The captain could barely save any money, and on top of that it was difficult to hire and keep good drivers.

> *2. Well, my feet raised corns and blisters and the mules but raised a stink,*
> *I took and threw them twisters into the dirty drink,*
> *I thought I'd give up drivin' and the Cap he thought so, too,*
> *He said, "Hire out a divin' or go bowin' a canoe."*

The lyric in the third verse mentions the heel path ("I was sittin' on the heel path watchin' boats haul up and down") and brings up the difference between the two sides of the canal. One side was the towpath, and the opposite side was the heel path. The towpath did not always stay on the same side. Natural or man-made obstructions, such as towns or rock cliffs, required a change to the opposite side of the canal. The usual means of changing sides was the change bridge—a bridge that worked somewhat like the modern highway cloverleaf, allowing the mules to change sides of the canal without being unhitched. In the photograph of the Whipple Iron Truss Change Bridge, the towpath is on the left until the canal reaches the Schenectady Bluffs. Here the mules would cross the bridge, the towline sliding over the unobstructed bridge railing. Upon reaching the far side of the canal, the team would turn right and follow the circular path down and under the bridge, where they would continue on the towpath, which was now on the right side. An observant viewer might notice that the path seems to continue under the bridge on the left side of the picture. The path is part of the cloverleaf, which is not visible on the far side of the bridge. This cloverleaf would be used by teams going in the opposite direction.

> *3. I was sittin' on the heel path watchin' boats haul up and down,*
> *A-shiverin' from the first good bath I got since I left town,*
> *When a boat hauled in the basin at the wood dock for the night,*
> *And I lost no time to hasten 'round to ask them for a bite.*

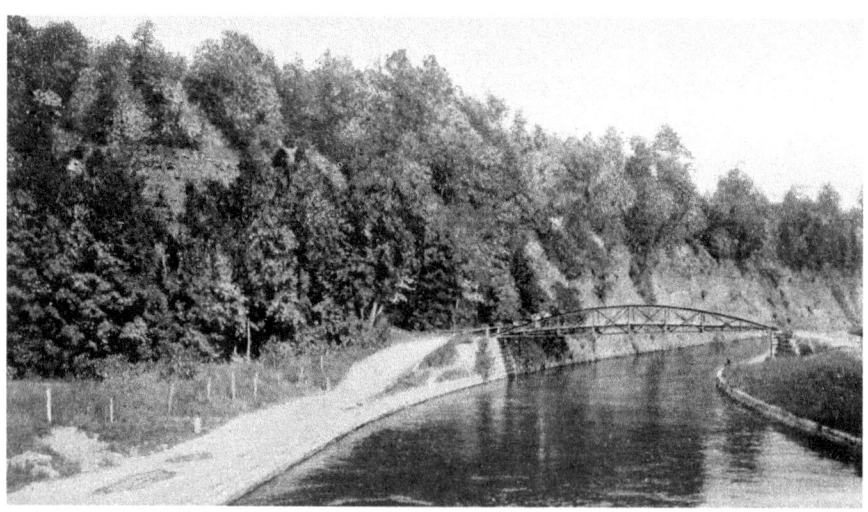

Erie Canal change bridge, Schenectady Bluffs, circa 1900. *Author's collection.*

The singer of this song has now graduated from line barn worker to driver to steersman. He considers this quite a promotion, but his unfamiliarity with a bullhead boat could cause the steersman, "watching the driver hoof," potential problems.

> *4. Well, they filled me up with beans and shote and offered me a cob,*
> *They asked if I could steer a boat and they offered me a job,*
> *The next mornin' I was boosted to the stern cabin's roof,*
> *To the tiller there I roosted and I watch the driver hoof.*

The position of the steersman on "the stern cabin's roof" is a clue to why this job was more dangerous than most. A note in a canal diary relates that not only were the crew in some danger but also the passengers. "Some serious accidents have happened for want of caution. A young English Woman met with her death a short time since, she having fallen asleep with her head upon a box, had her head crushed to pieces."[104] The passengers and the steersman, who usually stood in a well, were required to duck when approaching a bridge.

> *5. The boat she was a bullhead decked up to the cabin's top,*
> *Many canallers now are dead who had no place to drop,*
> *When the bowsman he forgot to yell, "Low bridge, duck'er down,"*
> *The bullhead steersman went to Hell with a bridge-string for a crown.*

The lyrics also mention the cargo the bullhead boat is hauling—salt ("We were loaded up with Star Brand salt"). Salt was an important commodity, because before refrigeration salt was needed to cure meat for storage. The "Salt City" (Syracuse, New York) supplied most of the salt used in the United States. The Erie Canal was called "the ditch that salt built." Salt tax revenues paid for half the cost of constructing the canal. It was no accident that the first section of canal curved south from Rome to Salina (Syracuse).[105]

> *6. We were loaded up with Star Brand salt, the Captain was loaded, too,*
> *I wouldn't say it was all his fault but what's a man to do?*
> *The bridge was only a heave away when I saw it 'round the bend,*
> *To the Cap a word I didn't say while tumblin' end o'r end.*

Many occupational songs warn of dangers, offer advice, or have a moral. This song warns of the dangers of bullhead boats and low bridges and offers the advice that the canal worker would have been better off foregoing all the "promotions" and keeping his original job. The moral might be "beware of what you wish for."

> *7. So canallers take my warnin', never steer a bullhead boat,*
> *Or they'll find you some fair mornin' in the E-ri-e afloat,*
> *Do all your navigatin' from a line barn filled with hay,*
> *Low bridge you won't be hatin' and you'll live 'til Judgment Day.*

"Boating on a Bullhead" tells about the job to be done by each member of the crew, the type of canalboat, what it takes to be successful (or in this case unsuccessful), the cargo and the dangers of the job. The singer starts as a worker in a line barn and ends up right back there after his ill-fated journey on a bullhead boat.

Another type of canalboat was the sectional boat. The sectional boat, or hinged boat, consisted of two or three separate, watertight sections hinged at the sides and were necessary on canals with inclined planes and tight, narrow bends. Hinged boats were unnecessary on the Erie, and there are no Erie Canal songs that refer to them. However, they were found in New York State on the Delaware and Hudson Canal, where they were referred to as "squeezers." The name was thought to have come from a lemon squeezer—an implement with two handles hinged together.

> *'Round and 'round the Wurtsboro bend,*
> *The big boat chased the squeezer,*
> *Pat Flax's boat had passed them both,*
> *Slicker than a weasel, Slicker than a weasel.*[106]

The hinged boats were also sung about on the Lehigh Canal and the Morris Canal. Lehigh boats continuing on the Morris Canal required hinges to accommodate the inclined planes.

> *Pete was at the hinges and Patsy at the bow,*
> *Mike was at the tiller, showing them how.*[107]

Three-part hinged boats were used on Pennsylvania's Main Line Canal to accommodate the boats being hauled over the Allegheny Portage Railroad, which consisted of ten inclined planes.

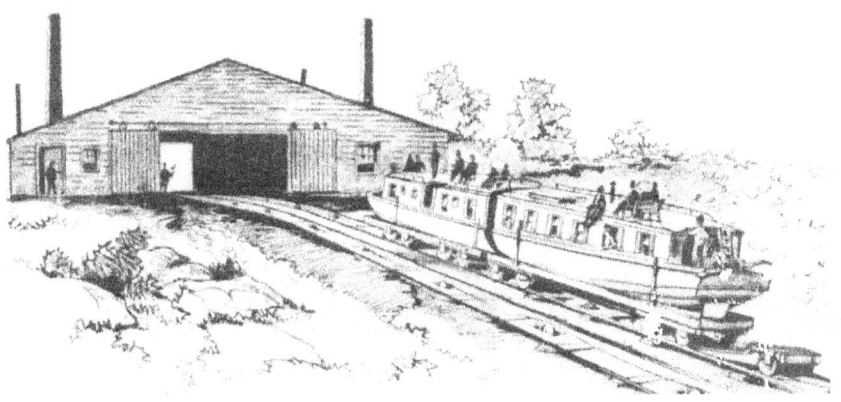

Two sections of a canalboat on inclined plane no. 6, Allegheny Portage Railroad, 1839, from a drawing by George Storm. *Reproduced by the author.*

MULE POWER

Of course, one of the big differences between canallers and Great Lakes sailors was the way the boats were propelled. Sailors referred to canallers as "horse-ocean sailors." A more accurate term might be "mule-ocean sailor," since canallers preferred mules to horses for work boats. Many of the occupational songs of the canal were about the mule—"Der Mule," "Simon Slick," "Runaway Mules," "Going Down to Cooper's," "Go Along, Mule," "Never Take the Hindshoe from a Mule" and "My Old Canal Mule." Canallers dealt with mules daily and relied upon mules for their living. Almost every canal had at least one song complaining about a mule. Here is one from the Morris Canal:

"Go Along, Mule"[108]

I've got a mule, she's such a fool,
She never pays no heed,
I'll build a fire beneath her tail,
And then she'll show some speed.
    Chorus:
Go along, mule,
Don't you roll them eyes,
You can change a fool but a doggone mule,
Is a mule until she dies.

Another mule is even blamed for breaking the towline in a verse from the Lehigh Canal song "Going Down to Cooper's." The "seventeener" is a long level (seventeen miles without locks) after the boat crosses the Delaware River and goes into the Morris Canal.

> *Going down the seventeener, doing mighty well,*
> *The mule broke the towline and the boat she went to Hell.*[109]

The only advantage the horse had over the mule was speed. That was why horses were used to pull packet boats. Mules, despite being hard to handle, were the draft animal of choice. The mule team was often mentioned in canal songs, and the lyrics described their position in the team:

> *The driver was lame, and the shaft mule was blind.*
> *The lead mule had a corncob sticking out behind.*[110]

When two or three mules were hitched together in a line, the shaft mule was the second mule in the line behind the lead mule. Hitching mules in a line was considered a more efficient way of towing by some canallers, but the side-by-side method of towing was also used.

> *Our Nell has got the blind staggers,*
> *And Maude has got the heaves,*
> *Black Tom has thrown his off shoe,*
> *And our driver's got the weaves.*[111]

The off shoe (line 3) is one of the shoes on the mule on the outside of the towpath, away from the canal. Likewise, when mules were in pairs, side by side or in a line, the off mule was the mule on the outside, while the nigh mule was on the inside, closest to the canal. Depending on the size of the canal and the canalboats, two-, three-, four- and even five-mule teams were used. The three-mule team in "The E-ri-e" dates this song to the period after the Erie Canal was enlarged (1836–62). Instead of 30-ton boats, pulled by two mules, the canal now accommodated up to 240-ton loads which required at least three-mule teams (Nell, Maude and Black Tom).

One of the hazards encountered by canallers that the Great Lakes sailors did not face was being kicked by a mule. Mules did have two troublesome traits: stubbornness and a propensity to kick. "Der Mule" describes both of them.[112]

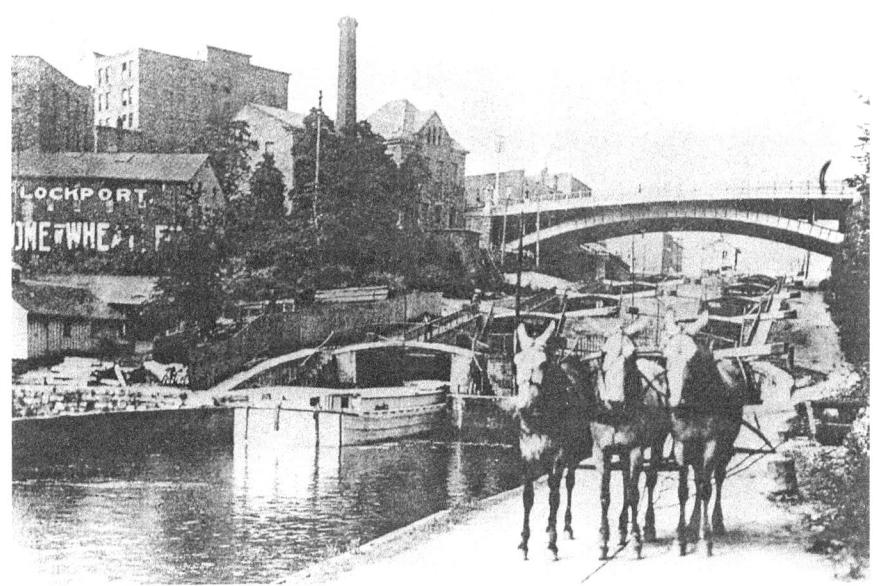

Canalboat towed by three mules. *Courtesy of Frank E. Sadowski Jr.*

Der mule sthoot on der canalboat deck, fur de towpath he wouldn't dret.

and

Den game a kick off dunder sount, off dis boy you needn't botter,
Ask off der wafes dat far aroundt, behelt him in de watter.

"My Old Canal Mule," from the Ohio and Erie Canal, describes both of the bad traits, the stubbornness and the kicking, in a single verse:

He was in the army and there you obey,
But he was like others got smart by the day,
He sure could act stubborn, would balk, kick and reel,
And want to kick you at most every meal.[113]

Mules were slower than horses but were much more sure-footed and less likely to be frightened by noises and things they saw. "My Old Canal Mule" contains an "old wives' tale" that a mule could be prevented from kicking if it could not raise its tail.

"My Old Canal Mule"[114]

He sure could act stubborn, would balk, kick and reel,
And want to kick you at most every meal.
So soon we all became tired of his pranks,
For when he felt like it would run break the ranks,
He'd bray like a wild ass, on mountain and vale,
'Til a surgeon got wise, cut the nerve in his tail.

Does this actually work? It is not very long before the listener finds out if cutting the nerve in a mule's tail prevents him from kicking:

One day he did plaster me, where I'll not say,
But over the bank for a while I did lay,
The boat came to search, I said, groaning, "Some pal,"
"He can sure lift his heels, even if he can't lift that tail."[115]

Apparently, a mule lifting its tail is not a prerequisite for kicking. There seem to be no end to the canal songs dealing with a stubborn, kicking mule. From the D&H Canal, "Simon Slick," which shares common verses and a chorus with "Whoa, Mule" and "Kicking Mule," is all about the trials of dealing with a stubborn, kicking mule.

"Simon Slick"[116]

I know an old canaller, his name is Simon Slick,
He had a mule with dreamy eyes, Lord how that mule could kick,
He'd wink his eye and wag his tail, and greet you with a smile,
Then gently telegraph his legs, and send you half a mile.
　　Chorus:
Whoa, mule, whoa, why don't you hear them holler?
I'll tie a knot right in your tail so you won't slip through your collar,
Why don't they put him on a track, why don't they let him go?
And every time he comes around, shout, "Whoa there, mule, whoa."

There is a common chorus among the kicking mule songs that links all of them together. "Simon Slick," "Whoa Mule" and "Kicking Mule" demonstrate this connection. This is how many canal songs came about. A well-known song, whatever its title, is quickly adapted by changing a word

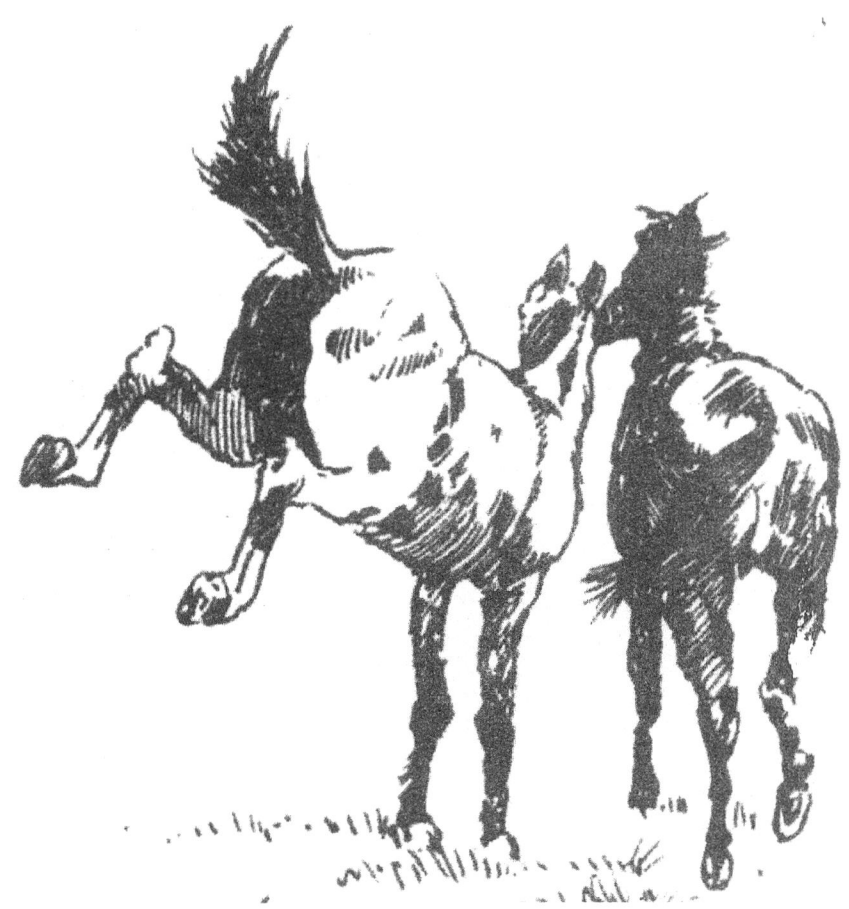

Drawing of kicking mules. *Author's collection.*

or two. The titles hardly matter, since oral transmission provided the song but rarely a title. "The Flop Eared Mule" and all of these songs are related to another song called "The Kicking Mule," which shares a number of "floating verses" and similar chorus.

"Whoa, Mule"[117]

Well it's Whoa, mule, whoa. Don't you hear him holler?
Tie a bow-knot in his tail or he'll jump through the collar.
Why don't you take him to the track? Why don't you let him go?
Every time I turn around, it's Whoa, mule, whoa.

Sometimes the same name keeps reappearing. There is very little difference between "The Kicking Mule" and "Simon Slick," except the title of the song.

"The Kicking Mule"[118]

There was a man, lived in this town
His name was Simon Slick
He had a wandering cross eyed mule
'N' how that mule would kick
He'd flop his ears, he'd switch his tail
He'd meet you with a smile
And when he'd stretch those hind legs out
He'd send you a half-a-mile
  Chorus:
Whoa mule, whoa
Whoa mule, whoa
Every time he looked 'round
It was, whoa mule, whoa
Whoa mule, whoa
Whoa mule, whoa
Every time he looked 'round
It was whoa, mule, whoa.

"Simon Slick" (Missouri version)[119]

There was a farmer's little son
His name was Simon Slick
He owned a rat-tail kickin' mule
O, how that mule could kick.

It seems likely that all of these songs, which have been collected all over the United States, were derived from "The Kicking Mule" or "The Flop Eared Mule." Since canallers were prone to parody just about any song they heard, it is probable that the owner of the mule evolved from "a man in town" to a "farmer's little son" to a "canaller" to "Simon Slick."

With these two troublesome characteristics, stubbornness and kicking, and the fact that mules were slower than horses, why would canallers prefer mules? Well, according to the humor in at least one canal song, a kicking mule was a good thing "to have around to tame your mother-in-law."[120] A mule was also valuable in case of a fight; "Once a man named Mike McGinty tried to put it over Sal / now he's way down at the bottom of the Erie Canal."[121] On a serious side, mules did have some good traits other than taking care of your mother-in-law and Mike McGinty. Mules are a hybrid obtained from a female horse and a male donkey, and they inherit most of the good traits from these two animals. Most of the professionally written songs inspired by the canal were about mules, and the majority were about the good traits of a mule. The most famous canal song, "Low Bridge, Everybody Down," centers on the mule and revealed a number of the reasons why mules were the draft animal of choice.

I've got a mule her name is Sal, Fifteen years on the Erie Canal.

That line could never be sung about a horse. The working life of a horse was twelve years or less. The working life of a mule was from fifteen to thirty.

We've hauled some barges in our day, filled with lumber, coal and hay.

Mules could pull heavier loads over a longer period of time than horses. It is said that a pair of mules hauling iron ore would outlast seven horses in a lifetime.

Eats a bale of hay for dinner, and on top of that my Sal, tries to drink up all the water in the Erie Canal.

Mules ate less than half the rations required for a horse. They were also less susceptible to diseases than horses. Another show tune, "Oh! Dat Low Bridge," speaks to one of these conditions:

There's freckles on the children, glanders on the mules.

This line mentions the disease glanders, caused by an animal ingesting contaminated food or water. However, horses were much more likely to contract glanders than mules.

When I drove a pair of spavined mules on the E-ri-e Canal.

Mules were much less likely to develop enlargement of the hock, a condition called spavined, than horses. Even though the lyric mentions mules as spavined, it is much more likely that it was used in the general sense of the word, meaning old, tired or worn out. When all was said and done, mules had more good traits than bad, and that is why they were preferred by canallers.

WORK

Once on their boats with their mules in tow, the canallers sang of the work they did. If the boat traveled day and night, the crew usually consisted of four members who shared jobs in six-hour shifts: the steersman, the bowman, the cook and the driver. The driver's job might seem like just a walk on the towpath, but in fact, there was constant activity dealing with the towline.

"A Trip on the Erie"[122]

> *Haul in your towline and take in your slack,*
> *Take a reef in your breeches and straighten your back,*
> *Mind what I tell you and don't you forget,*
> *To tap the mules gently when the cook is on deck.*

A simple line from the lyrics of the canal song "A Trip on the Erie" such as "haul in your towline, and take in your slack" might be almost overlooked by a person who has never handled a towline. To a canaller, especially a driver or towpath boy, the towline meant hard work and knowing what to do in a variety of situations. The average length of the towline was about one hundred feet, and the rope was usually soaked with water. The driver did not just hitch up the mules in the morning and start down the towpath. Starting the boat off meant overcoming the inertia of thirty to sixty tons of boat and cargo. If the driver did not take in the slack, the jolt caused by coming to the end of a slack line might injure the mules or even pull them into the canal. The driver had to haul in wet towline and play it out while positioning the mules on the towpath. And how many times in a six-hour shift did the driver "haul in the towline"?

For boats going in opposite directions to pass, one boat had to stop. Both mule teams used the same towpath. The yielding driver stopped the mules on the outside of the towpath, letting the towline go slack. In the illustration, the mule team in the distance is stopped, letting the towline of the boat in the foreground go slack. After the approaching team walked over the slack towrope on the ground and the approaching boat floated over the sunken towline in the canal, the driver had to haul in part of the soaked towline, take in the slack and start the team up. On a crowded day in the height of the canal era, this happened repeatedly.

When the boat reached a lock, the process of hauling in the towline and taking in the slack was repeated for each lock. This was challenging work

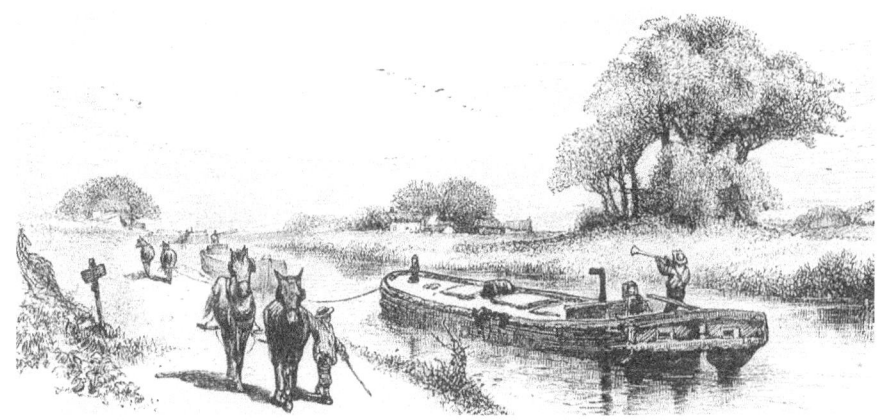

Grain-Boat on the Erie Canal. From America Illustrated, *edited by J. David Williams (Boston: DeWolfe, Fisk & Co., [1883]); reproduced by the author.*

in good weather. The following canal song, from the Ohio and Erie Canal, gives the listener a vivid picture of what it was like to "haul in the towline" in bad weather, especially late in the season:

> *"Last Trip in the Fall"*[123]
>
> *Window-glass ice everywhere,*
> *We handled lines with gloves,*
> *They soon were wet, our hands so cold,*
> *And that nobody loves.*

When overtaking another boat going in the same direction, someone on deck had to drag the towline up and lift it over the top of the boat being passed:

> *So, haul in your bowline.*[124]

and

> *Whoa back! Get up! And tighten up your line.*[125]

So, when the driver sang, "Haul in your towline, and take in your slack," a simple line in a canal occupational song, he was singing about a chore he did time and time again, thousands of times a season.

CANALLERS' RECREATION

Canallers sang about recreation on the canal, most of it created by themselves: playing music and games, dancing, swimming and, after the canal closed for the winter, sledding and skating. The canallers played portable musical instruments such as the harmonica, concertina, banjo and fiddle. They danced on the weighlock platforms: "One night in Cleveland we had a dance / On the weighlock platform we did prance, / Some would clog, and others buck and wing, / But the old square dance beat anything."[126] William Totten wrote about the canallers playing instruments, singing and dancing in his poem "The Rhyme of the Old Canal":

> *And they danced the double shuffle,*
> *And the clog with heel and toe,*
> *And passed around the latest jokes,*
> *From the "Free and Easy" show.*
> *Oft in the summer's twilight hour,*
> *The wheezy accordion's note,*
> *Droned its doleful melody,*
> *From the deck of the passing boat.*

According to Alvin Harlow (author of *Old Towpaths*), many packet boats had a small organ in the cabin where "the voices of men and women mingled with the soft, swelling tones of a parlor organ, and the less musical clicking of several sewing-machines." In *Old Towpaths*, Harlow mentions a singing session around an old pump organ aboard a packet boat where the passengers sang "Come Haste to the Wedding." Harlow also said that passengers on their way west sang, "Away, we're bound away, across the wide Missouri," the song known as "Shenandoah."[127]

> *Oh, Shenandoah, I long to hear you*
> *Look away, you rollin' river,*
> *Oh, Shenandoah, I long to hear you,*
> *Look away, we're bound away*
> *Across the wide Missouri.*

The canal era coincided with the popularity of minstrel shows and the songs of Pittsburgh composer Stephen Foster. Harlow relates that passengers made up their own version of "Oh! Susannah" that went something like this:

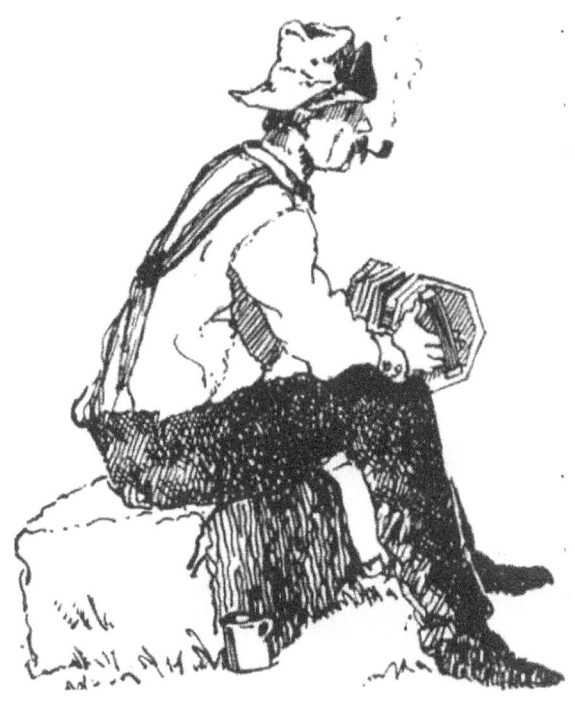

Left: Canaller playing a concertina. *Author's collection.*

Below: *Life on a Lumber Raft*, *Harper's Weekly*, October 8, 1873, 873. *Public domain.*

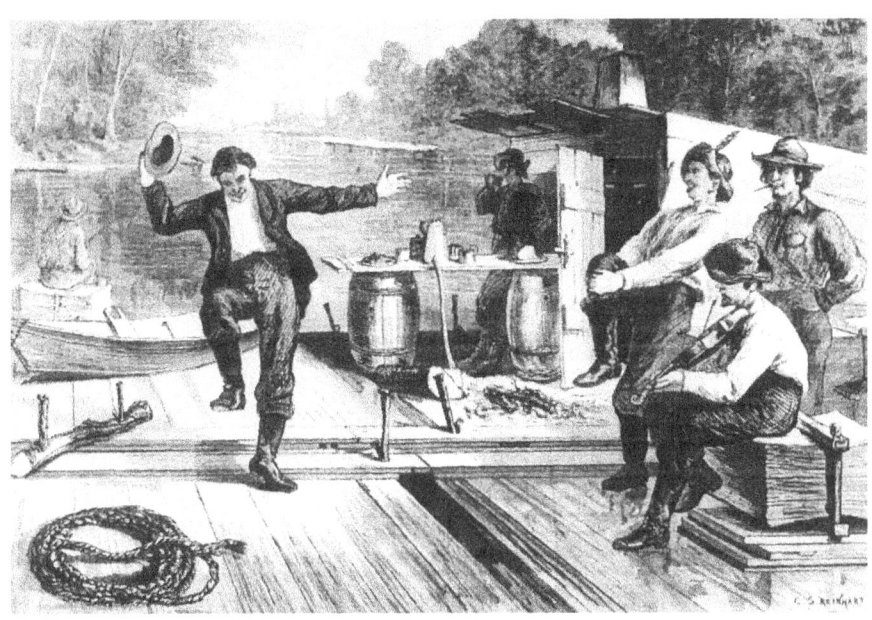

Oh! Susannah, Oh don't you cry for me,
I'm off to Minnesota, with a banjo on my knee.

Harlow also gives two stanzas of a Michigan classic, first heard in 1837, called "Michigan-i-a."[128] The song makes fun of New Yorkers for providing an easy way for travelers to get to Michigan:

Then there's the State of New York where some are very rich,
Themselves and a few others have dug a mighty ditch.
To render it more easy for us to find a way,
And sail upon the waters to Michigania,
Yes, yea, yea, in Michigania.

Ice skating was popular, and travelers created their own games on the ice, such as the "Flying Dutchman," where, according to Captain Nye, one child would be the "mule's tail" and the others would hold on to one another and spin around on the ice. The song they sang for this game was "Mulie, Keep Your Tail Up," sung to the tune of the eighteenth-century German folksong "Ach du lieber Augustin":

"Mulie, Keep Your Tail Up"[129]

Mulie, keep your tail up, your tail up, your tail up,
Oh, mulie keep your tail up, Oh, please hear my song.
I ride forward, backward, stride, and sideways, too,
So mulie keep your tail up, so I can hold on.

Another winter favorite was riding down the towpath on a "go-devil." A line from the song "The Old Go-Devil" is another example of canallers referring to the canal as the horse-ocean:

"The Old Go-Devil"

On the horse-ocean, we have a thing,
that makes folks shout, whistle and sing,
for up and down, we weave and swing,
as we ride the old go-devil.[130]

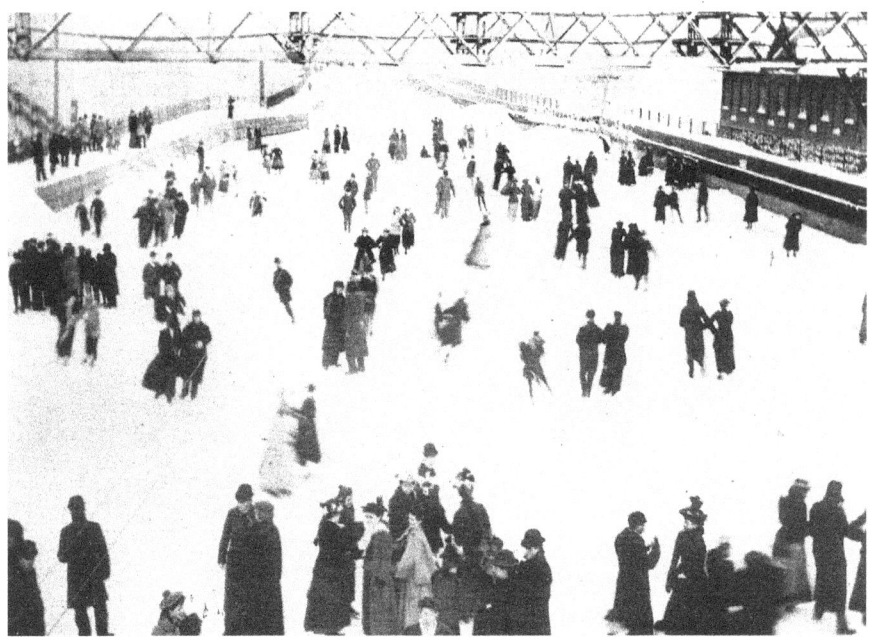

Ice skating on Erie Canal, Rochester, New York. *Courtesy of Frank E. Sadowski Jr.*

The go-devil was a simple one-horse sled used to haul logs out of the woods. It was short but could haul long logs out of heavily forested terrain. The go-devil only supported the leading edge of the log to keep it from digging into the ground or catching on ruts and low brush. The two hardwood runners were independent of each other, and there was considerable play in the runners. When a go-devil was used for recreation on the towpath, riders hung on for dear life.

CANALLERS' DIET

"From Buffalo to old New York they fed it to dear old me, then they boiled up the barrel and the rest of the pork and we had it all for tea."[131] The musical diaries told about the canaller's diet, and that line, from the canal song "Black Rock Pork," refers to a staple of the canaller's diet when crops were not available along the canal, such as early in the spring and late in the fall. Black Rock, north of Buffalo, New York, lost its bid to be the western terminus for the Erie Canal. However, Black Rock was famous for Black Rock pork, a necessary but much maligned product. Old-time canaller Albert Lavender, a former canaller from Holley, New York, said that "crews sometimes tired of too much Black Rock turkey," which was canalese for salt pork with a "streak o' lean and a streak o' fat."[132]

"Black Rock Pork"[133]

I shipped aboard of a lumber boat,
Her name was Charles O'Rourke,
And the very first thing that they rolled onboard,
Was a barrel of Black Rock Pork.

They fried a chunk for breakfast,
And a chunk for luncheon, too,
And it did not taste so goody, good,
And it was hard to chew.

From Buffalo to old New York,
They fed it to dear old me,
Then they boiled up the barrel and the rest of the pork,
And we had it all for tea.

A number of canallers spoke about the long-held belief that farmers along the canal left the first rows of their crops for the canallers. This may or may not be true, but it is certain that at least some of the canallers took advantage of this ready supply of fresh fruit and vegetables. There is reason to believe that this "privilege" also extended to stray ducks and chickens. One story involves a towpath boy who was constantly chased by a large gander as he passed by a farm along the canal. Finally, he devised a plan to rid himself of the aggressive fowl by placing a piece of corn on a hook at the end of a line. As he approached the farm, he started to drag the line, and sure enough, the gander took the bait and swallowed the corn. The boy ran down the towpath practically dragging the hooked gander until he was out of sight of the farm. Then he slit the gander's throat. That night the crew had a feast, and the boy's problem was solved. Once again, William Totten, a former towpath boy, writes about this practice:[134]

Woe to the thrifty farmer man,
Whose apples and pears looked fine,
Woe to the ducks that chased the boat,
On the end of a hook and line.
For the strictest rules of etiquette,
Were sometimes forgot,
When boatman had fair visions,
Of those steaming in a pot.

TAUNTS

There are songs that might be called "occupational hazard" songs. The towpath boy/girl heard canal songs made up by local lads who stood at a safe distance and teased him. Other times, boys would actually hinder the operation of the boat by swimming out into the canal and sitting on the tow rope or hanging on the rudder. Some of these songs, in the form of taunts, were collected on the canals in New York, New Jersey and Pennsylvania and show a pattern of treating canalboat crews as outsiders:

Canaller, canaller, you son-of-a-bitch,
You work on Sunday, you'll die in the ditch.

or

You Rusty Old Canaller, you think you're mighty nice,
Standing by the tiller blade, picking off the lice.

or

You Rusty Old Canaller, you'll never get rich,
You'll die in your cabin, you son-of-a-bitch.[135]

or

Hoggee on the towpath five cents a day,
Picking up horse manure to eat along the way.[136]

In James Lee's interview with Isabella Lenstrohm Mann, Mann relates that on the Morris, kids used to swim out to the boat and hang on the rudder so her father, Peter, could not steer. She also said that they would throw all kinds of things off the bridges onto the deck of the boat.[137] These incidents and taunts just serve to demonstrate that the canallers, even though welcomed for their business, were still a subculture of the area through which they traveled. "The canaler and his culture represented a…definite, separate social grouping, one apart from the mainstream of society. He was both mobile and caught."[138] Because of the seasonal nature of the work, canallers were considered outsiders, just passing through. A song from the Ohio and Erie Canal that expresses this point of view from the canallers' perspective is "We Stick Together." Canallers viewed themselves as "a tribe of strange people," "clannish" and "in a world of our own":

"We Stick Together"[139]

1. We're a tribe of strange people, this world does not know,
Most free, independent, wherever we go,
Yes, happy, contented, whatever our run,
And we all stick together in fight or in fun.

2. Of course we are clannish, and we do not bend,
Our freedom, rights, home, you bet we defend,
For much we see and know in all of our runs,
So we stick together in fight or in fun.

3. We will stick together, one family are we,
In a world of our own, we are happy and free,
We are not aggressive but will stand our ground,
When the battle is over, there we always are found.

4. Yes, we all stick together and aim to be fair,
Our oaths, obligations, make blood brother dear,
So don't go too far, oft our language is smiles,
You'll find us united on the dear old canal.

Because they were outsiders, canallers considered themselves "blood brothers," "one family" and "united." There may have been fights between canallers for position at locks, but when it came to dealing with non-canallers, they would always "stick together." Another verse from "The Rhyme of the Old Canal" confirms this:

And woe to the men that challenged them,
Whether by day or night,
For ashore they would jump "at the drop of
a hat," To stand or fall in fight.
And from the deck box, stove wood flew,
Likewise potatoes and coal,
And many a fighting fellow knew,
A smashing blow to his jowl.

Canallers at work had to contend with their boats, their mules, the towline, the weather, the food and the taunts. In an interview with James Lee, Isabella Mann said that her father found a way to deal with boys who swam out and held onto his rudder blade. Peter was a tobacco chewer, and he would send a mouthful of tobacco juice down on an unsuspecting miscreant. "They soon learned to leave him alone."[140] Those canallers, transporting coal from Pennsylvania, probably knew that old mining song:

My sweetheart's the mule in the mines,
I drive her without any lines,
On the bumpers I sit and tobacco I spit,
All over my sweetheart's behind.[141]

Long-distance canallers, who made trips on the Pennsylvania Main Line Canal, the Erie Canal and the Ohio and Erie Canal, were often considered outsiders. They went weeks before returning to the same towns again. Canal songs from shorter canals, such as the forty-mile Farmington Canal in Connecticut, provide a different picture of the interaction between canallers and local residents. The Farmington Canal went from the port at New Haven, Connecticut, inland to Farmington, Connecticut. Later, it connected to the Hampshire and Hampton Canal in Massachusetts for a total of eighty miles. When a canalboat tied up in one town two or three times a week, canallers were treated more like locals than outsiders. "Old Captain Dick"[142] (Captain Dick Norton) tells about tying up at Whiting's Dock in Plainville (about thirty miles from New Haven), where they unloaded cargo at Edna Whitin's general store and socialized with locals:

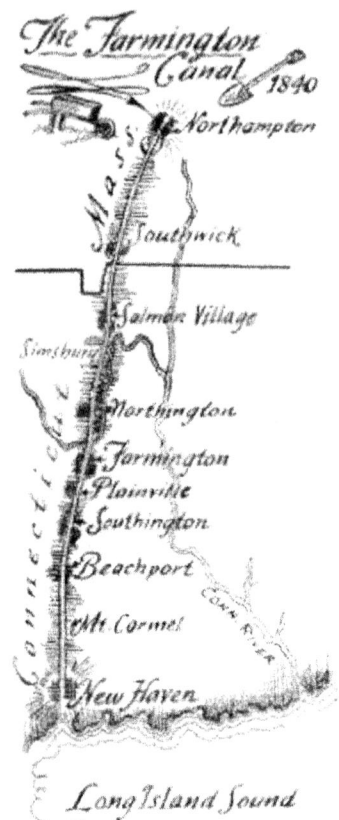

Map of Farmington Canal.
livinghistorymilitaryengineer.blogspot.
com/2011/03/.

The boat ties up at Whitin's Dock,
Two, three times a week, 'bout four o'clock,
Out comes Adney and old Eb, too,
Gub, Homer, Bela, and the rest of the crew.
They pull and haul and cuss and swear,
Unload the cargo and then repair,
To the store to licker up and smoke,
Tell tall tales, swap lies, and joke.

Taunts influenced the songs that the canallers borrowed. The idea that Great Lakes and deep-sea sailors looked on them as "dry-land sailors" or "horse-ocean sailors" bothered canallers. Canallers thought of themselves as sailors. This is evident in the number of canal songs borrowed from the sea. Some are parodies, such as "I'm Afloat on the Raging Canal" and "A Life on the Raging Canal." These involved changes in the lyrics. There are other "borrowed" songs that took few adjustments to change from one situation to another. To change the sea song "The Dark-Eyed Sailor" into a canal song required the change of only one word: *sailor* for *canaller.*

"The Dark-Eyed Sailor"[143] falls into the category sometimes known as the "broken token" songs. The plot, at least as old as Shakespeare, involves a couple who are separated for a long time. The man comes back, but his ex-lover does not recognize him. He decides to test her by trying to convince her to forget her long-lost love and go away with him. She rejects him and he unfolds a token, usually a ring, that they broke in half before his departure as a symbol of their love and the couple is reunited. Here are a few verses of "The Dark-Eyed Sailor" as "The Dark-Eyed Canaller":

"The Dark-Eyed Canaller"[144]

1. It was a comely young lady fair,
Was walking out to take the air,
She met a [sailor] *canaller upon the way,*
So I paid attention, So I paid attention,
To hear what they did say.

2. "Fair maid," said he, "Why do you roam alone,
The night is come and the day's far gone."
She drew a dagger and then did cry,
"For my dark-eyed [sailor] *canaller, for my dark-eyed* [sailor] *canaller,*
Though he may live or die."

3. "His coal-black eyes and curly hair,
His flattering tongue my heart ensnared,
Genteel was he, no rake like you,
To advise a maiden, to advise a maiden,
To slight his jacket blue."

4. "It is three long years since he left our boat,
A gold ring he took and gently broke,
He left this token—here's half you see,
And the other he's keeping, and the other he's keeping,
To remind him oft of me."

5. When William did his ring unfold,
She seemed too struck with joy and woe,
"You're welcome William, I've land and gold,
For my dark-eyed [sailor] *canaller, for my dark-eyed canaller,*
So manly true and bold."

"The Clever Skipper[145] is another canal song, collected from Captain Pearl R. Nye of the Ohio and Erie Canal, with origins on the ocean as "The Bold Boaster" (a song variously known as "The Charleston Merchant," "The Boatsman and the Chest," "Jolly Boatman," "The Wealthy Merchant," "The Jolly Boatswain," "The Tailor in the Tea [Sea] Chest," "The Boatswain and the Chest," "The Sailor and the Tailor" and "The Boatswain and the Tailor"). Only a few place names needed to be changed to adapt it from sea song to canal song. The tale the song tells goes all the way back to the medieval era and possibly earlier. Its author, Giovanni Boccaccio (1313–1375), borrowed most of the stories in *The Decameron* from earlier sources. The theme was also carried on in Geoffrey Chaucer's *Canterbury Tales*.

The tale is of the age-old love triangle. A wife, thinking her husband away on a voyage, meets with her lover. They are surprised by a knock on the door, and the wife locks the lover in a trunk belonging to her husband. Her husband comes in and announces that he needs his trunk, and two sailors carry it out. They soon discover the man inside the trunk and take him onboard. Here are a few verses to show how close the songs are:

"The Bold Boaster"	"The Clever Skipper"
1. There was a bold boaster	*1. There was a clever skipper,*
And in Dublin he did dwell.	*And in Akron he did dwell,*
He had a lovely woman,	*He had a lovely woman,*
And the tailor she loved well.	*And a tailor she loved well.*
Come a rally tally dally,	*Come a rally tally dally,*
Come a rally tally day	*Come a rally tally day.*
2. She was a walkin'	*2. She was a walkin',*
Up Dublin Street,	*Up South Howard Street,*
Who but the tailor,	*Who but the tailor,*
Did she chance forth to meet?	*Did she chance forth to meet?*
Come a rally tally dally,	*Come a rally tally dally,*
Come a rally tally day	*Come a rally tally day.*
3. They took him on board,	*3. They took him on board,*
And for England they did steer,	*And for Portsmouth they did steer,*
And that is the last,	*And that is the last,*
Of the tailor we do hear	*Of the tailor we do hear.*
Come a rally tally dally	*Come a rally tally dally,*
Come a rally tally day.	*Come a rally tally day.*

Other canal songs use the melodies of sea songs but have few similarities in lyrics. "The Dreadnought" (sea song), "Red Iron Ore" (Great Lakes song) and "Attend, All Ye Drivers" and "The George C Finney" (canal songs), all use the tune called "Derry Down." Ivan Walton, in his book *Windjammers*, said that as soon as the song "The Dreadnought" reached the Great Lakes, it "became a platform upon which sailors built other songs."[146] The *Dreadnought* was a clipper ship built in Newburyport, Massachusetts, in 1863. It sailed for the Red Cross Line and was known for the fastest passage between New York and Liverpool, England.

"The Dreadnought"

Oh, there is a flash packet, Flash packet of fame.
She hails from New York, And the Dreadnought's her name.
She's bound to the west, Where the stormy winds blow.
Bound away in the westward, To the Dreadnought we'll go.
Derry down, down, down, Derry down.

"Red Iron Ore" is about the voyage of the *E.C. Roberts* from Chicago to Cleveland. The *Roberts* was a schooner built in Cleveland, Ohio, in 1856.

"Red Iron Ore"

Come all you bold sailors that follow the Lakes,
On an iron ore vessel your living to make.
I shipped in Chicago, bid adieu to the shore,
Bound away to Escanaba for red iron ore.
Derry down, down, down Derry down.

"Attend, All Ye Drivers" was collected on the Champlain Canal, and the song "The George C Finney" from the Oswego Canal in New York State.

"Attend, All Ye Drivers"[147]

Attend all ye drivers, I sing of my team,
They're the fleetest and strongest that ever was seen,
There's none that will toil with such speed down the creek,
Or start at the word of the driver so quick.
Derry down, down, down, Derry down.

The canal schooner *George C Finney* was built in Oswego, but its home port was Buffalo. The *Finney* was lost in a storm on Lake Erie in November 1891 on a trip from Toledo, Ohio, to Buffalo.

"The George C Finney"[148]

Come all ye old sailors who follow the lakes,
And in a canal vessel your living do make.
The Finney is lying at the salt dock.
The boys and the girls to her deck they do flock.
Derry down, down, down Derry down.

Along with sharing the same tune, "The George C Finney" and "Red Iron Ore" also share a few similarities in the lyrics, known as "floating verses." The first two lines of the first verse and the last verses are almost the same.

"The George C Finney"	*"Red Iron Ore"*[149]
Come all ye old sailors who follow the lakes,	*Come all you bold sailors that follow the Lakes,*
And in a canal vessel your living do make,	*On an iron ore vessel your living to make.*
The Finney is lying at the Salt Dock,	*I shipped in Chicago, bid adieu to the shore,*
The boys and the girls to her deck they do flock,	*Bound away to Escanaba for red iron ore.*
Derry down, down, down Derry, down,	*Derry down, down, down Derry down.*
7. Now the Finney's in Chicago, made vast stem and stern,	*7. Now the Roberts is in Cleveland, made fast stem and stern*
We'll go to Pete Kemmer's and spin a long yarn,	*And over the bottle we'll spin a big yarn.*
To the health of Jack Preston who gave us a treat,	*But Captain Harvey Shannon had ought to stand treat,*
For arriving in Chicago ahead of the fleet	*For getting to Cleveland ahead of the fleet.*
Derry down, down, down Derry, down.	*Derry down, down, down Derry down.*

Still another canal song with the same melody as a sea song is "I'm a Little Canaler." The melody to which it is sung is identified as "Sailing over the Sea." A song by this name, written in 1882 by D'adhe'mar, does not fit the lyrics. The tune could be the Canadian song "Sailing over the Ocean" or the U.S. children's song "Sailing, Sailing" ("Over the Bounding Main"). Both songs fit the lyrics better. There is a recording of "I'm a Little Canaler" in the Library of Ohio State University, and it uses the tune to "A Life on the Ocean Wave" by Henry Russell.[150] Regardless of which tune is intended, they are all examples of the adaptation of a melody from a sea song.

Another sea song known to river raftsmen and lumbermen in New York State as well as canallers is "Shove around the Grog." The Toronto Morris Men sing this version, called "Shove around the Jug." Most of the places mentioned are on the Erie Canal (Albany, Amsterdam, Rome, Syracuse, Liverpool,) and it is told from the perspective of an Irish immigrant working on the Erie Canal.

"Shove Around the Jug"[151]

Chorus:
Shove around the jug, boys,
The chorus around the room,
For we're the boys that fear no noise
Although we're far from home!
1. Well, I courted a girl in Albany,
One in Montreal,
One in Philadelphy,
But the best in Lewiston Falls.
2. When you get to Albany
Give the girls a call.
There's not a tart to be compared,
With the ones from Lewiston Falls.

3. When I came on from Ireland
I was just a lad.
But working these canal boats
Is the only life I've had.
4. A dollar in a tavern,
Is very easy spent.
If I had it in Ireland,
I'd have to pay down rent.
5. A drunkard in the tavern,
A fish is in the sea!
The cork is in the bottle,
But the whiskey is in me!
6. Amsterdam or Liverpool,
Rome or Syracuse,
If you've ever been to Lewiston Falls,
It's the only place you'd choose.

Along with the other adapted sea songs, they all point to the canaller's desire to see himself as a sailor, despite the differences and despite the derision of Great Lakes sailors. Many canal songs were born directly from the taunts the canallers had to withstand. "With their imaginations whetted by boredom and scorn that can naturally arise between different breeds of men, the sailor-composer reached his crowning achievement for creativity and sarcasm while bumping along the canal."[152]

8

THE RAGING CANAL

Come listen to my story, ye landsmen one and all,
I'll sing to you the story of that raging canal,
For I am one of many who expects a watery grave,
I've been at the mercy of the wind and of the wave.
—"The Raging Canal," Pete Morris (1844)

The "raging canal" expression is a good example of how songs and print media quickly spread popular trends and information along the canals and beyond, but where did the expression originate? The first documented raging canal songs were parodies of two songs by Henry Russell. Both songs belong to the phenomenon of raging canal references and songs that spread across the canals and across the country. In an interview with canaller Butch Sullivan, Ivan Walton learned that sailors and canallers held no love for one another and often brawled in the bars on Canal Street in Buffalo, New York. Walton asked if Sullivan remembered any of the songs pertaining to insults by Great Lakes sailors: "Although Sullivan couldn't recall any of the songs in particular, he said that sailors sometimes joked about his navigating skills and sang about the great storms, bad shoals, and even pirates that he and his canallers faced in the big ditch."[153]

Great Lakes sailors making jokes about "the great storms" on the canal may have been the spark that set the "raging canal" songs and expressions echoing up and down the canals. Ivan Walton speculates that the original idea of the storm-tossed raging canals may have come from Great Lakes sailors. As it turns out, there were numerous canal songs that mentioned the jokes recalled by Sullivan. The most far-fetched of these is when "The Good Ship Called Danger" is attacked by pirates. This verifies the fact that canallers heard the joke about pirates on the canal enough to actually mention them in a song.

At two days out we struck a fog,
No land could we espy,
And a pirate boat bore down on us,
With a goddamn wicked eye.[154]

Pirates on the canal turned out to be no joke. Canallers were attacked by marauders who lay in wait at remote places or who jumped aboard from bridges onto the deck of the canalboat. The following newspaper accounts confirm that canallers were confronted by robbers on the canal:

"Arrest of Canal Boat Robbers"

We learn from Detective Donohue, who returned from Lockport this morning, that night before last while a canal boat was passing near Medina, five men jumped on board and demanded the money from the captain. The robbers were resisted by the crew, and two of them arrested. One of the prisoners gave his name as Haley and said he was from Lockport; the other, whose name did not transpire, is said to belong to Buffalo.
—Buffalo (NY) Commercial,
Saturday, November 14, 1868

"Canal Robbery"

Officer Tolls succeeded in arresting on Wednesday afternoon and evening, three men charged with committing several felonies on canal boats, principally between Rochester and Albany. A large portion of the property has been found in this city and some in Rochester. The fellows were traced to three different lurking places by our indefatigable officer, and arrested separately. They were taken to Rochester by Mr. Tolls yesterday and fairly committed.
—Buffalo (NY) Commercial,
Saturday, May 28, 1853

More of Butch Sullivan's comments are confirmed by two newspaper articles that report the same types of gibes he remembered being directed toward canallers. The first article, from the *New York Times*, says, "Upon this difficult and embarrassing point, is a little pleasant badinage and some amusing jokes about injured affections and the 'raging canal.'" The second article, from the *Logansport Pharos-Tribune*, jokes about a boat being wrecked in a storm on the raging canal.

We have appealed to the Atlas, *and are answered by gibes. The most we can extract from that authority, upon this Difficult and embarrassing point, is a little pleasant badinage and some very amusing jokes about injured affections and the "raging canal."*

—New York Times,
Friday, September 24, 1852

Folks think that a canal boat sailor is something to make fun of, and they always like to get off their little jokes about being wrecked in a storm on the raging canal.

—Logansport (IN) Pharos-Tribune,
Thursday, January 28, 1892

Other canal songs refer to jokes about the shoals and "running aground on a lump of coal that wasn't marked down in the chart." However, it was the storm-tossed canal that turned out to be the inspiration for a half century of songs and articles during the canal era. The expression "raging canal" became a part of the canallers' vocabulary and soon found its way into "raging canal" songs. Based on early newspaper accounts, the first canal song, and the first use of the words "raging canal" published in a newspaper, were parodies of Henry Russell's "A Life on the Ocean Wave."[155]

"A LIFE ON THE OCEAN WAVE"

English composer Henry Russell, who lived in Rochester, New York, from 1833 to 1841, wrote the widely popular "A Life on the Ocean Wave" in 1838. It quickly spread along the canal from Buffalo to Albany and on to New York City with the help of broadsides and newspaper accounts. In fact, the first newspaper account of a performance of the song in a public concert was only months after it was first published. The *New York Evening Post* announced a concert in which the song was to be performed on Monday, October 8, 1838. The program features "A Life on the Ocean Wave" and other Russell songs. Numerous newspaper accounts of performances appear in 1838 and the following year.[156]

It was not long after its original publication that "A Life on the Ocean Wave" was parodied on the canal and became the first documented "raging canal" song. Although the parody of Russell's song has no date, the popularity and widespread dispersion of this song up and down the canals and two newspaper accounts of performances in Buffalo in 1843 would suggest that the canal song was being sung even earlier, much closer to the 1838 date "A Life on the Ocean Wave" was published. The following comparison of the choruses of both songs reveals how close they were.

"A Life on the Ocean Wave"[157]	*"A Life on the Raging Canal"*[158]
A life on the ocean wave	*A life on Raging Canal,*
A home on its rolling deep,	*A home on its muddy deep,*
Where the scattered waters rave,	*Where through summer, spring and fall,*
And the winds their revels keep.	*The frogs their vigils do keep.*

The two 1843 programs printed in the *Buffalo Commercial* called the song "The Raging Canal." Is this the parody "A Life on the Raging Canal"? "A Life on the Raging Canal" was known on the Ohio and Erie Canal as "The Raging Canal" and collected by John Lomax as "The Raging Canal."[159] Also, Pete Morris's famous song, known as "The Raging Canal," was not published until 1844. "The Raging Canal" listed in the newspaper is most likely "A Life on the Raging Canal," as it would have been in circulation even before 1843.

The *Buffalo (NY) Commercial*, Monday, June 5, 1843, page 2. *Public domain.*

THE RAGING CANAL

Only one year later, a second raging canal song appeared. The most famous raging canal song of all, and the one that inspired any number of spin-offs, was "The Raging Canal" by Pete Morris. This song was published by C.G. Christman in 1844. Harold Thompson said that "the one canal ballad which you are likely to find in any songster printed before the Civil War is 'The Raging Canal.'"[160] *The American Vocalist* (1853) printed a version with twenty-four verses. The original sheet music of Pete Morris's song had six verses, and the lyrics contain more sea-related terms than canal terms, with lines like "We put our helm hard a port"; "We carried away our mizzen mast"; "We had to reef our royals"; and "Hallowed to the driver to take in more sail." Along with the image on the sheet music cover, the song suggested a sailing ship with a mast and sails surviving waves a mountain high.

"The Raging Canal"

1. Come listen to my story, ye landsmen one and all,
I'll sing to you the story of that raging canal,
For I am one of many who expects a watery grave,
I've been at the mercy of the wind and of the wave.

2. When we left New York harbor it was the middle of the year,
We put our helm hard a port and for Buffalo did steer,
But when we got sight of Alba'y, we met a heavy squall,
And we carried away our mizzen mast on that Raging Canal.

3. She minded her helm just like a thing of life,
The mate got on his knees uttering prayers for his wife,
We throwed the provisions overboard it was blowing such a squall,
And we were put on short allowance on that Raging Canal.

4. It seemed as if the devil had his work in hand that night,
For all our oil was gone, and our lamps they gave no light,
The clouds began to gather and the rain began to fall,
And we had to reef our royals on the Raging Canal.

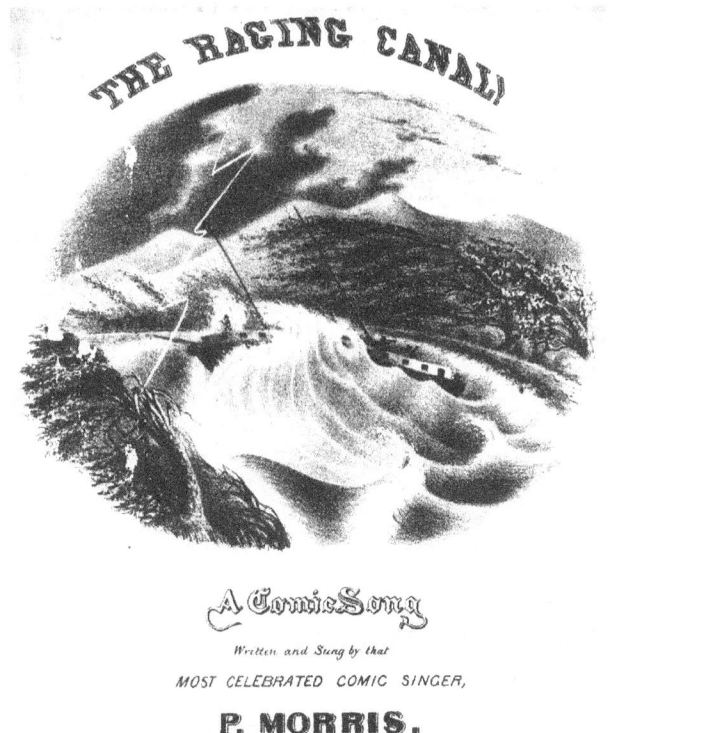

"The Raging Canal" sheet music cover. *Reproduced by the author.*

5. Loud roared the dreadful thunder, the rain in deluge showered,
The clouds were rent asunder, by lightning's vivid powers,
The bowsman gave a hollow and the cook she gave a squall,
And the waves run mountains high on that Raging Canal.

6. The Captain came on deck and then he began to rail,
He hollowed to the driver to take in more sail,
The driver knocked a horse down and then gave a bawl,
And we scudded under bare poles on that Raging Canal.[161]

By the time "The Raging Canal" was published in broadsides and songsters, it was growing exponentially. It kept gaining verses from anonymous sources. A broadside in the Union College Library,

Schenectady, New York, has fifteen verses. *The Negro Forget-Me-Not Songster* has twenty-three verses, and a set of twenty-four verses for "The Raging Canal" are in a broadside in the New York State Library.[162]

"I'M AFLOAT ON THE RAGING CANAL"

The next raging canal song is a parody of another Henry Russell song, "I'm Afloat" (1843). The parody, "I'm Afloat on the Raging Canal," was published in the *Utica Daily Gazette* in April 1845.[163] Eliza Muggins, a former cook, was given credit for the lyrics, but this turns out to be a joke since the original lyricist for Henry Russell's song was Eliza Cook. By July 1845, the song had reached the Hudson River and New York City and was published in the *Poughkeepsie (NY) Journal*, the *New York Post* and the *Brooklyn (NY) Evening Star*. Eventually, the song reached Pennsylvania through the print media, where it was published in the *Raftsman's Journal*. Within a few years of the first raging canal song, "I'm Afloat on the Raging Canal" became the third. Raging canal songs were appearing every year (1843, 1844 and 1845).

"I'm Afloat on the Raging Canal"

I'm afloat! I'm afloat on the Raging Canal
Its wave is my home and my scow beats them all,
Off! Up with your hats, give three cheers, now three more,
I'm afloat! I'm afloat! After four months on shore.

The raging canal songs are not just hyperbole but add to the story of the canal era. How long did it take to travel by canal on those first twenty miles from Albany to Schenectady? A raging canal song gives us the answer and provides a good example of how personal experiences and references attached themselves to canal songs.

I left Albany harbor 'bout break of day,
And if I rightly remember, 'twas the second day of May,
We trusted to our driver, although he was but small.
For he knew all the winding of that raging canal.

2. It seemed as if the devil had his work in hand that night,
For all our oil was gone and our lamps they gave no light,
The clouds began to gather and the rain began to fall,
And I wished myself off of that raging canal.

3. The Captain told the driver to hurry with all speed,
And his orders were obeyed for he soon cracked up his lead,
With the fastest kind of driving, he allowed by twelve o'clock,
We should be in Old Schenectady, right bang against the dock.[164]

The lyrics of this song may be hyperbolic when it comes to conditions on the canal, but they are absolutely correct in assessing how long it took a canalboat to travel from Albany to Schenectady. "I left Albany harbor 'bout break of day…With the fastest kind of driving, we allowed by twelve o'clock, we'd be in old Schenectady, right bang against the dock." Was that twelve o'clock noontime or twelve o'clock midnight? That all-day trip involved twenty-seven locks, and it is the reason most passengers chose a different mode of transportation to get to Schenectady. In the early days, they traveled by stage, later by train, rather than endure the all-day trip on the canal. It required an average of twenty hours, no matter how favorable the conditions, to make the twenty-seven-mile trip from Albany to Schenectady.

Juncta, or what became the city of Cohoes, also was a central gathering site at the junction of the Erie Canal and the Champlain Canal. It was the spot reached after climbing the staircase of locks passing Cohoes Falls. Here, weary passengers were accosted by "runners" hired for packet boat lines and boardinghouses. The runners quickly grabbed the dazed passengers' luggage and headed for their assigned locations. The boardinghouses and "hotels" were nothing more than grog shops on the lower level and sleeping rooms on the upper level. The accommodations in one such establishment were described as a room with four poles from floor to ceiling. Around each pole was a circular platform that held twelve men with their feet to the pole and their bodies radiating outward like the spokes on a huge wheel. There is a song about just such a hotel, aptly named "The Cohoes Hotel." In this hotel, instead of forty-eight to a room, there were eighty-three.

"The Cohoes Hotel"[165]

It's one cent for coffee, it's two cents for bread,
It's three for mince pie, and five cents for a bed.
There're eighty-three boarders all packed at my door,
And they paid their five cents to sleep on the floor.

Another piece of information found in one of the added verses in a songster tells why escape cuts were made in the sides of the canal in places like Cohoes Falls and the Niagara escarpment. Animals who stumbled or were pulled off the towpath into the canal needed a means to get out. Where that was not possible, many animals drowned.

The horses gave a stumble and the driver gave a squall,
And they tumbled head over heels into the raging canal.
The Captain came on deck, with a voice so clear and sound,
Saying, "Cut the horses loose, my boys, or else we'll all be drowned,"
The driver swam ashore, altho' he was but small,
And the horses sank to rise no more in the raging canal.[166]

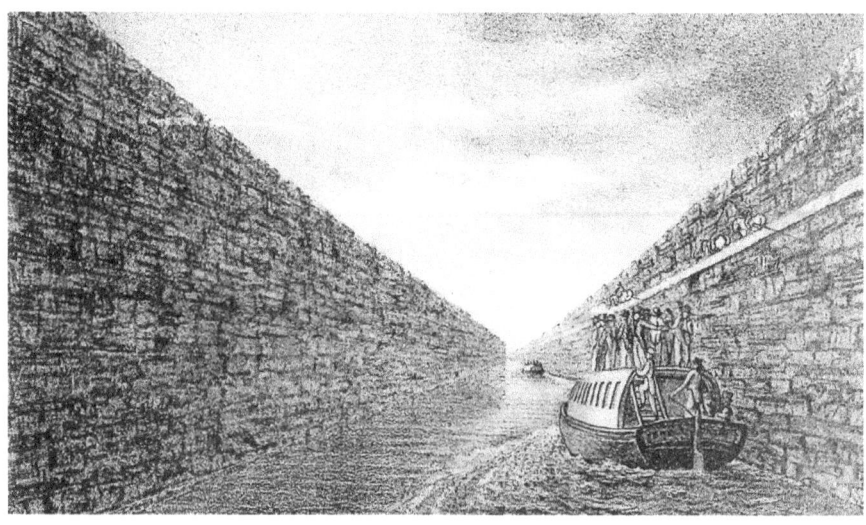

Deep Cutting Lockport [looking west]. *From a memoir by Cadwallader D. Colden (New York: Printed by order of the Corporation of New York, 1825), 299; reproduced by the author.*

THE RAGING CANAL IN NON-CANAL SONGS

The use of the term *raging canal* was so pervasive that it appears in songs that are not that closely related to canals. One such song is "The Blue Eagle Jail" (1850), written by Dan Rice only six years after "The Raging Canal" was printed. Rice was a famous nineteenth-century circus clown and entrepreneur who was arrested in the village of Pittsford, near Rochester, New York. Despite coming up with a promissory note guaranteeing his bail, he was incarcerated in the Monroe County Jail for a week. Rice, who generally stayed a few blocks away at the Eagle Hotel, referred to the Monroe County Jail as the "Blue Eagle Jail" when he wrote the lyrics to this song on his jail cell wall. The final verse mentions Rice's "ups and downs on the raging canal":

"The Blue Eagle Jail"

Kind Ladies, here, and good gentlemen all,
I now must close up my song,
Of my ups and downs on the raging canal
And how I've been getting along.
But one word I must say, before I go away,
And then my song is at an end,
If you would avoid going astray,
never trust too much to a friend.[167]
[emphasis added]

In *Rochester History*, historian Blake McKelvey notes, "That ditty, sung on frequent occasions in Rochester, supplied an enduring name and won the Monroe County Jail a secure place in Rochester history."[168] Dan Rice continued to sing the song on the New York and Pennsylvania canal systems.[169]

A play-party song, "Hello, Sally Brown" (also known as "Coffee Grows on White Oak Trees," "Four in the Middle," "Two in the Middle," "Oh, She's Gone, Gone, Gone"), has verses and a chorus that end with the line "the raging canal." The raging canal was even adopted for the title.

"The Raging Canal (Two in the Middle)"[170]

Coffee grows on white oak trees, rivers flow like brandy, O,
Go choose someone to go with you, as sweet as 'lasses candy, O,
There's six in the middle and I can't catch Josie,
Six in the middle and I can't get around,
There's six in the middle and I can't catch Josie, Hello, Susan Brown.
Singing, railroad, steamboat, river and canal,
I lost my love on the raging canal.
Let her go, go, go, Let her go, go, go,
Let her go for to stay on the raging canal.
Now she's gone, gone, gone, Now she's gone, gone, gone.
Now she's gone for to stay on the raging canal.

The play-party was a southern invention to get around religious restrictions barring the use of instruments and dancing. Here participants sang the accompaniment to their activity, which usually involved circle or line games. This play-party song must have moved north (possibly through Pennsylvania) and acquired the raging canal addition, which by then was a generic term for every canal. A newspaper article would announce the opening of "the raging canal" in the spring, and unless you looked at the location of the newspaper, it was impossible to identify the canal.

STEPHEN FOSTER'S USE OF "THE RAGING CANAL"

"The Raging Canal" was so famous that none other than composer Stephen Foster and author Mark Twain made mention of it in their works. Foster wrote "Song of All Songs" (1863), in which the lyrics consisted of the titles of well-known (at the time) songs. Foster's verse referring to the Pete Morris song goes like this:

There was "Abraham's Daughter" "Going Out Upon a Spree,"
With "Old Uncle Snow" "In the Cottage by the Sea";
"If Your Foot Is Pretty, Show It" "At Lanigan's Ball";
And "Why Did She Leave Him" "On The Raging Canawl?"
Old songs! New songs! Ev'ry kind of song,
I noted them down as I read them along.[171]

A Canal Song Using "The Raging Canal" Tune

Not only did lyrics to "The Raging Canal" inspire composers and writers, but the tune was so well-known that it also began to be used for other songs. A canal song that uses the tune to "The Raging Canal" is "The Girl from Yewdall's Mill."[172]

It is of a girl from Fairmount, that I am going to sing,
Her cruel, sad misfortune, tears to your eyes will bring,
She was a cotton dolly and she wrought at Yewdall's Mill.
She loved a gallant boatman who always dressed to kill.

"The Raging Canal" in Books

There is a reference to "The Raging Canal" in a book by American author Mark Twain. Twain includes an epic poem called "The Aged Pilot Man" in his book *Roughing It* (1872). The poem describes a wild trip from Albany to Buffalo on the raging canal (see appendix C for complete poem).

On the Erie Canal it was, all on a summer's day,
I sailed forth with my parents, far away to Albany.
From out the clouds at noon that day, there came a dreadful storm.
That piled the billows high about and filled us with alarm.[173]

Mark Twain said that the idea for this poem was probably inspired by the old song "The Raging Canal."[174] Some of Twain's lines closely resemble those of Pete Morris, such as "we throwed the provisions over board."

The Raging Canal Appears in Other Canal Songs

The term *raging canal* became so common that it appeared in verses of other canal songs not of the raging canal genre. Sometimes it was only one verse or one line, but canallers started using the term more and more. Two versions of the canal song called "The E-ri-e" have a verse about the raging canal.

The wind began to whistle,
And the waves began to roll
And we had to reef our royals
On the raging canal.[175]

The E-ri-e was a raging,
And the gin is a-getting' low,
And I scarcely think I'll get a drink,
'Til we get to Buffalo.[176]

"The Er-i-e" is not the only canal song to pick up the phrase. "The Prickly Heat," sometimes called "The Canaller's Lament," has a verse referring to the raging canal.

"Let go the lines," the mules are hitched,
To take the boat in tow,
We're off upon the raging canal,
We're bound for Buffalo.[177]

The newspaper accounts of the "raging canal" quickly spread across the whole country. The "raging canal" appeared in articles in every year between 1845 and 1900. A sample of some of these newspapers are: *Public Ledger*, Philadelphia, Pennsylvania (1845); the *Raleigh Register*, Raleigh, North Carolina (1845); *Lancaster Post*, Pittsburgh, Pennsylvania (1848); the *Natchez Weekly Courier*, Natchez, Mississippi (1850); the *Portsmouth Inquirer*, Portsmouth, Ohio (1851); the *Louisville Daily Courier*, Louisville, Kentucky (1853); the *Belvidere Standard*, Belvidere, Illinois (1855); *Cooper's Clarksburg Register*, Clarksburg, West Virginia (1858); the *Daily Milwaukee News*, Milwaukee, Wisconsin (1859); *Weekly Mountain Democrat*, Placerville, California (1861); *Dawson's Fort Wayne Daily Times*, Fort Wayne, Indiana (1862); the *Hickman Courier*, Hickman, Kentucky (1880); and the *Mail*, Hagerstown, Maryland (1899).

There is little doubt that through oral transmission, songsters, song sheets, newspapers, magazines and books, information flowed quickly from one canal to another throughout the country. The contribution of the canallers themselves to the vitality of the folk tradition is evident in the number of parodies and additional lyrics supplied to popular songs. The canallers turned the tables on their tormentors and made the "raging canal" a badge of honor.

William Rideing, a writer for *Harper's New Monthly Magazine*, boarded a canalboat in New York Harbor that was towed, along with other canalboats, up the Hudson River. Rideing then traveled across the Erie Canal and wrote an account of the trip called "The Waterways of New York." He gives an eyewitness account of a singing session in the cabin of a canalboat that goes as follows:

> *His musical acquisitions included a stock of ballads, which he rendered with marvelous nasal inflections and in varying measures. It was in the sentimental that Jack excelled and a ditty that described the perils of canal life, the first stanzas we append, invariably brought tears to the eyes of the auditors.*
>
> *Come, sail-i-ors, landsmen, one and all.*
> *And I'll sing to you the dan-gi-ers of the raging canal,*
> *For I've been at the mer-i-cy of the windless and wave,*
> *And I'm one of the merry fellows what expects a watery grave.*
>
> *We left Albany about the break of day,*
> *As near as I can remember 'twas the second day of May,*
> *We depended on our driver, though he was very small,*
> *Although we knew the dan-gi-ers of the raging canawl.*[178]

Because Rideing provided us with two verses of the song, there is no doubt that this is Pete Morris's song "The Raging Canal." The first two verses of the original Pete Morris song are:

> *1. Come listen to my story, ye landsmen one and all,*
> *I'll sing to you the story of that raging canal,*
> *For I am one of many who expects a watery grave,*
> *I've been at the mercy of the wind and of the wave.*
>
> *2. When we left New York harbor it was the middle of the year,*
> *We put our helm hard a port and for Buffalo did steer,*
> *But when we got sight of Alba'y, we met a heavy squall,*
> *And we carried away our mizzen mast on that Raging Canal.*[179]

This is a good demonstration of the process of oral transmission, because another version of this song is even closer to the one Rideing heard on his excursion:

We left Albany harbor 'bout break of day,
And if I rightly remember 'twas the second day of May,
We trusted to our driver, altho' he was but small,
For he knew all the windings of that raging canal.[180]

This eyewitness account proves that canallers did sing "The Raging Canal" and continued to add their own changes to the original. Indeed, this is an excellent example of a published canal song that went into oral tradition and was perpetuated by the canallers themselves (not all of them were). Canallers took the raging canal joke and turned it into a canal-era anthem.

9

SUPERSTITION

Superstitions can be a stimulant to drive a person into unusual activity. Therefore, to fail to take into account this level of human motivation and to properly gauge it is to ignore a vital segment of human life.
—*Ray Browne,* New York Folklore Quarterly *17, no. 3 (Autumn 1961)*

C anallers might have been adept at turning gibes into humorous songs, but there was no joking about the mysterious forms of Civil War soldiers in the mist or a ghost carrying a lantern across an aqueduct. By association with deep-sea and Great Lakes sailors, canallers adopted long-held superstitions. However, canallers, especially the towpath drivers, did not need any additional superstitions to add to the many they themselves conjured up. William Totten mentions a number of superstitions and haunted places in his poem "The Rhyme of the Old Canal": "And loud were the cries of terror / And fearful the sound and harsh / Of victims borne on spectral wings / O'er Montezuma's marsh."[181]

The Cayuga Marsh had a haunted house, and on the towpath between Canastota and Wampsville was an unseen mass that could be felt. Somewhere beyond Amsterdam (New York), a "haunted house" is adjacent to the towpath: "It war a woman who put a ghost into that house; least ways I've hearn it war."[182] There were enough haunted lock-tender's houses, ghostly locks, cemeteries and swamps to terrify those on the towpath for miles. On the Chesapeake and Ohio Canal, according to

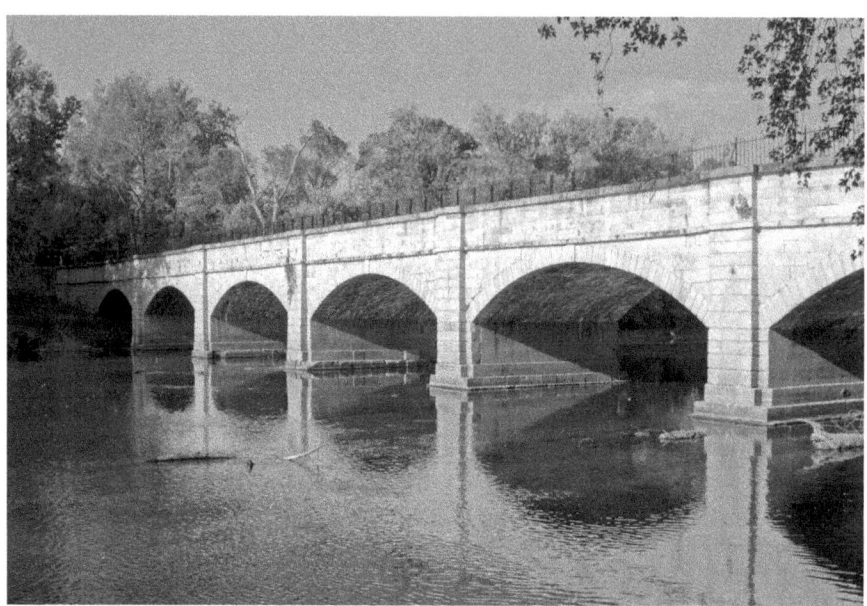

Monocacy Aqueduct. *National Park Service.*

Thomas Hahn in his *Towpath Guide*, canallers saw a headless man in the Paw Paw Tunnel. Canallers avoided tying up at these places at night.

At Haunted House Bend, the ghosts of Civil War soldiers could be seen in the mist hanging over the Potomac, and the ghost of a Civil War soldier was seen "from time to time on moonless nights crossing the Monocacy Aqueduct carrying a lighted lantern."[183] The Ohio and Erie Canal had its Haunted Rogues Bridge and the ghosts of Lock 4. The Pennsylvania canals had their share of haunted spots as well.

Superstition among the boatmen in those days was great, and one or two incidents at a particular spot could spawn a legend. The drowning of a canaller on the Schuylkill Navigation during an accident launching his boat prompted many workmen to quit their jobs and leave for other fields of work. It was then believed that after many years, nearly a quarter of a century, the canaller came back to haunt those whom people now believe were responsible for his death.[184]

A ghost comes back to haunt her lover in the Schuylkill Canal song "The Girl from Yewdall's Mill." After being spurned by her lover, "the girl who wrought at Yewdall's Mill" kills herself and

Every night at twelve o' clock, on top of Fairmount Hill,
The ghost of Bedelia may be seen gazing down on Yewdalls Mill.[185]

Along with home-grown superstitions, canal songs adopted a superstition legacy from the sea. A variety of sights and sounds figure into sailors' superstitions. Sightings of phantom ships, St. Elmo's fire and sounds of singing sirens, waves and tolling bells all brought various consequences to the crew who saw or heard them. The phantom ship the *Flying Dutchman* is one of the most often seen and quoted in literature.

PHANTOM SHIPS

In a study of fifteen phantom ships, Ralph Childs reports a number of characteristics that he says apply to phantom ships everywhere.[186] One characteristic is that phantom ships tend to sail against the wind or at high speeds with no wind at all. A second is that the ships either have no crew or a crew that is ghost-like and inactive. A third characteristic is that phantom ships are prone to appear after suffering disasters. And lastly, they are under an age-old curse of never making port.

The *Flying Dutchman* seems to fit all of the characteristics described by Ralph Childs. Sailors report seeing the *Flying Dutchman* traveling at very high speeds into the wind, or with no wind at all, as spray flies over the rails. The ship is either unmanned or has a ghost-like crew. The captain, Vanderdecken, ignores the pleas of his crew to seek shelter in Table Bay. Captain Vanderdecken (often referred to as Van Dyke) curses God for creating the storm and, after it is too late, attempts to turn into Table Bay but cannot. The ship is lost and is cursed to ply the seas for eternity. Sighting of the *Flying Dutchman* is considered a bad omen.

Here comes The Flying Dutchman now, fast through the hissing spray,
And proceeded by the tempest he heads for Table Bay,
With bird-like speed he's borne along before the howling blast
But he never can cast anchor there, for the bay, alas, he's passed.[187]

There is certainly a precedent for phantom vessel lore. Numerous literary figures wrote poems and stories about phantom vessels. There is even a Wagner opera, *Der Fliegende Holländer.* We also have the high school

English class standard *The Rime of the Ancient Mariner*, by Samuel Taylor Coleridge. Such noted authors as Whittier, Longfellow, Poe, Marryat and Washington Irving wrote about phantom ships. Respectively, the titles are, *The Dead Ship of Harpswell*, *The Phantom Ship*, *The Narrative of Arthur Gordon Pym of Nantucket*, *The Phantom Ship* and *The Flying Dutchman on Tappan Sea*.

What about phantom canalboat songs? The canal song "The Cruise of the Bouncing Sally" presents a real conundrum for the collector of canal songs. For one, it is the only canal song collected so far about a phantom vessel, and secondly, it is far better poetry than most canal songs. Its use of literary devices sets it apart from anything else in the canal song canon. There also is a great deal of mystery surrounding the origin of "The Cruise of the Bouncing Sally." It was reported to have been collected by Henry Shoemaker, a Pennsylvania folklorist and author.[188] However, a search of Shoemaker's papers and publications reveal no source for this song.[189] The only clues to where it might have been collected are given in the song itself— "where the Schuylkill flows in beauty" and "we were bound for Penn's fair city" (Philadelphia). This would place the song in eastern Pennsylvania, somewhere along the Schuylkill River or Schuylkill Canal. "The Cruise of the Bouncing Sally" has all the characteristics of the classic phantom ship with spray flying over the rails (quite a feat for a canal boat traveling at four miles an hour), a phantom crew and never seems to arrive at any destination.

"The Cruise of the Bouncing Sally"[190]

1. The boat has slipped her moorings, the mules have whisked their tails,
While the Captain grasps the tiller, as the spray flies o'er the rails,
Of the trim-built Bouncing Sally, On the waters free and bright,
Where the Schuylkill flows in beauty, through the starry, cloudless night.

The lyrics in the first verse of "The Cruise of the Bouncing Sally" foreshadow a canalboat that is not all it seems to be. "The boat has slipped her moorings" is the first indication that something is not right. The canalboat is not launched. It is not untied by a crew but "slips her moorings," as if it just floated out onto the canal with no help from an earthly crew. "While the Captain grasps the tiller, as the spray flies o'er the rails" sounds eerily familiar to the *Flying Dutchman* legend. Most accounts of the *Flying Dutchman* describe the ship charging through the water at a high rate of speed with spray flying over the rails. At three miles an hour, a mule-drawn canalboat, even in bad weather, could not produce "spray flying o'er the rails."

> *2. We were bound for Penn's fair city with a cargo from the mines,*
> *And the crew were staunch and steady with "Chief" Bangs to hold the*
> *lines.*
> *O'er the leader gay and frisky on the towpath winding fair,*
> *While the mule bells drowsy tinkle sang a ditty strange and rare.*

The second verse foreshadows another ominous sign: "The mule bells drowsy tinkle sang a ditty strange and rare." Something is not right about this "strange and rare" canalboat. This verse uses another literary device that also appears in *The Rime of the Ancient Mariner*, personification: "the mule bells...*sang* a ditty."

> *3. The "Chief" was a sunburned cowboy, aged ten, or thereabouts,*
> *And his looped and windowed apparel, flipped lazily in and out,*
> *Sometimes slept in the saddle, sometimes by the leader's side,*
> *He awoke and slept alternately nor recked of time and tide.*

The third verse describes a seemingly normal crew and voyage but leads us to another much-used literary device, alliteration. The line about Chief Bangs as he "sometimes slept in the saddle, sometimes by the leader's side" is a special type of alliteration called sibilance. In the fourth verse of the lyrics, we get "the twang of the tightened towrope" and "glittery drops that gleamed like gems in glistening moonlight."

> *4. The mellow sound of the boat horn, as it rang from the mountainside,*
> *Echoed from crag to valley or in lingering cadence died.*
> *The twang of the tightened towrope, the glittery drops that gleamed,*
> *Like gems in glistening moonlight and in filmy radiance beamed.*

Along with personification, "The Cruise of the Bouncing Sally" also gives us simile, such as the one in the previous paragraph—"glittery drops that gleamed like gems." There also is the use of onomatopoeia in the words "tinkle," "tinkling" and "twang." This verse introduces the sounds heard from the phantom boat—a boat horn, echoes, the twang of the tow rope and the tinkling of bells. These sounds are an indication that the canalboat is heard, not seen, and like other phantom vessels, the *Bouncing Sally* never reaches its destination.

> *5. They seemed to come from a phantom vessel, on the waters free and bright,*
> *Where the Schuylkill flows in beauty through the starry, cloudless night,*
> *With a phantom crew to man her and a phantom captain bold,*
> *With a phantom sunburned driver who cared not for storm or cold.*
> *And this phantom boat went drifting o'er the waters free and bright,*
> *With the phantom mule bells tinkling, through the clear and silent night.*

In the fifth and final verse, suspicions are confirmed that this is not a normal canalboat. It is brought home with plenty of repetition when the lyrics tell of "a phantom crew, a phantom captain, a phantom driver, a phantom boat and phantom mule bells," and as first foreshadowed when "the boat slipped her moorings," "the phantom boat went drifting o'er the waters." Despite the mystery surrounding the origins of "The Cruise of the Bouncing Sally," it remains a unique and beautifully poetic canal song and deserves to be sung often to whatever tune the singer chooses.

A possible second phantom canal song comes from the Erie Canal. It is an ominous sign when a canaller signs up to work on a canalboat named the *Prickly Heat* and the captain's name is Scratch. The canaller seems unaware that folklore, and blues legend, refer to the devil as Scratch. Almost immediately after coming aboard, the canaller perceives an uncanny resemblance to the phantom ship *Flying Dutchman*, whose captain, Vanderdecken, "cursed and swore and ranted 'round" and refused to seek shelter in a raging storm. This sounds like the canalboat from Hell!

"The Prickly Heat"[191]

> *1. The name she bore was The Prickly Heat,*
> *The captain's name was Scratch.*
> *He bawled and cursed and ranted 'round,*
> *The world held not his match.*

> *2. His voice was like an old foghorn,*
> *His eyes like one gone mad,*
> *He never tied up in a raging storm,*
> *I tell you he was bad.*

The Great Lakes and deep-sea sailors had no swamps, cemeteries and haunted houses. What they had was a world of unpredictability and events governed by the laws of chance. As a consequence, sailors' myths and superstitions contain references to sly transformational creatures—mermaids, mermen and silkies—and superstitions involving people with unusual physical characteristics; cross-eyed, red-haired or flat-footed. Surviving at sea depended on the sailor's ability to recognize what was not ordinary. Kitteridge believes that "surviving depended on the sailor's ability to see what was really going on, not what was supposed to be going on. Myths and superstitions help the sailor see by disassociating the sensibilities or fracturing the ordinary."[192] Evslin proposed the question, "What if imagination is viewed as an uncanny form of insight?"[193] This could be applied to superstition. Instead of superstition being looked upon as an unreasoned fear of the unknown, what if superstition is viewed as an uncanny form of insight? Sailors had to be aware of everything around them and distinguish what things were out of the ordinary. Observing unusual physical characteristics may have been more a survival skill than superstition.

PEOPLE TO AVOID

Superstition warned sailors to avoid encounters with people with certain physical characteristics. While heading to the ship to leave on a journey, sailors tried to steer clear of people with flat feet, crossed eyes and red hair. One canal song collected by John Lomax about these personal characteristics is "The Ballad of the Erie Canal."[194] The song refers to "a cross-eyed gal named Sal" and "a red-headed son-of-a-gun." The term *son-of-a-gun*, which refers to a male child born on a seagoing vessel, is another reference to the sea. "My Old Canal Mule" also uses this nautical expression.

"*Ballad of the Erie Canal*"

Once I was a brakeman on the E-ri-e Canal,
I met, fell in love with a cross-eyed gal named Sal,
She shook me for the driver, a red-headed son-of-a-gun,
And left me here and you may see, a poor old bum.

"A Trip on the Erie," found on both the Erie Canal and the Ohio and Erie Canal, is another canal song that contains references to red-haired and cross-eyed people. In this instance, the canalboat cook has "fiery red hair" and "she's cross-eyed."

"A Trip on the Erie"[195]

The cook she's a daisy, she's dead gone on me,
With her fiery red hair, *and she's twice twenty-three.*
She's cross-eyed *and freckled, a dumpling and a pet,*
And we use her for a headlight at night of the deck.

Red-headed people find their way into other canal songs:

Sandy Dan, he had red hair,
Sunday night he went to see Red-headed *Sal.*[196]

Although the people mentioned in these songs are already onboard, the references to cross-eyed and red-haired people are, most likely, vestiges of seafaring superstitions.

FEAR OF FRIDAY

Sea songs are filled with cautions to never leave for a voyage on Friday, and there are many inland waterway songs that include this superstition. Supposedly, this superstition came about because Friday was the day Jesus was crucified. However, some writers believe it can be traced back even farther. Rappoport believes that the notion may date back to pagan days, "For the dread of Friday is not at all limited to Christians. Friday derived its name from Freya or Frigga, the wife of Ode."[197] Sailing songs speaking to this superstition include "The Mermaid" and "Swell Me Net Full." The belief in the superstition about not leaving for a voyage of Friday was so strong that an urban legend appeared about the efforts of the Royal Navy to dispel this belief among its sailors. It goes something like this:

The British Admiralty had the keel of a ship laid on Friday, named the ship HMS Friday, *and launched her on Friday. They gave the command to a captain named Friday, and the ship commenced its maiden voyage of a Friday. Neither the ship nor the crew were ever heard from again.*[198]

In the Irish canal song "The Ballad of the 13th Lock," brought to the Erie Canal by Irish workers, the boat and its captain are doomed because they left on Friday, not to mention the unlucky number for the lock and the fact that the captain jeered at the ghosts on the dock. Boatmen on Ireland's Grand Canal believed that the thirteenth lock (just west of Dublin) was haunted because a graveyard was removed to build the lock. This tale became the subject of a poem by Arthur Griffith, "The Spooks of the Thirteenth Lock," and the inspiration for this song:

"Ballad of the 13th Lock"[199]

Every night of the week, 'round the 13th Lock,
The ghosts and the spooks of the Draferteen flock,
Sit swaying their bodies all this and that way,
And mournfully singing right tor-a-li-ay.

Chorus: Singing tor-a-li-or-i-li-or-a-li-ay,
Tor-a-li-or-i-li-or-a-li-ay,
Sit swaying their bodies all this and that way,
And mournfully singing right tor-a-li-ay.

2. There once was a Captain so gallant and bold,
He scoffed at advice from the young and the old,
"Do you think I'm afeared?" he would often say,
"Of any dead ghosts singing 'tor-a-li-ay.'"

3. On Friday morning we left from Athy,
The Captain looked back as 13th lock we passed by,
And he jeered at them ghosts sitting there on the quay,
a-mournfully singing right tor-a-li-ay.

JONAH

I fear I am the Jonah on board. Just tip me over into the deep, deep sea.
We thought this our last wreck. We chartered a line boat of Capt. John W.
Stephens, at Akron. We got as far as Johnny Cake Lock, when all the water
ran out of the raging canal and left us high and dry.
—Summit County Beacon *(Akron, OH) Wednesday, October 2, 1889*

Another sailing superstition that apparently carried over to the canal
was that of the Jonah. This superstition is based on the Old Testament
story of the prophet Jonah, the man swallowed by the great fish, who
angered God by ignoring his order to go to Nineveh and preach against
wickedness. Instead, Jonah fled to Joppa and attempted to sail to Tarshish.
A great storm threatened the ship, and Jonah told the men to throw him
overboard. The storm abated, and Jonah was swallowed by a great fish,
made his amends to God, and was saved. Typically, a Jonah is anyone
who causes bad luck, especially onboard a boat. In the newspaper article
about a canalboat experiencing a series of mishaps, a passenger suspects
that he is the Jonah and says, "Just tip me over into the deep, deep sea."

FOR WHOM THE BELL TOLLS

Sounds were the subject of many sailing superstitions: whistling, the
singing of sirens and the tolling of bells. If the sailors heard a church bell
chime at sea, it was an omen that someone would die. One canal song,
"The Cruise of the Calabar," an Irish canal song popular on American
canals, contains a reference to a town clock chime. It turns out that this is
the Albert Clock Tower situated at Queen's Square in Belfast, Northern
Ireland, on the Lagan Canal. Although not officially a church bell, its
chime foretells the boat's utter destruction: "Then all became confusion
and the raging winds did blow." Of course, as it turns out, the boat is not
out at sea, as we are at first led to believe, but in a canal. This is another
canal song in which the canallers refer to themselves as "dry-land sailors"
("Come all ye dry-land sailors and listen to me song"):

"The Cruise of the Calabar"[200]

Come all ye dry-land sailors and listen to me song,
It's got a thousand verses but I won't detain you long,
It's all about the adventurers of this sou' Lisburn lad,
As he sailed as a man before the mast on the good ship Calabar.

2. Now, a few days after we set sail, the weather it being sublime,
We passed beneath a railway bridge and I heard the "Albert" chime,
We were going along by the gasworks straight, a very dangerous part,
Where we run aground on a lump of coal that wasn't marked down in
the chart.

3. Then all became confusion and the raging winds did blow,
The bosun slipped on an orange peel and fell into the hold below,
"Put on more steam," the captain cried, "For we are sorely pressed,"
But the engineer from the bank replied, "The horse is doing his best."

Even though sea songs have the greatest number of references to superstition, the more protected life of a canaller still resulted in the reflection of some of the deep-sea sailors' superstitions. Canallers were superstitious and created their own canal superstitions in addition to adopting them from the sea. It is likely that some of the adopted superstitions were not even recognized for what they were. The superstition references in canal songs were, at times, taken lightly. Canallers could laugh a bit more where superstition was involved, but nevertheless, sailing superstitions were present even in the protected environment of the inland waterways.

10

THE MINSTREL SHOW
COMES TO TOWN

lmost all canal songs were based on the melodies to popular songs of the day. Popular music's influence on canal songs is greater than its influence on other occupations that were more isolated. Although canal occupational songs have some things in common with those of the cowboy, the lumberjack and the coal miner, there is one big difference—outside influences. Cowboy songs were born from the cattle drives in which they drove herds of cattle across wide, barren stretches of open land. When they did come to town, it was usually not a major city, as back east, but a small frontier town. The cowboys' association with popular music was limited. The same can be said for lumberjacks, who plied their trade in the lumber camps isolated in places like the Adirondacks or the Catskill Mountains of New York State. Their contact with other people or cities was limited. Again, the miners had much the same situation of being more or less isolated in company mining towns in the mountainous areas of Pennsylvania, Maryland and West Virginia. Contact with the cities, people other than themselves and the latest popular music was limited. Korson asserts, "Until modern conditions broke down the barriers, the mine patch or coal camp was as much a closed town as any feudal village in the Middle Ages."[201] The songs of cowboys, coal miners and lumberjacks are far less likely to reflect the popular music of the day. Canallers were bound to hear and be exposed to more popular music than someone out on the range, in a remote Adirondack lumber camp or nestled in an isolated company coal town in northern Pennsylvania. Canal boatmen, for example, had direct connections to New York City, Philadelphia, Washington, D.C., and Pittsburgh. One trip on the Erie Canal could take a canaller to Albany, Utica, Rome, Syracuse, Rochester and Buffalo. Even on canals that covered less distance, canallers were constantly on the move and visiting populated areas. William Rideing described a trip in which they started in New York City and were towed up the Hudson and across the Erie Canal, visiting the major cities along the canal.[202] The population centers tended to grow along the canals. This accounts for the large number of parodies on popular songs and the number of canal songs using popular melodies of the day. This also accounts for the dissemination of canal songs over a wider area. Only the fact that the canal era occupied such a brief period of time limited the collected repertory to a relatively small number of songs.

The protected environment of the inland waterways was responsible for canallers having more contact with popular culture than many professions. Canallers traveled constantly between large population centers, not occasionally, as Great Lakes or deep-sea sailors, but every day. They participated in music sessions in the cities and towns they visited and heard popular music on a regular basis. They had daily access to the latest songs being sold in music stores and published in newspapers in communities along the canal.

What was the music they saw and heard? It was the music of Dan Emmett, Stephen Foster, James Bland, Charles White and L.V.H. Crosby. The canal era coincided with the era of the minstrel show (1840–80), so a great number of minstrel songs show up as melodies for canal songs and popular songs sung by the canallers. Almost every famous minstrel show composer was parodied at some time during the canal era or there was a canal song being sung to one of his tunes. Minstrel songs by Emmett, Foster, Bland, White and Crosby were well known, and if anyone wanted to borrow a singable melody that everyone knew, minstrel music was tops. At this time, it was almost impossible to find anyone connected to the canals who did not know "Oh! Susanna," "Camptown Races," "Old Dan Tucker" or "Golden Slippers."

The man given credit for starting the first minstrel group was Dan Emmett. Emmett, along with Billy Whitlock, Dick Pelham and Frank Brower, formed the Virginia Minstrels in 1843, not in Virginia but New York City. Daniel Decatur Emmett (1815–1904) was perhaps best known as the composer of "Dixie." Emmett wrote two songs for the Virginia Minstrels,

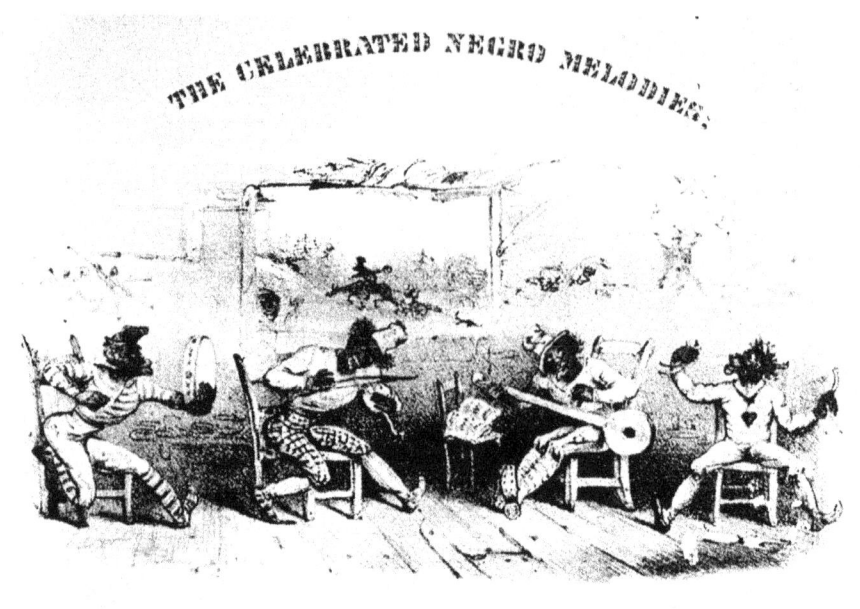

Virginia Minstrels, reproduced from the sheet music by the author. *Public domain.*

"De Boatman Dance" and "Old Dan Tucker," that became part of the canal song repertoire. Emmett's "De Boatman Dance" became the "Canal Boatman Dance."

"De Boatman Dance"[203]
Dan Emmett

De boatman dance, De boatman sing,
De boatman do 'most anything,
And when de boatman get on shore,
He spends his cash and works for more.
    Chorus:
Dance, boatman, dance, dance, boatman, dance,
Dance all night 'till de broad daylight,
Go home wid de gals in the morning.
Hi, ho, de boatman row,
Sailing down the river on de Ohio,

Hi, ho, de boatman row,
Sailing down the river on de Ohio.

"The Canal Boatman Dance" is a parody of the minstrel song, and the lyrics to the choruses are similar. It is a joyful celebration of the opening of the canal in the spring. It retains the dialect from the minstrel version, and the first verse reflects its minstrel stage origin with the line "ol' winter's walked his chalk so nice," a reference to chalk marks on the stage to guide the performers to where they should stand. Some canal songs have similar characteristics of minstrel songs, resulting in the use of dialect and hints of slavery, as reflected in the line "and Massa Sun's unfriz the ice."

"The Canal Boatman Dance"[204]

Old winter's walked his chalk so nice,
And Massa Sun's unfriz the ice,
Canal's wide open wid de Spring,
Canal boat people dance and sing.
   Chorus:
Wake up, canal boy, wake.
Wake up, canal boy wake,
Pull off your coat and load de boats,
Get ready to go in de mornin'.
Heigh Ho! We'll steer and haul,
Our boats, up and down de long canal.
Heigh Ho! We'll steer and haul,
Our boats, up and down de long canal.

Dan Emmett's "Old Dan Tucker," written for the Virginia Minstrels in the 1840s, became a canal song by Captain Pearl R. Nye. In the song, Nye mentions Nelsonville, a town on the Ohio and Erie Canal, and compares "big Sil Blan" to a mule. Most canallers used the names of real people in their songs, so Big Sil was probably a resident of Nelsonville.

In Nelsonville, 'Twas big Sil Blan,
He was more like a mule than he was like a man,
But he was good natured, wore a golden smile,
And he seemed to capture the whole canal.[205]

STEPHEN FOSTER

Stephen Foster songs found their way onto the canal as well. Stephen Foster (1826–1864) was one of America's most popular songwriters, with such hits as "Oh! Susanna," "Camptown Races" and "Old Folks at Home." Foster's "Old Black Joe" was used as the melody for the "Ballad of the Erie Canal."[206]

> *Once I was a brakeman on the E-ri-e Canal,*
> *I fell in love with the cook, a cross-eyed gal named Sal.*
> *She shook me for the driver, a red-headed son-of-a-gun.*
> *And left me here as you may see, a poor old bum.*
> > *Chorus:*
> *I'm going, I'm going, for I know my time has come,*
> *And to the workhouse I must go, a poor, old, bum.*

Stephen Foster's "Oh! Susanna" was used as the tune for the following song, "Runaway Mules":

"Runaway Mules"[207]

> *The mules ran off and I fell down,*
> *I really thought I'd croak,*
> *A bullfrog yelled, "Look out there, Boy,*
> *I'll jump right down your throat,"*
> > *Chorus:*
> *That night was a hummer,*
> *Old Fear was there in style,*
> *But I looked beyond his capers,*
> *For I love the Old Canal.*

L.V.H. CROSBY

L.V.H. Crosby, who is given credit for being the first "middle man," or "Mr. Interlocutor," in a minstrel show, was also the organizer of the Harmoneons, an early (1845) Boston minstrel troupe. He composed songs for the Harmoneons and recognized the connection the audience would have to a song about the canal. In 1845, Crosby wrote "I'm Sailing on De

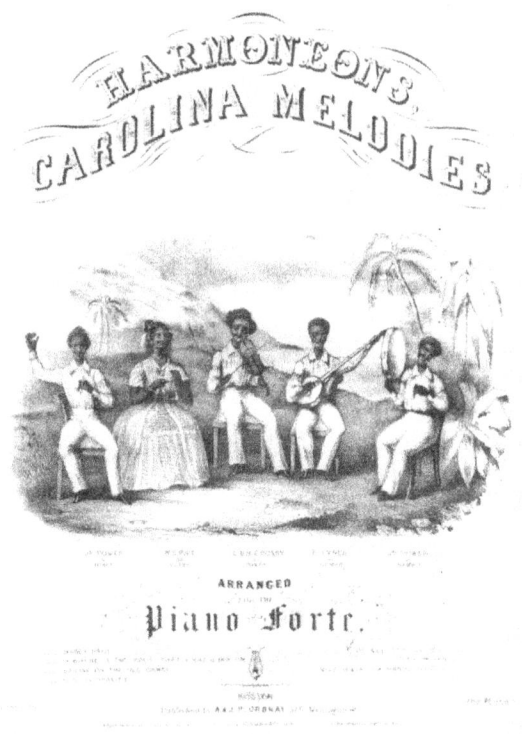

Crosby, L.V.H., "I'm sailin' on de old canal." African American Sheet Music. *Brown Digital Repository. Brown University Library.*

Old Canal."[208] The minstrel shows influenced canal songs, and the canal influenced minstrel songs—more on that subject in the next chapter.

"I'm Sailing on de Old Canal"

O! yes dear Fanny I'll be dar soon.
You're handsome as dat ole new moon;
Your form is as fair as any spring wedder,
So jump on board and we'll sail off togedder.
    Chorus:
I'm sailing on de ole canal,
Tra la la la la la la la la,
I'm sailing on de ole canal.
Tra la la la la la la la la

Although Crosby's song was written only one year after "The Raging Canal," none of the verses mentions the raging canal or any particular canal.

CHARLES ALBERT WHITE

Charles White (1832–1892) was one of America's earliest popular music composers and one of the first songwriters to establish a successful music publishing company, the Boston firm of White, Smith & Perry. White's song "Marguerite," published in 1882, sold over one million sheet music copies. Russell Sanjek, in his book *American Popular Music and Its Business: The First Four Hundred Years*, puts White's copyrighted pieces at over 1,500. White wrote a number of minstrel songs, including "I'se Gwine Back to Dixie,"[209] which became the inspiration and the tune for the song "I'm Going Back to the Canal."

"I'se Gwine Back to Dixie"	*"I'm Going Back to the Canal"*[210]
I'se gwine back to Dixie, no more I'm gwine to wander	*I'm bred and born a canaller, My heart is always yearning,*
I'se gwine back to Dixie, can't stay here no longer	*To see the old boat yonder, So now I am returning.*
I miss the old plantation, my home and my relations	*The sound so won'drous pretty, Far grander than a city,*
My heart's turned back to Dixie and I must go	*I'm more happy than a kitty, For I'm going back to the canal.*
Chorus:	*Chorus:*
I'se gwine back to Dixie, I'se going back to Dixie	*I'm going, yes, I'm going, I'm hauling, running, towing,*
I'm going where the orange tree blossoms grow	*With the good things growing with a smile,*
I hear the children calling, I see the sad tears falling	*The breezes soft are blowing, While milk and honey flowing,*
My heart's turned back to Dixie and I must go	*All along so I am going, To my old boat on the canal.*

JAMES BLAND

James Bland (1854–1911) was known in his day as "The World's Greatest Minstrel Man," "The Greatest Ethiopian Songwriter" and the "Black Stephen Foster." He wrote over seven hundred songs and

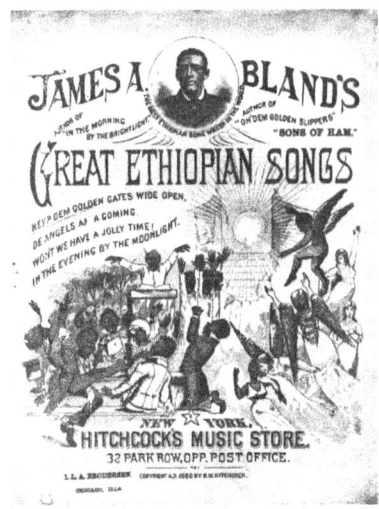

James Bland sheet music cover.
Reproduced by the author.

is generally acknowledged to be the first commercially successful black songwriter.[211] The composer Charles Albert White's Boston music company published the earliest compositions of James Bland. Bland is known for such tunes as "Golden Slippers," "In the Evening by the Moonlight" and "Carry Me Back to Old Virginny." All three of these tunes made their way into the canal song repertoire. "Golden Slippers" became "Oilskin Slickers."

Canallers did not have the luxury of steering the boat from a nice dry cabin or treading the towpath under an umbrella. The whole crew was out in the weather, no matter how bad, for long periods of time, sometimes day and night, and relied on a material known as oilcloth to protect them from the elements. Oilcloth, or oilskin, was fabric treated with tar or oil to make it waterproof.

"Oilskin Slickers"[212] *Tune: "Golden Slippers"*

When a storm comes up we don our skins,
To keep us dry and warm within,
But when those sheets or torrents poured,
In our oilskins we were safely moored.
    Chorus:
Oh, those oilskin slickers, Oh, those oilskin slickers,
Hat, coat, breeches, rubber boots, We can keep dry let torrents shoot.
Oh, those oilskin slickers, Oh, those oilskin slickers,
As we gaily move along, Upon the old canal.

"In the Evening by the Moonlight" was turned into "In the Evening in the Summer," and "Carry Me Back to Old Virginny" was transformed into one of Captain Nye's "Chanties."

"In the Evening in the Summer"[213] *Tune: "In the Evening by the Moonlight"*

In the evening in the summer, you could hear canallers singing,
On the decks or in the hatches, banjos, fiddles would be ringing,
How the whole crew would enjoy it, well as those along that listened,
As we sang in the evenings, on our canal boats.

"Chanty"[214] *Tune: "Carry Me Back to Old Virginny"*

Oh, how I love my silver ribbon,
No place in all the world that's half so dear to me,
There I am free as the birds in the wildwood,
There shall I live and die will always be my plea.

The minstrel show with its stereotyped blackface characters was dying out just at the time when most of the canals were doing the same. As the minstrel era gradually changed over to vaudeville, ragtime and other musical styles, the canal era ended in much the same way, with canals shutting down gradually over a period of time and the canal era giving way to new styles of transportation—motors and the railroad. The Farmington Canal closed in 1847. The Beaver and Erie Canal closed in 1871. The Pennsylvania and Ohio Canal closed in 1872. The North Branch of the Pennsylvania Canal system ceased operation in 1872. The Chenango Canal closed in 1878, and the Union Canal followed in 1881. Most of the Pennsylvania West Branch closed in 1891. The Delaware and Hudson Canal shut down in 1899. And, just as the minstrel show continued on a local, amateur basis into the twentieth century, individual canal systems hung on into the twentieth century as well. The Schuylkill Navigation shut down gradually from 1872 until 1931. The Ohio and Erie ended operation in 1913. Finally, the Chesapeake and Ohio Canal came to an end in 1924, and the Lehigh followed in 1931. Now we hear an occasional song by Stephen Foster, Dan Emmett or James Bland just as we hear an occasional canal song to remind us of a bygone era:

Lay me down, Carolina, lay me down,
Don't wanna wake up in the mornin' no more,
Sing me one slow, sad song for this one last old time,
Before they close the minstrel show.
—Bob Coleman, "Before They Close the Minstrel Show"

160

IV

AN ERA HAS ENDED
BUT THE MELODY LINGERS ON

*Nostalgia—a wistful or excessively sentimental yearning
for return to some past period or irrecoverable condition.*

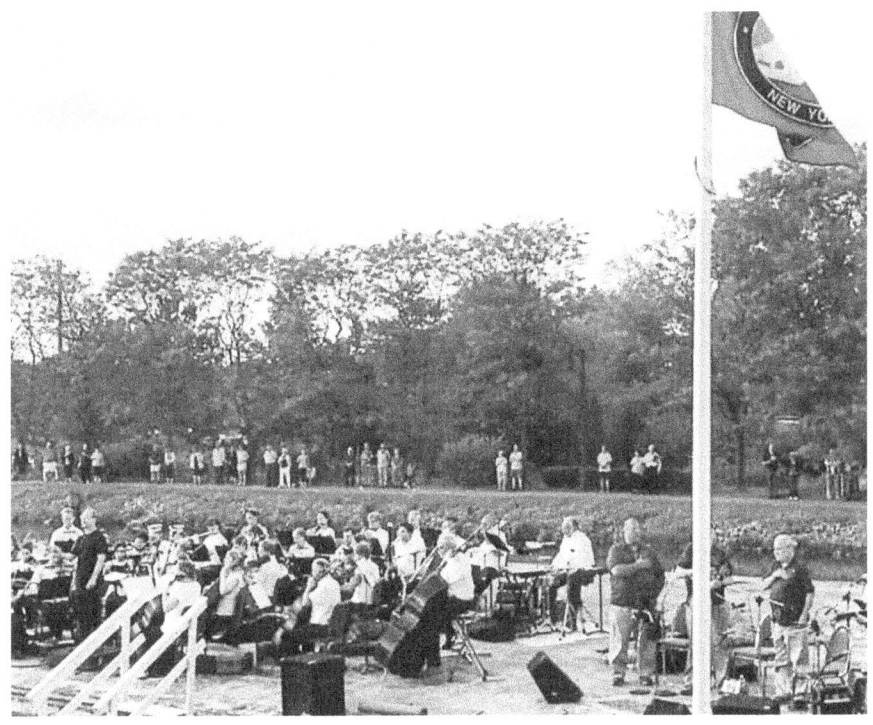

Water Music, the Albany Symphony and the Golden Eagle String Band, July 2017.
Photograph by Paul Minor, used with permission.

THE CANAL COMES TO THE STAGE

If you want to make good in a Broadway show,
You must have a song that is sure to go.
A pretty little ditty that they whistle 'round the city,
And they play ev'rywhere, ev'ry day, ev'rywhere.
—"Down by the Erie Canal," George M. Cohen

By 1912, after most canals were closed, people along the Erie Canal had become aware that the old canal was slipping away. Even though New York State decided to keep its canal system, the era of towpaths and mules was giving way to motors, larger boats and the use of natural waterways. Cities such as Rochester and Syracuse were bypassed, and landmarks like aqueducts, weighlocks and some locks were becoming obsolete. Nostalgia for the "good old days" was building along the canal.

In 1912, "The Rhyme of the Old Canal" (appendix A) and "Low Bridge, Everybody Down" (appendix B), a poem and a song, respectively, were published, captivating the sentiment of the time. They may have been written about the Erie Canal, but they soon became synonymous with the entire canal era. The composer of "Low Bridge, Everybody Down" first saw the Erie Canal in 1910.[215] The author of "The Rhyme of the Old Canal" was born along the Erie Canal and is reported to have worked on the canal.[216]

The song "Low Bridge, Everybody Down" consists of five verses and five choruses, which is quite long for the normal popular song of that era and unusual in that all the choruses are different. (Edward Meeker recorded the entire song, minus the fifth verse, in his 1913 Edison recording.) The popularity of the sentiment surrounding this song is reflected in the fact that violinist and composer Thomas S. Allen's "Low Bridge, Everybody Down" was widely recorded. Billy Murray recorded "Low Bridge, Everybody Down" for Victor on the day it was copyrighted—November 18, 1912. The Peerless Quartet recorded the song for Columbia less than a month later (December 6, 1912), and Edward Meeker recorded the song for Edison a month after that in January 1913. Record companies remained interested in the song long after Thomas Allen's death. In 1929, Vernon Dalhart recorded the song twice: electronically under his own name on January 16, 1929 (Columbia 15378-D), and acoustically under the pseudonym Mack Allen on January 21, 1929 (Harmony 831-H and Velvet Tone/Viva labels).[217] The song was also used in the 1935 movie *The Farmer Takes a Wife*, and it is still being recorded in the twenty-first century by such artists as Bruce Springsteen and Suzanne Vega, one hundred years after it was written.

While "Low Bridge, Everybody Down" comes from a Tin Pan Alley songwriter with only a slight connection to the canal, the author of "The Rhyme of the Old Canal" is someone quite familiar with canalling. William Totten was born in 1858 in New London, New York, a village in the town of Verona, situated on the Erie Canal. John and Alan Lomax, in their book *American Ballads and Folksongs*, state that William D. Totten sang canal songs "while working as a towpath boy out of Buffalo from 1871 to 1877."[218] The poem draws upon the popularity of Coleridge's *Rime of the Ancient Mariner*; in fact, Totten even refers to his subject as the "ancient captain." "The Rhyme of the Old Canal" is more regular in its structure, but it does adapt the four-line verses and rhyming scheme of the first sections of Coleridge's poem (lines two and four of a quatrain are rhymed). Even some of the subject matter hints at a connection between the two poems. Totten writes, "And loud were the cries of terror / and fearful the sound and harsh / of victims borne on spectral wings"; "and groaning ghost beneath the boat";[219] "Over the mystic river, / with spirit hand at the helm, / they've passed away forever, / into the Silent Realm."[220]

The two canal pieces provide some insight into the public's feelings about the end of an era and why a song like "Low Bridge, Everybody Down" came to be written and recorded so frequently. Although it did not enjoy the same popularity as the song, the poem provided its readers with the same nostalgic feeling. At least two newspapers (the *Newark (NY) Courier* and the *Lyons (NY) Republican*) in towns along the Erie Canal thought that their readers would identify with a nostalgic poem about the end of the canal era, and a publisher and several record companies thought the same of the song.

The canal era was a slower, more peaceful time, when canalboats moved along at three miles an hour and animals provided the power to transport people and things. It was a time of great prosperity. Canals opened up the interior of the United States to settlement, transported goods, stimulated trade and produced economic growth that would have been impossible without them. "Low Bridge, Everybody Down" was not about one canaller and his mule looking for another job but about a monumental change in people's lives and the way transportation and the country would go forward.

Many people were not sure they liked the change. New technology powered by machines, not animals, took over the transportation system. Things moved faster. Instead of three miles per hour, the world moved at a frightening speed. The quiet pastoral scene of the canal gave way to the roar of trains racing down iron rails. People looked back on the canal era as a source of comfort. A number of artists recognized this and began to produce nostalgic works that helped people reflect on a bygone era.

Public interest and nostalgia for the canal era were recognized by professional songwriters before the twentieth century. "Low Bridge, Everybody Down" was not the first nostalgic song about the canal or the first to use the expression "low bridge" in song. It became evident to Broadway composers that a sure way to sell a show was to have a song about the canal. David Braham and Edward Harrigan composed a song for their show *The Grip* (1885) that foreshadows Thomas Allen's song in many respects. Not only does it use the term "low bridge" in the title but also in other prominent places in the lyrics. Braham and Harrigan also foreshadow Allen's song by the use of call and response. Although that technique was already common in work songs and minstrel shows, it was out of place in canal songs. In Braham and Harrigan's song for *The Grip*, the use of call and response goes beyond the first two lines and repeats the technique in the chorus, again repeating "low bridge."

The Grip takes place in New York City, where Patrick Reilly (Edward Harrigan) is proprietor of the Canteen, a saloon frequented by canallers. In the show, a canal captain, in blackface (the reason for the dialect), sings "Oh! Dat Low Bridge," accompanied by other members of the cast.[221] Was this the song witnesses in the Haviland-Doubleday lawsuit heard prior to 1912? Those witnesses may not have remembered the tune but recalled the references to "low bridge," "bulky mule" and "Buffalo."

"Oh! Dat Low Bridge"[222]

It's many miles to Buffalo, Oh! dat low bridge,
Bulky mule he travel slow, Oh! dat low bridge.
Dars gravel on de towpath, Dars hornets in de sand,
Oh, pity poor canallers dats far away from land.
    Chorus:
Den look out dat low bridge, Look out dat low bridge,
Look out dat low bridge, Look out dat low bridge,
De Captain, cook and all de crew, Oh, duck your head way down,
De fastest boat in all de fleet, Two Sisters come to town.

By the time Broadway came around to recognizing the canals, the canal era was all but over. The songs played upon the nostalgic reaction of the audience.

David Braham and Edward Harrigan wrote another song for a Broadway show that produced an entirely different result. "Never Take the Horseshoe from the Door," written for the show *The Mulligan Guards' Surprise* in 1880, did not have anything to do with the canal, yet it ended up as a canal song. In the show, a recurring character, Dan Mulligan, played by Ed Harrigan,

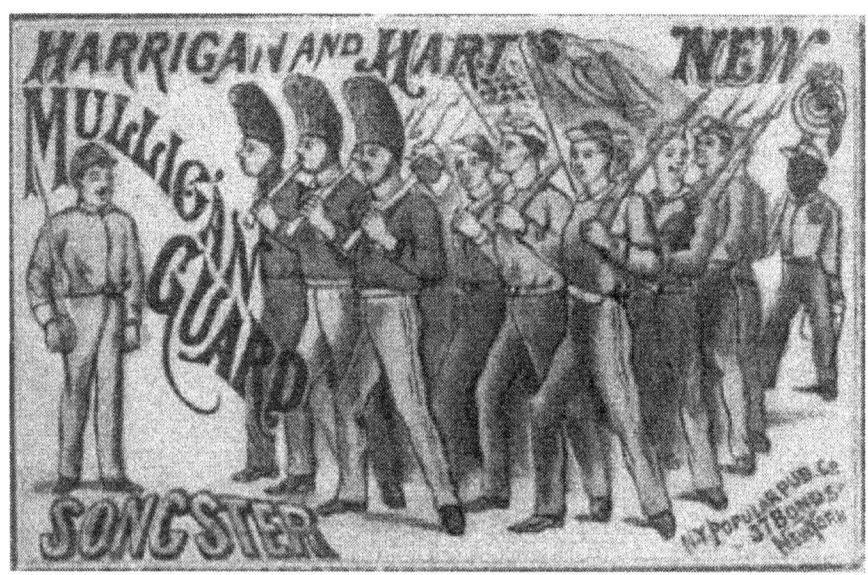

The Mulligan Guard songster. Buffalo-Erie County Library.

166

throws a surprise party and one of the guests presents Dan with a horseshoe, which becomes the theme of a song.[223] "Never Take the Horseshoe from the Door," and its subsequent parody, "Never Take the Hindshoe from a Mule," were popular with the public and on canals in New York and other states. We know the parody was sung by canallers, but it is possible that the parody was not the product of canallers but professionally composed. It was included in a Harrigan and Hart songster in 1882.[224] This was not the first song from the canal included in Harrigan and Hart songsters. An early version of the canal song known today as "The E-ri-e Was A'risin" appeared in Harrigan and Hart's *The Mulligan Guards' Songster* (1873), simply titled "Buffalo."[225] While the original intent of "Never Take the Horseshoe from the Door" was not to create a canal song, the composers recognized the popularity of the parody by publishing it themselves.

> "*Never Take the Horseshoe from the Door*"[226]
>
> *There's a story handed down in Irish history,*
> *Far, far beyond the days of King Borhue.*
> *That the best of luck is always waiting on you.*
> *If you pick up on the road a horse's shoe.*
> *Then gather the family 'round me Sunday morning.*
> *Let the babies roll upon the floor.*
> *So, one and all I give ye timely warning,*
> *Never take the horseshoe from the door.*
>
> "*Never Take the Hindshoe from a Mule*"[227]
>
> *A story has come down from old Mathusam,*
> *I learned it when I was a boy in school,*
> *You'll make a big mistake and don't forget it,*
> *If you bother 'round the hind parts of a mule.*
>   *Chorus:*
> *So, never tickle a mule when he's reposing,*
> *If you disturb his slumber, you're a fool,*
> *If you don't want to visit the undertaker,*
> *Never take the hindshoe from a mule.*

Braham and Harrigan were not the last commercial songwriters to compose a nostalgic canal song for a Broadway show. George M. Cohan,

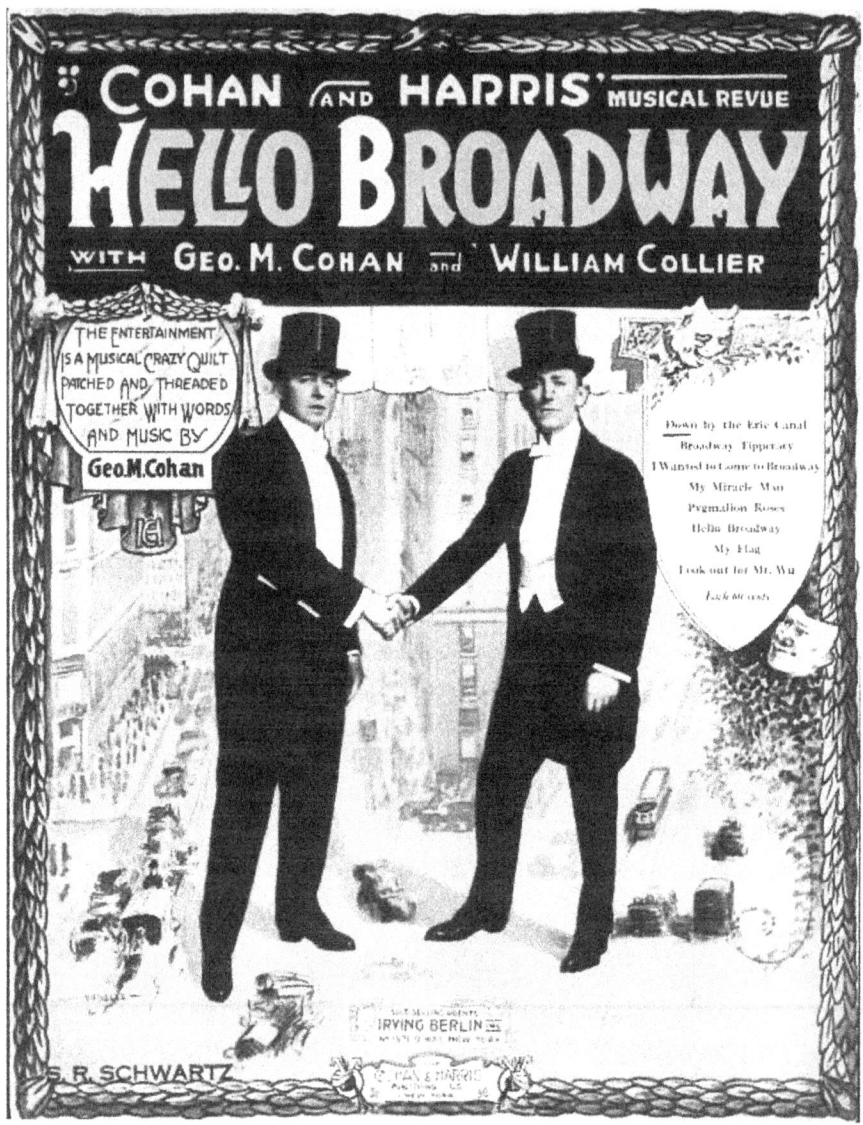

Hello Broadway sheet music cover. *Reproduced by the author.*

the "Yankee Doodle Dandy," was already a star on the New York stage when he followed with his own nostalgic piece about the Erie Canal. Cohan was a bit more sarcastic and a little less nostalgic when in 1915 he wrote "Down by the Erie Canal" for the show *Hello Broadway*. It seemed to be Cohan's intent, if the words are any indication, to put an end to songs about the canal on the New York stage. Motors and technology had already put an end to songs on the canal.

Apparently, the influence of the canal on the New York stage was prevalent enough to raise the ire of the new generation of songwriters and performers. In his song, Cohan lambasted the producers on Broadway for the cliché song choruses they required to sell a show. The patter-like verse, filled with sarcasm, is followed by a deliberately bad chorus about the Erie Canal.

"Down by the Erie Canal"[228]

If you want to make good in a Broadway show,
You must have a song that is sure to go.
A pretty little ditty that they whistle 'round the city,
And they play ev'rywhere, ev'ry day, ev'rywhere,
A regular, popular, tin pan song,
The kind of melody that can't go wrong,
A catchy refrain, the sort of strain that gives you a pain.
It's usually sung by the female star.
The publisher gives her a motor car.
And the chorus goes something like this:

Down by the Erie, there waits my Pal,
Tho' the days are long and dreary,
He declares he'll ne'er grow weary,
Poor John O'Leary, I'm afraid you've lost your gal,
For I've left you flat my dearie, by the Erie Canal.

The irony is that "Down By the Erie Canal" was not the end of Erie Canal songs on Broadway, as Cohan's song is still being sung in the musical *George M!*. So, despite Cohan's best intentions, he did not manage to eliminate the influence of the canal from the New York stage or the hearts of those who longed for memories of a bygone era.

FROM BUFFALO TO TROY

W here did canal songs originate? Examples in previous chapters give examples of canal songs that originated from parodies of popular songs, were borrowed from folk songs, were improvised to familiar melodies and were composed by professional songwriters. In a discussion of the origins of canal songs organized by the New York Folklore Society at the Erie Canal Museum in Syracuse, New York, one of the panelists suggested that we cannot be sure of the lyrics or tunes to any canal song because there were so many versions sung at any one time. There is some truth in this view, but because other folk songs have been handed down for hundreds of years with similar lyrics and tunes, it is also possible that canal songs with similar lyrics and melodies survive as well. Even taking into account the "folk process" of changes in words or variations in melody, there are countless examples of folk songs, much older than canal songs, handed down to us in essentially the same form. There are folk songs from Ireland and Great Britain found in New York and elsewhere in the United States that survived a transatlantic journey and were still passed from generation to generation in an almost identical version. Thus, it seems possible that some canal songs evolved from a common source and remained relatively unchanged over a 150-year period.

There is evidence to suggest that one such canal song is "From Buffalo to Troy." Harold Thompson printed words to the song in *Body, Boots and Britches* and said that it was sung "in the Alhambra Varieties on Commercial Street in Buffalo during the 1880s" by an entertainer named Johnny Bartley.[229] Lionel Wyld wrote that it was a "canal song of which there are numerous versions."[230] John and Alan Lomax publish two similar versions of the song collected from N.E. Bugbee of Cortland, New York, and D. Gillespie from Buffalo, New York. They also restate the claim that it was "sung by Johnny Bartley in the eighties, at the Alhambra Varieties on Commercial Street near the Erie Canal."[231] Folklorist Frank Warner sang a version using nearly the same words Thompson printed and a melody similar to Great Lakes songs known in the Buffalo area.[232] George Ward sings a version using similar words and a similar tune strain.[233]

"From Buffalo to Troy"[234]

I've travelled all around this world, and Tonawanda, too,
I've been cast on desert isles and beaten black and blue,
I fought and bled at Bull Run and wandered as a boy,
But I'll never forget the trip I took from Buffalo to Troy.
   Chorus:
Whoa Back! Get up! And tighten up your line,
And watch the playful flies as on the mules they climb,
Whoa back! Duck your nut! Forget it I never shall,
When I drove a pair of spavined mules on the E-ri-e Canal.

Did Johnny Bartley write the song or, as Thompson and Lomax suggest, merely perform it? Advertisements in the Buffalo newspapers list Johnny Bartley as the manager of the Alhambra Theater, not an entertainer, although both are possible. The date for the song could be later than the 1880s given by Thompson. When almost every Erie Canal song sings about Buffalo to Albany, why does this song sing about Buffalo to Troy? This is the only canal song that gives Troy as the eastern entrance to the canal. Typical lyrics either mention Albany, Buffalo or both.

I left Albany harbor about the break of day. ("The Raging Canal")
We were forty-nine-miles from Albany. ("The E-ri-e")
And every inch of the way we know, from Albany to Buffalo. ("Low Bridge, Everybody Down")

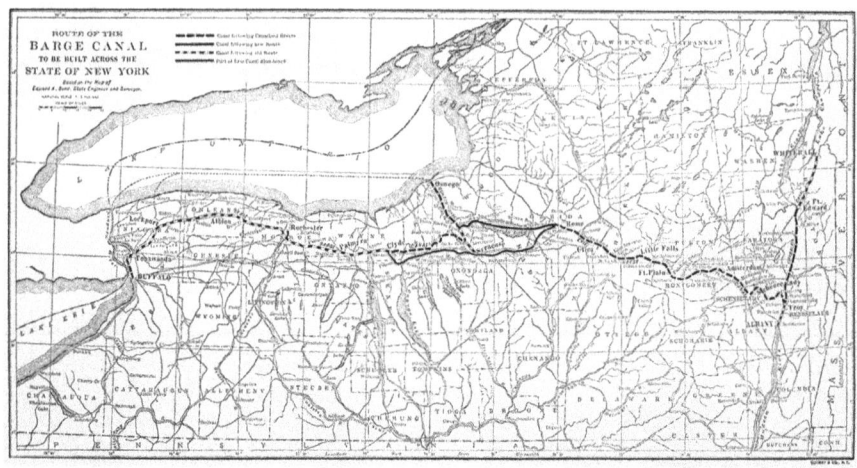

A 1905 map of the Erie Canal showing Troy as the eastern end. *eriecanal.org.*

If the title were the only reference to Troy, it could be ignored because titles of songs are rather arbitrary. However, the Buffalo to Troy reference is found in the lyrics: "And I'll never forget the trip I took from Buffalo to Troy." How did Troy figure in this? Albany was the eastern end of the Erie Canal, unless boats at Juncta (Cohoes) followed the Champlain Canal route and used the side cut at Waterford to enter the Hudson River. In 1903, the State of New York made plans to modernize the canals into what it called the New York State Barge Canal System. It was during this time, 1903–1916, that the Troy Federal Lock became the entrance to the Erie Canal from the Hudson River, and the locks in Waterford were numbered starting with E2.

Could this be the reason that this song is titled "From Buffalo to Troy" instead of "Buffalo to Albany"? If so, it may have been composed later than the 1880s. The origins of the song are worth examining to try to place this song in a general time frame and discover the evolution of the melody and lyrics. If Bartley did write this song, what was his inspiration and where did this canal song originate?

Buffalo, New York, is a logical place to start, and there is a great deal of circumstantial evidence that points to Buffalo. The title and lyrics of the song point to Buffalo. The song contains references to places familiar to people from Buffalo. Buffalo is a port on the Great Lakes and connected to New York City by the Erie Canal, and obviously, theater managers or entertainers like Johnny Bartley (the possible author of this song) and others would have heard Great Lakes songs, canal songs and popular songs in this gathering place of all three. Harold Thompson places the canal song in Buffalo. Also, the lyrics suggest a Buffalo origin. The first line of the first verse would have brought a laugh to an audience in Buffalo: "I've traveled all around the world and Tonawanda, too." Tonawanda is one of Buffalo's nearest neighbors (twelve miles to the north) and not a destination for many world travelers, but it was on the Erie Canal.

The song was recorded by New York folk song collector Frank Warner and others. Most of those recorded examples, although slightly different in some respects, seem to come from a common tune strain. The tune suggests a Buffalo origin for "From Buffalo to Troy" because it shares a melody with a well-known Great Lakes song. There is a relationship, both in the lyrics and the melody, between "From Buffalo to Troy" and the Great Lakes' song "The Bigler." Every chorus in "The Bigler" ends with the line "on our passage down to Buffalo from Milwaukee." "The Bigler" had a closer connection to Buffalo than any port on the Great Lakes. The *Bigler*'s entire purpose was to haul lumber from the Midwest to Buffalo.

The other connection with Buffalo may be one word in the chorus of "The Bigler" that has sparked some debate—*juberju*. Bernard DeVoto, in his book *Mark Twain's America*, ties that word to slave dances and their adaptation to the minstrel show by Edwin Christy in Buffalo circa 1843.[235] One such dance was the Juba, which contained a step called the Jubal Jew. An account of the dance describes the dancers, with one leg lifted, dancing counterclockwise in a circle. It does not take much imagination to transform Jubal Jew into juberju, and the high leg lift might have given rise to "jump up on her juberju."

"From Buffalo to Troy" is a canal song with ties to a Great Lakes song, a popular song and a sea song,

"From Buffalo to Troy" (Canal)	"The Knickerbocker Line" (Popular song)
Whoa back! Get Up!, *And tighten up your lines*	*She's a rig! She's a Jig!* *She's a ripperty-skipperty dig*
"The Bigler" (Great Lakes)	"The Grimsby Fisherman" (Sea song)
Watch her! Catch her! *Jump up on her juberju*	*Then watch us, twig us,* *We're a popular juba-ju,*

The melody commonly used for "The Bigler" and all of these songs is similar but not quite the same as Warner's version of "From Buffalo to Troy." This melody belongs to a tune strain well traced by Cazden, Haufrecht and Studer in their book *Folksongs of the Catskills*.[236] They go back to an entertainment song called "The Knickerbocker Line." "The Knickerbocker Line" uses a melody for the verse that is similar to "The Bigler" and a chorus that could have inspired the chorus in "The Bigler." They all have similar melodies and choruses to "From Buffalo to Troy."

Dating the songs is difficult, but not impossible. We know that the *Bigler* was commissioned in Detroit in 1866 and that it sank in 1884. This tells us that the song, "The Bigler," most likely did not exist before 1866. There is a copy of the broadside of "The Grimsby Fisherman" in the Bodleian Libraries in Great Britain that is undated but has been identified as approximately 1880.[237] It is possible that the Great Lakes song "The Bigler" came before "The Grimsby Fisherman."

"The Knickerbocker Line" was written about an omnibus line (a trolley car pulled by horses) that ran between 1830 and 1860 in New York City. However, there is no reason to believe that the song had to be written during those years; it does not show up in songsters until the 1860s. A parody called "The Stage Driver on the Knickerbocker Line" has been dated as early as 1859.[238] Obviously, you cannot have a parody before the song exists, so "The Knickerbocker Line" was probably being sung before 1859. "The Knickerbocker Line" was most likely the source of a British music hall song that inspired "The Grimsby Fisherman" or, as it was alternately known, "The Dogger Banks." There also is a British variant of "The Knickerbocker Line" estimated to stem from the 1860s, in which the setting is transferred to the London Bristol railway line and the tailoress becomes a pickpocket, stealing a watch. The song was popularized in British music halls.

The final verse of "Dogger Banks" contains a reference to "The Knickerbocker Line":

> *So it's watch her, twig her,*
> *It's down the street she came;*
> *With high heels and painted toes*
> *Good Jilly is on the game*
> *She is one of them flash girls,*

Can't she cut a shine?
She can do a double shuffle
On the Knickerbocker Line.[239]

The British music hall version, in which the woman becomes a pickpocket:

I took her up to town one day, to the theater we did go,
To see them all a-staring at her, you'd think she was the show,
When coming out she stopped me, and particular asked the time,
Then skidaddled with my ticker down The Knickerbocker Line.[240]

This would place "The Knickerbocker Line" as the earliest, and the possible origin, of all the other versions. All of the versions of "The Knickerbocker Line" predate the *Bigler*, which was commissioned in 1866. The version of "The Bigler" published in the Lomax's *Our Singing Country* was collected from a Captain Asel Trueblood, who claimed to have walked the decks of the *Bigler*.[241] If his version of the song came from the time the *Bigler* was in service, that would date it before 1884 (the year the *Bigler* sank). "The Grimsby Fisherman" probably followed along after this. (The broadside copy was printed approximately 1880.) In fact, Roy Palmer, in his book *The Oxford Book of Sea Songs*, states, "'The Grimsby Fisherman' seems to be an English parody of a song of the North American lakes, 'The Cruise of the Bigler'."[242] This does seem to be likely, given the fact that they both have "juberju" or "juba-ju" in their choruses.

"The Cruise of the Bigler"

Chorus: Oh, Watch her, and catch her, Jump up on her juba ju,
Oh, give her sheet and let her rip, We're the boys'll put her through,
You ought to seen her howling, When the wind was blowing free,
On our passage down to Buffalo from Milwaukee.

"The Grimsby Fisherman"

Chorus: The watch us, twig us, We're a popular juba ju,
Give her sheet and let her rip, We're the boys to put her through,
You ought to see her rally, And the wind a-blowin' free,
On the passage from the fisher bank to Great Grimsby.

Palmer goes on to say that "this in turn derived from, or gave rise to, 'The Knickerbocker Line'."[243] Given the approximate dates of "The Knickerbocker Line" and the version of "The Dogger Banks," it is probable that "The Bigler" and "The Grimsby Fisherman" were derived from "The Knickerbocker Line."

If there is a missing link between all of these songs and "From Buffalo to Troy," it could be a version of "The Bigler" collected in the early twentieth century by Carl Sandburg. Sandburg obtained "The Bigerlow" from a friend who worked for the *Cleveland Plain Dealer* around 1905.[244] Since "The Bigerlow" was a corruption of "The Bigler," it might well have become popular after the *Bigler* was no longer on the Great Lakes (1884). Harold Thompson said that "From Buffalo to Troy" was sung in Buffalo in the 1880s. This, however, is undocumented, and the 1905 date for "The Bigerlow" and the use of the Troy lock at the eastern end of the canal (1903) would suggest a later date for "From Buffalo to Troy."

"The Bigerlow"[245]

Twas one October morning, That I seen a wondrous sight,
'Twas the timber driver Bigerlow, A-hailin' from Detrite,
   Chorus:
Watch her! Catch her! Jump up in her ju ju ba ju,
Giver her sheet and let her go, We're the boys to see her through,
You shoulda' heard her howlin', When the wind was blowin' free,
'Twas on the trip to Buffalo from Milwaukee.

However, there is a problem with "The Bigerlow." The form seems flawed. Of all the versions of "The Bigler," "The Bigerlow" is the only song with a verse that has only two phrases. The chorus has four phrases. It is possible that this particular version is unique, but this does not seem right. In fact, the words to phrases 1 and 2 ("'Twas one October mornin', that I seen a wondrous sight / 'Twas the timber drover Bigerlow a-hailin' from Detrite") are the words to the third and fourth phrases in every other version of this song. Even the melody indicates that these are the third and fourth phrases rather than the first two phrases. It may be that in collecting this song, the first two phrases of the verse were left out, either due to a lapse in memory of the informant or lost in copying versions of the text prior to publication. It was also one of the last versions of "The Bigler" collected, and the lines may have been lost in oral transmission.

"From Buffalo to Troy" solved the problem of the form. The verse contains four phrases. If the canal song was derived from "The Bigerlow," it might have been learned from an informant who had a better memory for the song. Or, of course, "The Bigerlow" could have been a later folk song that was influenced by the commercial song sung in the Alhambra Varieties. It really is impossible to prove, but both songs could have come along at about the same time.

Much like biological evolution, there often are problems dating items and filling in links, and sometimes the sequence in the evolutionary process is open to speculation. However, given the facts, and using some musical intuition, the evolution of our canal song could have the following timeline:

"The Knickerbocker Line" ➡ *"The Bigler"* ➡ *"The Grimsby Fisherman"* ➡ *"The Bigerlow"* ➡ *"From Buffalo to Troy"*

It certainly was not uncommon for canal songs to be born from popular songs. Henry Russell's "A Life on the Ocean Wave" and "I'm Afloat! I'm Afloat!" are two examples. The geography seems right, with the canal connecting New York City to the Great Lakes and the mixing of sailors from the canal and the Great Lakes in Buffalo.

At the risk of really incurring the wrath of folk song collectors, and knowing the criticism leveled at the Lomaxes for exactly the same thing (combining verses from many sources into one version of a song), a reworked version of "The Bigerlow," adding two phrases from "The Bigler," is given here. The verse seems much more normal and is symmetrical with the four phrases of the chorus (as are all of the other related songs).

This may just seem like an attempt to make "The Bigerlow" and "From Buffalo to Troy" seem a better match, but using musical intuition to "fix" the problem with the "The Bigerlow" provides a much more musical version of the song. Since it is impossible to prove an original version of either one of these songs, musical intuition is all anyone can go on.

COMPARISON OF "FROM BUFFALO TO TROY" AND THE REVISED "BIGERLOW"

"From Buffalo to Troy"

I've travelled all around this world, and Tonawanda, too,
I've been cast on desert isles and beaten black and blue,
I fought and bled at Bull Run and wandered as a boy,
But I'll never forget the trip I took from Buffalo to Troy.
  Chorus:
Whoa Back! Get up! And tighten up your line,
And watch the playful flies as on the mules they climb,
Whoa back! Duck your nut! Forget it I never shall,
When I drove a pair of spavined mules on the E-ri-e Canal

"The Bigerlow"

Come all you boys and listen, And a song I'll sing to you,
It's all about the Bigerlow and of her jolly crew,
'Twas one October morning, That I seen a wondrous sight,
'Twas the tinber driver Bigerlow, A-hailin' from Detrite,
  Chorus:
Watch her! Catch her! Jump up in her juberju
Giver her sheet and let her go, We're the boys to see her through,
You shoulda' heard her howlin', When the wind was blowin' free,
'Twas on the trip to Buffalo from Milwaukee.

Before leaving the subject, there is a song collected in Buffalo by Ivan Walton, John and Alan Lomax and others that appears to be yet another canal song based upon this same tune strain. "The Good Ship Called the Danger" has the same type of chorus, has floating verses from both "The E-ri-e" and "From Buffalo to Troy" and fits the structure of the tune strain.[246]

"The Good Ship Called the Danger"

I just came down from Buffalo on the good ship called the Danger,
A long, long trip on the Erie boys and I feel just like a stranger,
Fearful storms and heavy fogs, forget I never shall,
For I'm every inch a sailor boy on the E-ri-e Canal.

Chorus:
Stand by your bowline boys, Stand by your sorrel mule,
It's low bridge duck your head, Don't stand there like a fool,
The E-ri-e's a-risin' and the gin's a-gettin' low,
And don't think I've had a drink since we left old Buffalo.

"From Buffalo to Troy" provides a good example of a canal song derived from many of the same influences as dozens of other canal songs that came before and after. Those influences, ranging from its location, its date and its use of the popular and folk songs of the era, combine to create the songs of the horse-ocean sailors. It also provides us with an example of a surviving canal song with little change in melody and lyrics for over one hundred years. "From Buffalo to Troy" may come at the end of a long list of canal songs, but the actual date of the song itself is somewhere in the last two decades of the nineteenth century or the first decade of the twentieth century. Either way, it comes along late in the canal era when most of the canals were but a memory. Another canaller was singing, "I'll never forget the *last* trip I took from Buffalo to Troy."

13

THE SINGING CONTINUED

When it comes to reminiscences of the canal era, there is no one more important than a canalboat captain from the Ohio and Erie Canal. His repertoire of songs was never fully documented and is thought to be over seven hundred.[247] Those songs not only document life on the canal but also folk and popular songs commonly sung on the canals. Captain Nye is mentioned quite frequently in previous sections of this book and is a prime source for canal songs and information about life on the canal. The Library of Congress recognized Captain Nye's importance by digitizing its holdings on Nye for all to see (and hear). Nye's influence goes far beyond the Ohio and Erie Canal.

During the canal era, Captain Nye knew songs common to other canals ("A Trip on the Erie," "The Raging Canal" and "A Life on the Raging Canal"), and some of his songs were known on the New York canal system. (Nye had two brothers who worked on the Great Lakes and the Erie Canal.) Nye said that he "wrote songs on all subjects...and they were sung on all the canals because they were in canal language."[248]

Ironically, the Ohio and Erie Canal closed after a disastrous flood in 1913, the same year "Low Bridge, Everybody Down" was published. The New York Canal System continued to function, but the era of canal transportation was all but over. After the canal era, Captain Nye remained an influence by recording canal songs for collectors and appearing in folk festivals. As one article states, he was "an informant in search of a collector."[249] No other informant from any of the other canal systems promoted the collection of songs sung on the canals with the enthusiasm of Captain Nye. Only a few songs from scattered individual informants were collected from other canals. The best single source of songs from the canal era is Captain Nye.

Pearl Robert Nye was born on the canalboat *Reform* on the Ohio and Erie Canal in 1872 and spent forty years on the canal. "He came to know the Ohio scene intimately, as only a person who has crossed the state again and again in all seasons and weather could know it."[250] Nye was part of a large family (eighteen children) who were singers, and he

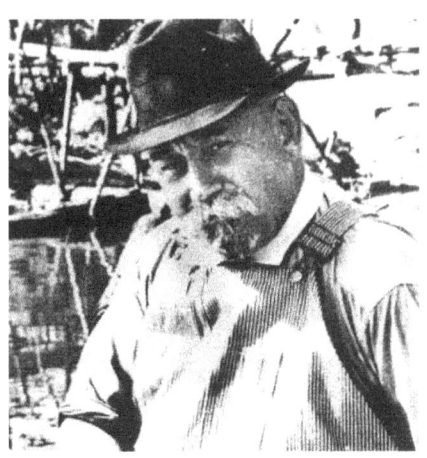

Captain Pearl Robert Nye. *From* Captain Pearl R. Nye: Life on the Ohio-Erie Canal, *Library of Congress.*

himself, until late in his life, was a strong singer. He learned songs from his parents, his grandparents and his great-grandparents. In transcribing the songs from the recordings, it is obvious that Nye has a remarkable sense of pitch. He sings, unaccompanied, a dozen or more verses and ends on the same pitch he started on at the beginning of the song.

In June 1937, John Lomax recorded thirty-three of Nye's songs, with commentary, for the Library of Congress.[251] In November 1937, Alan and Elizabeth Lomax recorded thirty-nine more songs.[252] In September 1938, Ivan Walton recorded three canal songs: "The Old Skipper," "Take a Trip on the Canal" and "We're Going to Pump Out Lake Erie," which are duplicates of those recorded by John Lomax.[253] Captain Nye recorded seventy-two songs for the Library of Congress and fifty-three for Ohio State University (although at least one other source says fifty-two). The discrepancy in the number of songs recorded may be because one of the songs, "What Trouble I've Had," is recorded twice. Rebecca Schroeder, in her 1973 article, "An Informant in Search of a Collector: Captain Pearl R. Nye," says that the Ohio State University recordings have been lost."[254] Apparently, they were subsequently found because recordings made by the author from those in the library at Ohio State University since then have fifty-three songs with the duplicate. Some of the songs are duplicates of the Lomax recordings, and of course, some are not canal songs. Between the two recordings, there are forty canal songs. Of the forty canal songs on the two recordings, there are some duplicates, but it appears that there are twenty-five unique canal songs.

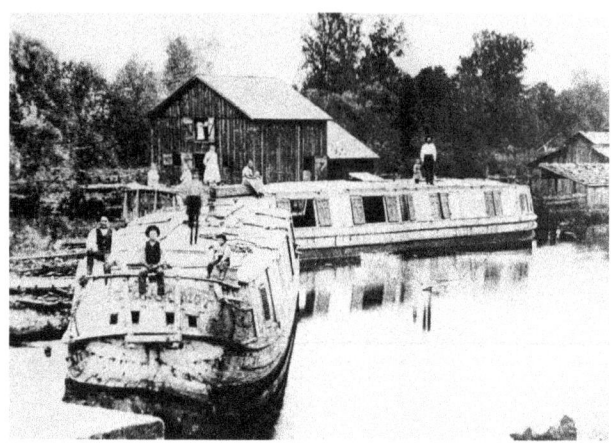

Nye family canal boats, including the *Reform*. *From* Captain Pearl R. Nye: Life on the Ohio-Erie Canal, *Library of Congress*.

John and Alan Lomax were most likely more interested in collecting Child Ballads than canal songs. As stated earlier, of the seventy-two songs collected by the Library of Congress, only ten (not counting duplicates) were canal songs. The other songs consisted of Child Ballads, "The House Carpenter" (#248), "Barbara Allen" (#84), "Lord Vaniford's Wife" (#87), "Lord Lovele" (#75), "The Jew's Daughter" (#155) and "On the Banks of Salee" (#112) (which Rebecca Schroeder says is a unique Ohio version of "The Baffled Knight") and other American folk songs, including "Perry's Victory," "Jones Hospital" (a version of "The Unfortunate Rake"), "When I Was Single," "The Cumberland's Crew," "The Roving Gambler" and "The Dying Cowboy."

Lomax did say that many of Nye's songs were popular songs of the era, and he was not interested in collecting those. He was interested in the songs handed down in oral tradition, not songs that were published or available in printed copies.[255] Nonetheless, Lomax was able to document a valuable informant. In addition, Captain Nye wrote down the lyrics and identified tunes to hundreds of songs in a manuscript, described by John Lomax "as many sheets of yellow lined paper all pasted end to end in one long scroll."[256] Cloea Thomas, who organized the Ohio State University recordings, transcribed and edited eight of the songs, and they were included in a booklet published by The Ohio State Archeological and Historical Society. The booklet, published in 1952, is called *Scenes and Songs of the Ohio-Erie Canal*. The songs taken from the recording and included in the booklet are "Get that Boat," "The Old Canal," "Last Trip in the Fall," "The Clever Skipper," "Erin's Green Shore," "Johnny and Mollie," "The Canal Dance" and "The Gospel Boat." This booklet is now out of print.[257]

Very few of the songs recorded by Ohio State University duplicate what John and Alan Lomax recorded for the Library of Congress. Of the ten canal songs on the Lomax recordings, five are unique and do not appear on the Ohio State University recording: "Scioto Valley Mills," "Little Sally Waters," "Down the River," "Canal Boat Wedding" and "Take a Trip on the Canal if You Want to Have Fun." The canal song Ivan Walton recorded as "Take a Trip on the Canal" is really a duplicate of "Take a Trip on the Canal If You Want to Have Fun." The songs Nye recorded for the Library of Congress can be heard by going to the following URL: www.loc.gov/collections/captain-pearl-r-nye-life-on-the-erie-and-ohio-canal/about-this-collection.

It might be easy to dismiss these canal songs, many of them highly romantic remembrances of Nye's former life on the canal, as just poorly written folk songs, much the way Francis James Child looked upon the broadside ballads as inferior literature. Even a comparison of Nye's versions of Child Ballads and his own canal songs exposes the literary differences. Nye gives us a look into the individual canal songs that must have existed all over the canal systems during the canal era. Most of the songs in an individual canaller's repertory were lost. Many canallers, unlike Captain Nye, moved on to other jobs and left the canal just as the fictional canaller in "Low Bridge, Everybody Down" ("Gotta look around for a job old pal").

A number of Nye's canal songs were written after the Ohio and Erie Canal closed in 1913 and are reminiscences of life on the canal. Nye's songs, written by a canaller, not a vaudeville songwriter, could easily be called "Low Bridge, Everybody Down" or "Forty Years on the Ohio and Erie Canal." In addition, we know that Captain Nye knew and borrowed songs from the Erie Canal and that some of Nye's songs were collected on the New York canals.

Not all of Nye's songs were written after the canal closed. He mentioned that his songs were known on other canals, and some of his songs were popular with audiences along the canal: "This was sung from one end of the canal to the other and all along. I 'canalized' it so every town and city could be 'localized' and they liked it—with laughter as a side line." Captain Nye took a popular favorite, "Shortnin' Bread," and "canalized" it by making it a part of the Ohio and Erie Canal. He went on to "localize" it by inserting the name of the town he happened to be in.

"Canal Towns"[258]

Shortnin' bread is a peppy food,
It makes you feel so fresh and good,
Portsmouth is our Rainbow Port,
Where we find many gay old sports.

It is not difficult to imagine the easy changes to the song anywhere along the canal:

Cleveland is our Erie Port,
Where we find good fun and sport,

This practice continues today. No matter where the Golden Eagle String Band plays along the canal systems, it "localizes" the song, and the locals do smile when they hear their town mentioned in song.

Nye wrote down his recollections of life on the canal in the form of songs. The canal songs serve as Captain Nye's personal "musical diaries." In these musical diaries, he presents us with a firsthand picture of what life was like on the canal: nature, food, work, play, places, people and attitudes. Nye's diaries are not a dry account of financial records or a list of chores he did every day but his impressions, observations, feelings and thoughts. He gives impressions of actual canallers and the people they meet along the way; observations of the beautiful scenery, nature and towns; and the attitudes of his fellow canallers, townspeople, superintendents, toll collectors and canal bullies. The music presents us with the jobs the canallers did, such as locking through, driving mules, adjusting the tension of the towline and loading and unloading cargo.

Just one of Nye's songs demonstrates how active the canaller's job actually was at times. Nye's lyrics in "Isabella: A Canal Cook" give some idea. Locks were numerous and involved not only knowledge of how to work the lock but also some physical labor. Lock tenders were not always available.

"Isabella: A Canal Cook"[259]

8. She could run the plan, Oh, yes, just like a skipper
Double locks, run the gates, snub, ease her up, she was a clipper,
She had a towpath swing, and of course knew everything
So good bye, Isabella, and be gone.

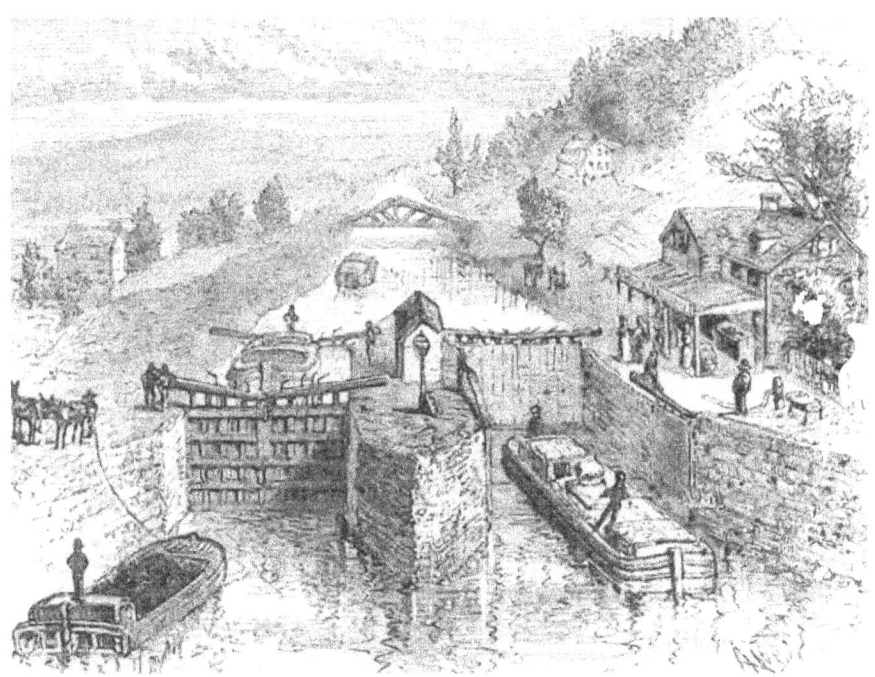

Canal boats in lock. *Erie Canal Museum, Syracuse, New York.*

To ascend in a lock, the boat would enter the lock chamber at the lower level. The boat would glide into the lock chamber and be brought to a stop by wrapping a rope around a snubbing post. The miter gates behind the boat would then be closed by pushing on the heavy balance beams attached to the gates. Then the paddles (or sluice gates) in the upper gates were cranked open using a lock key (windlass) to fill the lock chamber. Crew members then worked with lines to keep the boat from hitting the lock walls or gates as water rushed into the chamber and the boat rose. When the water in the lock chamber and the upper canal level were equal, the paddles in the upper gates were cranked closed and the gates themselves pushed open. The mules were reattached to the boat's deadeye (cleat) and pulled out of the lock and up the canal. All of this happened often. On a trip from Cleveland to Portsmouth (309 miles), there were 150 locks. It was necessary to have experience with the locking procedure to prevent injury. Canal manuals warn canallers of some of these lock-related dangers:

> *When you wind up the paddles don't leave the windlass on the paddle gear. The safety catch on the paddle gear could slip off and the windlass would*

spin rapidly and fly through the air. People have been badly injured by flying windlasses.[260]

All of this work, described by Nye in "Isabella," was done by the cook. This proved to be a problem for Captain Nye, because he disliked strong women who challenged his authority ("She could run the plan, Oh, yes, just like a skipper"). Thus, the line, "good-bye Isabella, and be gone." Isabella could "climb the gates." If the boat entered the lock from below, usually someone on shore such as the driver or a lock tender performed some of the lock chores from above. If no one is on shore, which sometimes happens (as the author can attest to), someone on the boat has to get to the top of the lock to do the chores. Climbing a wet, slimy, algae-covered lock gate is about the only solution, and it is a perilous ascent.

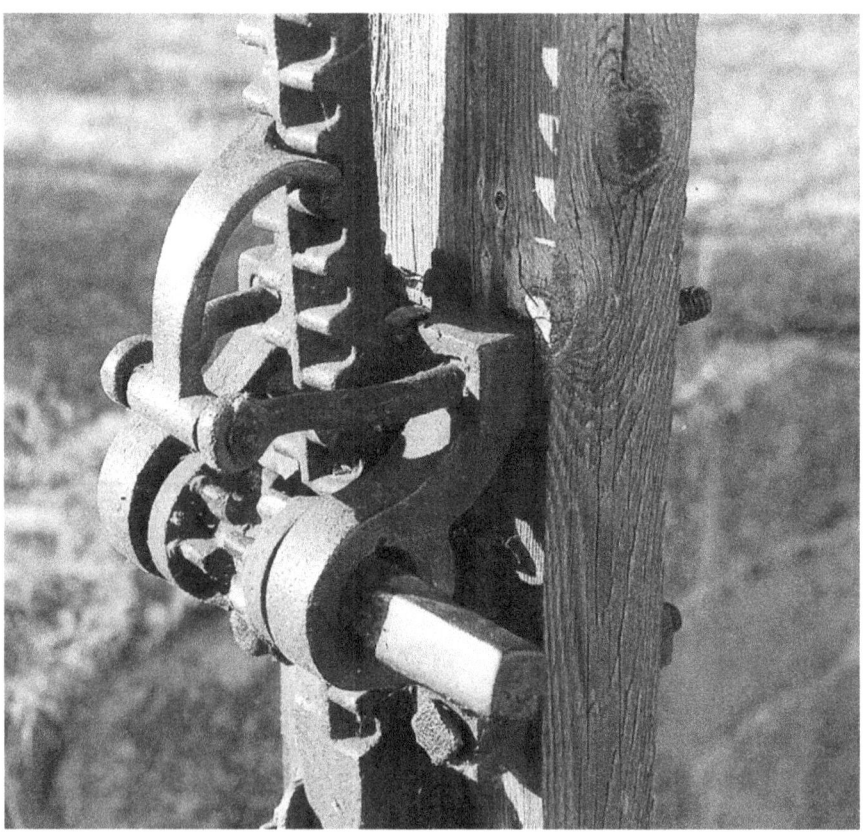

Paddle gear. *From* Guide to the Grand Canal: Ireland's Inland Waterways, *produced by the Departments of Arts, Heritage, Gaeltacht and the Islands, 1999.*

9. She could run a line, in or out, tie, splice a bowline,
Use a pry, jump them in, drive a stake, poling,
She could straddle up the stick, catch, throw the line so quick,
But, good bye Isabella, and be gone.

"Isabella: The Canal Cook" could "drop a line." To let another boat pass, coming from the opposite direction, the driver had to stop the mules and let the line drop so the other boats could pass over it. At the height of the canal era, when traffic on the canal was heavy, this would have happened many times every day. Isabella "could drive stakes." If the boat wanted to tie up in between locks or towns where there were no posts provided for this purpose, stakes had to be driven into the canal bank to secure the boat. In fact, Isabella was so handy she could: spring a paddle, run a double lock, run the gates, snub, run a line, splice a towline, pole a boat, vault with a pole from boat to shore, trim the coal, coil the lines, run the pumps and wash the decks.

16. She would trim the coal and run the pumps, yes, oft the water measure,
Coil the lines, run them out, wet decks with perfect pleasure,
Space forbids so many things, but with joy I sure can sing,
Isabella, I'm glad that you are home.

From the lyrics of Captain Nye's songs, we also learn about the geography of a canal. Examining a present-day map of the canal, or even a map from an earlier era, shows only a fragment of the canal geography. The lyrics identify "our Rainbow Port," "Rubber City" and other cities not found on any map. Also identified are such landmarks as "Three-mile Feeder," "Four-mile Basin," "Swamp Bug Island," "Cemetery Bend," Potato Patch Basin," "Soft Shell Turtle Bridge" and numerous other locations nicknamed by the canallers.

"Lockburne"[261]

Old Lockburne, she sure was a gay one,
There was Moneypenny's Distillery made things hum,
In Jake Eidel's Store, you could buy yourselves poor,
He had eve'ry thing and you were welcome.

We learn about the businesses the canallers patronized (Jake Eidel's Store, Effron's Tavern, Bob Shasteen's Store, Meeker's Grocery) and the businesses for which they hauled cargo (Moneypenny's Distillery, Percy Haden's Coal Mine, Seed's Mills, Klage's Ice House, Cleveland Brick Yard). Nye tells us in the lyrics what cargo they hauled (corn, wheat, tan bark, hoop poles, clay, coal, bricks, lumber, cord wood, stone and ice).

We learn about the people—not only their names but also their personal characteristics. ("Captain Bill Lovell had a fight at a lock just below Old Quadenhuttes where he knocked out seventeen men.") We learn about the food the canallers ate (berries, nuts, bran, roast chicken, stew, fish, turtles, frogs, pancakes), food preparation and the source of the food.

Captain Nye's musical diaries give us a view of nature: the flora and fauna, picturesque sites and even the insects. Nye relates the recreational activities, such as singing and playing sessions, cock fights, skating, sledding, tightrope walking on a rope stretched over the canal and games (Flying Dutchman, Who Has the Button?, Fox and Geese, Drop the Handkerchief and tag). We also learn a great deal about canal slang, from the names given to places along the canal to the food they ate: deadeyes (fish), groans (frogs), flappers (pancakes), darnic (biscuits). Nye includes many terms used to describe canallers, such as "dry land sailors" and "horse-ocean sailors."

Nostalgia, in the case of Pearl Robert Nye, is not a bad thing. It spurred him into action to preserve whatever he could from an era he loved and remembered and wanted to share with others. Nye's nostalgic look back on the canal era provides the most complete musical diaries of any informant yet found. The fact that Captain Nye chose to write his recollections in the form of songs demonstrates how important song is in telling the story of the canal era.

Purists, who reject anything that is not "authentic," often reject new folk songs. However, none other than the iconic folksinger and composer Pete Seeger thought otherwise. In an interview for the documentary *Adirondack Minstrel*, Pete said:

> *The old-time singers were always making up new songs. And, I think making up new songs is part of the tradition. Simply singing the old songs, you're not carrying on the tradition. You have to make up new ones. I tell people, "Make up a song." They say, "What do you make it up about? There are no more lumberjacks." Well, life is going on. Make it up about the life you know. It may be trying to save your town from the bulldozers. It might be about trying to get Washington to spend money on peace instead of war. But if it's something you're doing, something that's life. Make up a song about it.*[262]

For the Golden Eagle String Band, "something they're doing, something that's life," is singing about canals. The band members took Pete Seeger at his word and decided that the canal did need some new songs. Although the remaining canals have changed from what they once were when songs flooded the waterways, canals are still here and still have lock tenders, bridge tenders, maintenance boats, recreational boating and commercial shipping.

> *I believe that the presence or absence of parodies or local songs is a test of the vitality of a folk tradition. If singers do not make up new songs, or manipulate the old materials, we have one indication that the singing tradition in that area has become fossilized.*
> —*Herbert Halpert (1911–2000)*

It is not enough just to sing canal songs; folksingers must contribute to the making of a new repertory of songs, and that is another way to keep canal songs and interest in canals alive. Folksinger Jean Richie wrote a new canal song called "That Long Canal." Fred Gee composed an entire album of songs reminiscing about the Chenango Canal. George Ward contributes new canal songs, including his epic "Captain Billy and the Whale." The Golden Eagle String Band, aside from its usual adaptation of canal songs to particular locations and situations, is also committed to adding new songs as well. The band wrote a parody of a popular and much parodied song, "The Ship that Never Returned" (remember the MTA?). Henry Clay Work's song became "The Canalboat that Never Returned."

The band focused on Pete's words, "Make it up about the life you know." The song would not be a reconstruction of the past but a song about the present. Since the band began at The College at Brockport in Brockport, New York, they used local events, places, current canalboat names and names of actual people from the area to write the song. Brockport is on one of the "long levels." There is a stretch of canal from Rochester to Lockport without any locks, so that became a part of the song. Great Lakes Navigation ran an excursion boat called the *Emita (Emita II and Emita III* have now taken its place) that docks on occasion in Brockport. The captain of the *Emita* was a man named Peter Wiles Sr., an avid canal advocate. So, Peter and his *Emita* became part of the song. Only five miles east of Brockport is a place called Adam's Basin, named after an ancestor of the New York author Samuel Hopkins Adams. So, Adam's Basin earned its spot in the song. The song, being a parody of the original Henry Clay Work song, incorporates some of the original in the new version. Here is the song:

"The Canalboat that Never Returned"[263]

1. On a summer's day, when the waves were a-rippling,
With a quiet and gentle air,
The Emita set sail with people destined,
For a town that was so fair,
There were gay farewells, there were hands a-waving,
As Emita left Brockport Town,
But she disappeared along the "long level,"
And no one saw her go down.

2. They searched the banks and they searched the basins,
But they never found a soul,
No one was sadder that the Canal Commission,
Because they couldn't collect the toll.
Now Peter Wiles' ghost haunts Adam's Basin,
And to this very day,
People hear howls from the banks of the towpath,
"It's eerie," is what they all say.
    Chorus:
Did she ever return? No, she never returned,
And her fate is still unlearned,
And that last poor soul set off to the westward,
On the canalboat that never returned.

Since canal songs were known for their humor, the Golden Eagle String Band played a joke on Peter Wiles Sr. in the last verse—a joke they ended up regretting. A few days after writing the song, the band performed at the World Canal Conference in Rochester, New York, and was gleefully awaiting Peter's response to his ghost haunting Adam's Basin. Peter's son (Peter Wiles Jr.) approached the band and asked for a copy of the song. When asked about his father, he replied, "He died this past week."

A number of folksingers such as Jean Richie, Dave Ruch, George Ward, Fred Gee and others are carrying on the tradition and contributing new canal songs. A canal songwriting contest was recently introduced. "If it's something you're doing; something that's life; make up a song about it." If you listen carefully, it is still possible to hear the sounds of singing on the canals in America.

I was born and raised in the State of New York, in the town of Albany,
And my heart was gay 'till that fateful day, they opened the Erie.
   Chorus:
And oh, that day, that lonesome day, forget it I never shall;
For he's gone, he's gone, my love is gone, Gone on that long canal.
—"That Long Canal," Jean Richie, liner notes, Folkways/Smithsonian
Records, FW32318

Appendix A

"The Rhyme of the Old Canal"

William DeForest Totten (1912)

Harken back to the good old days,
When the Erie Canal was great,
And brought in store of golden toll,
To the coffers of the State.

(5) When from afar came floating down,
The wealth of the timbered plain,
Lumbered loads from the Saginaw,
And cargoes of western grain.

(9) Those were the days when boats ne'er stopped,
There never was time for rest,
Night and day they found their way,
From the lakes to the salt waves breast.

(13) All day long was the steady pull,
By the changes from "trek" to "trek,"
Always a span of mules ashore,
Another one under the deck.

(17) Through calm and storm they move along,
Though bad the night and black,

You could hear the song of the driver strong,
His tow line never slack.
Loud were the Steersman's stern commands,
And louder the Captain's call,
As they woke the echoes along the land,
On the line of the Old Canal.

(25) The driver trudged from day to day,
Weary and footsore, too,
With trembling limbs he made his way,
With gravel in each shoe.
He "tailed" the mules from boat to shore,
And drove till the bridge chains clanked,
Then, happily, with six hours o'er,
"Tailed" them in from the bank.

(33) And soon with stores of pork and beans,
Within his youthful frame,
He crawled to bunk with shirt and jeans,
Weary and sore and lame.
Far down in the forward cabin stayed,
The members of the crew,
Next to the cabin where beasts eh'sayed,
Their hay and oats to chew.

(41) And some of the bedding was musty,
And much of it alive,
With creeping, crawling, lively things,
Which found a way to thrive.
And noisy discord often came,
From the home of the restless mule,
Whose stamping feet and honking bray,
Made sleeplessness the rule.

(49) Many the barrels of beer they drank,
And many the casks of ale,
And under the belt, strong liquor felt,
As they faced the heat or the gale.
And many the fights on the towpath bank,

Enlivened the battle lust,
Of the brawny men who longed for rank,
And some of them bit the dust.

(57) And some would curse and others cry,
As they reeled 'neath blows in pain,
But all were bound their skill to try,
And the victory to gain.
The pennant graded the figure head,
Of the prow of the champion boat,
Whose crew in battle others led,
As the "smartest" crew afloat

(65) And woe to the men that challenged them,
Whether by day or night,
For ashore they would jump "at the drop of
a hat,"
To stand or fall in fight.
And from the deck box, stove wood flew,
Likewise potatoes and coal,
And many a fighting fellow knew,
A smashing blow to his jowl.

(73) Woe to the thrifty farmer man,
Whose apples and pears looked fine,
Woe to the ducks that chased the boat,
On the end of a hook and line.
For the strictest rules of etiquette,
Were sometimes forgot,
When boatman had fair visions,
Of those steaming in a pot.

(81) And many a happy hen roost,
Looked lonely every morn,
And many a green corn garden patch,
Of luscious things was shorn.
And oft were heard the fierce old yarns,
Of the panthers in Rome's dread swamp.
Carrying screaming drivers off,

To dismal regions damp.
(89) And loud were the cries of terror,
And fearful the sound and harsh,
Of victims borne on spectral wings,
O'er Montezuma's marsh.
And groaning ghost beneath the boat,
Wherever the eel grass grew,
Struck terror in the quaking souls,
Of every wondering crew.

(97) Listen again to the old time song,
How "Susie and Sal and Hank,"
Greased themselves with tallow fat,
And slid ashore on a plank.
How the "Erie was arising and the
Gin was getting low,"
And they did not think they'd get a drink,
"Till they got to Buffalo."

(105) And they danced the double shuffle,
And the clog with heel and toe,
And passed around the latest jokes,
From the "Free and Easy" show.
Oft in the summer's twilight hour,
The wheezy accordion's note,
Droned its doleful melody,
From the deck of the passing boat.

(113) Oft came mirth and laughter,
Often a song from the heart,
For the men who were meeting and passing there,
Knew they were soon to part.
And sometimes the lute and viol,
With music's sweetest tone,
Came while boatmen softly sang,
Of Mother, and Love, and Home.

(121) The bow lamp light, its yellow rays,
Through the gloomy darkness shed,

And the click of hoofs on the tow path stone,
Told of the power ahead.
And oft the stars, till dawn appeared,
Their light lent to the scene,
As the steersman found his course along,
Twixt banks of emerald green.

(129) The farm dog's bark, the night bird's cry,
The crow of the chanticleer,
Banished sleep from the weary eye,
And filled each heart with cheer.
So out of the harbor of Buffalo,
Off toward the ocean's tide,
Floating through orchards and meadowlands,
On, to the river side.

(137) Winding away on the sides of a hill,
Falling through adamant locks,
Crossing rivers in channels of stone,
Passing through rifts in the rocks,
Onward they went through valleys fair,
Scented with lily and rose,
Reaching a landscape rich and rare,
Where the lordly Hudson flows.

(145) Farewell, Farewell, ye ancient captain,
And the old time busy throng,
That met you at each landing,
And cheered your course along.
No more we hear your packet horn,
Your bowsman's task's o'er,
Though cities fair, and hamlet thrive,
Along the Erie's shore.

(153) Your craft that floated spick and span,
With colors gay and bright,
Now rests, her ribs beneath the soil,
Away from mortal sight.
Harken back to the good old times,

Here's a thought for men that were,
Whose active, tough, and ready lives,
Made business life astir.

(161) Over the mystic river,
With spirit hand at the helm,
They've passed away forever,
Into the Silent Realm.
Their calling was hard and humble,
But the sum of their labors great,
For they crowned as King of Commerce,
The dear old Empire State.

Appendix B

"Low Bridge, Everybody Down" (or "Fifteen Years on the Erie Canal")

Thomas S. Allen

First verse:
*I've got an old mule and her name is Sal, Fifteen years on the Erie Canal.
She's a good old worker and a good old pal, Fifteen years on the Erie Canal.
We've hauled some barges in our day, Filled with lumber, coal and hay,
And ev'ry inch of the way I know, From Albany to Buffalo.*

First chorus:
*Low bridge, ev'rybody down, Low bridge, We must be getting near a town.
You can always tell your neighbor, You can always tell your pal,
If he's ever navigated on the Erie Canal.*

Second verse:
*We'd better look 'round for a job old gal, Fifteen years on the Erie Canal.
You bet your life I wouldn't part with Sal, Fifteen years on the Erie Canal.
Giddap there gal, we've passed that lock, We'll make Rome 'fore six o'
clock,
So one more trip and then we'll go, Right straight back to Buffalo.*

Second chorus:

Low bridge, ev'rybody down, Low bridge, I've got the finest mule in town,
Once a man named Mike McGinty, tried to put it over Sal,
Now he's way down at the bottom of the Erie Canal.

Third verse:

Oh, where would I be if I lost my pal, Fifteen years on the Erie Canal.
Oh, I'd like to see a mule as good as Sal, Fifteen years on the Erie Canal.
A friend of mine once got her sore, Now he's got a broken jaw.
'Cause she let fly with her iron toe, And kicked him into Buffalo.

Third chorus:

Low bridge, ev'rybody down, Low bridge, I've got the finest mule in town,
If you're looking 'round for trouble, better stay away from Sal,
She's the only fighting donkey on the Erie Canal.

Fourth verse:

I don't have to call when I want my Sal, Fifteen years on the Erie Canal.
She trots from her stall like a good old gal, Fifteen years on the Erie Canal.
I eat my meals with Sal each day, I eat beef and she eats hay.
She ain't so slow if you want to know, She put the "Buff" in Buffalo.

Fourth chorus:

Low bridge, ev'rybody down, Low bridge, I've got the finest mule in town,
Eats a bale of hay for dinner, and on top of that, my Sal,
Tries to drink up all the water in the Erie Canal.

Fifth verse:

You'll soon hear them sing all about my gal, Fifteen years on the Erie Canal.
It's a darned fool ditty, 'bout my darned fool Sal, Fifteen years on the Erie Canal
Oh, ev'ry band will play it soon, Darned fool words and a darned fool tune,
You'll hear it sung ev'rywhere you go, from Mexico to Buffalo.

Fifth chorus:

Low bridge, ev'rybody down, Low bridge, I've got the finest mule in town,
She's a perfect, perfect lady, and she blushes like a gal,
If she hears you sing about her and the Erie Canal.

Appendix C
"The Aged Pilot Man"

Mark Twain (from *Roughing It*)

On the Erie Canal, it was,
All on a summer's day,
I sailed forth with my parents
Far away to Albany.

From out the clouds at noon that day
There came a dreadful storm,
That piled the billows high about,
And filled us with alarm.

A man came rushing from a house,
Saying, "Snub up your boat I pray,
Snub up your boat, snub up, alas,
Snub up while yet you may."

Our captain cast one glance astern,
Then forward glanced he,
And said, "My wife and little ones
I never more shall see."

Said Dollinger the pilot man,
In noble words, but few,—
"Fear not, but lean on Dollinger,
And he will fetch you through."

The boat drove on, the frightened mules
Tore through the rain and wind,
And bravely still, in danger's post,
The whip-boy strode behind.

"Come 'board, come 'board," the captain cried,
"Nor tempt so wild a storm;"
But still the raging mules advanced,
And still the boy strode on.

Then said the captain to us all,
"Alas, 'tis plain to me,
The greater danger is not there,
But here upon the sea.

So let us strive, while life remains,
To save all souls on board,
And then if die at last we must,
Let...I cannot speak the word!"

Said Dollinger the pilot man,
Tow'ring above the crew,
"Fear not, but trust in Dollinger,
And he will fetch you through."

"Low bridge! low bridge!" all heads went down,
The laboring bark sped on;
A mill we passed, we passed a church,
Hamlets, and fields of corn;
And all the world came out to see,
And chased along the shore
Crying, "Alas, alas, the sheeted rain,
The wind, the tempest's roar!
Alas, the gallant ship and crew,
Can nothing help them more?"

And from our deck sad eyes looked out
Across the stormy scene:
The tossing wake of billows aft,

The bending forests green,
The chickens sheltered under carts
In lee of barn the cows,
The scurrying swine with straw in mouth,
The wild spray from our bows!

She balances!
She wavers!
Now let her go about!
If she misses stays and broaches to,
We're all—then with a shout,
"Huray! huray!
Avast! belay!
Take in more sail!
Lord, what a gale!
Ho, boy, haul taut on the hind mule's tail!"
"Ho! lighten ship! ho! man the pump!
Ho, hostler, heave the lead!"

"A quarter-three!—'tis shoaling fast!
Three feet large!—t-h-r-e-e feet!—
Three feet scant!" I cried in fright
"Oh, is there no retreat?"

Said Dollinger, the pilot man,
As on the vessel flew,
"Fear not, but trust in Dollinger,
And he will fetch you through."

A panic struck the bravest hearts,
The boldest cheek turned pale;
For plain to all, this shoaling said
A leak had burst the ditch's bed!
And, straight as bolt from crossbow sped,
Our ship swept on, with shoaling lead,
Before the fearful gale!

"Sever the tow-line! Cripple the mules!"
Too late! There comes a shock!

Another length, and the fated craft
Would have swum in the saving lock!

Then gathered together the shipwrecked crew
And took one last embrace,
While sorrowful tears from despairing eyes
Ran down each hopeless face;
And some did think of their little ones
Whom they never more might see,
And others of waiting wives at home,
And mothers that grieved would be.

But of all the children of misery there
On that poor sinking frame,
But one spake words of hope and faith,
And I worshipped as they came:
Said Dollinger the pilot man,—
(O brave heart, strong and true!)—
"Fear not, but trust in Dollinger,
For he will fetch you through."

Lo! scarce the words have passed his lips
The dauntless prophet say'th,
When every soul about him seeth
A wonder crown his faith!

And count ye all, both great and small,
As numbered with the dead:
For mariner for forty year,
On Erie, boy and man,
I never yet saw such a storm,
Or one't with it began!'
So overboard a keg of nails
And anvils three we threw,
Likewise four bales of gunny-sacks,
Two hundred pounds of glue,
Two sacks of corn, four ditto wheat,
A box of books, a cow,
A violin, Lord Byron's works,
A rip-saw and a sow.

A curve! a curve! the dangers grow!
Labbord!—stabbord!—s-t-e-a-d-y!-so!—
Hard-a-port, Dol!—hellum-a-lee!
Haw the head mule!—the aft one gee!
Luff!—bring her to the wind!'

For straight a farmer brought a plank,—
(Mysteriously inspired)—
And laying it unto the ship,
In silent awe retired.

Then every sufferer stood amazed
That pilot man before;
A moment stood. Then wondering turned,
And speechless walked ashore.

NOTES

Preface

1. Schiff, "Scurvy Rascal."
2. Korson, *Pennsylvania Songs*, 284.

Chapter 1

3. Gioia, *Work Songs*, xi.
4. "African-American Spirituals, Work Songs and Ballads," Library of Congress, Archive of American Folk Song, recording AFS L3, 11A, track 1.
5. Walton and Grimm, *Windjammers*, 30–31.
6. Ibid., 76.
7. Anna Lynch, reminiscing about her childhood with Park Ranger Susan Fauntleroy, 1992, National Park Service, https://www.nps.gov/choh/learn/historyculture/canallerinterviews/htm.
8. Lomax and Lomax, *American Ballads*, 453.
9. Interviews by Park Ranger Susan Fauntleroy, 1992, National Park Service, https://www.nps.gov/choh/index.htm.
10. Totten, "Rhyme of the Old Canal," lines 85–88.
11. Ibid., lines 17–20.

12. Lomax and Lomax, *American Ballads*, 453.
13. Letter from Pearl R. Nye to John Lomax, January 10, 1938 (Library of Congress).
14. Cloea Thomas, ed., *Scenes and Songs of the Ohio-Erie Canal* (Columbus, OH: The Ohio State Archaeological and Historical Society, 1952).
15. "Paddy upon the Canal," Irish song, Chas. H. Keith, Boston, monographic, 1844, notated music, retrieved from the Library of Congress, www.loc.gov/item/sm1844.390820.
16. Thompson, *Body, Boots and Britches*, 223.
17. Wyld, *Low Bridge!*, 80.
18. Koeppel, *Bond of Union*, 319.
19. Reminiscences of the first railroad over the Allegheny Mountain read before the Historical Society of Pennsylvania, April 8, 1878, by Solomon W. Roberts.
20. Hullfish, *Songs*, 22–23.
21. Letter, Coldren to Major William E. R. Covell, with postscript endorsement by Grant, August 30, 1926, George Washington Memorial Parkway/C & O Canal file 500-10, National Capital Planning Commission, Record Group 328, National Archives, Washington, D.C. Collection.
22. "Canal Workers," National Park Service, www.nps.gov/choh/learn/historyculture/canalworkers.htm.

Chapter 2

23. Evslin, *Green Hero*, 7.
24. Barlow, *Vision of Columbus*, 246.
25. Bill Shank, "Canal Fever" in *Best of American Canals*, 3–6.
26. Koeppel, *Bond of Union*, 39.
27. Ibid., 45.
28. Jesse Hawley, "Essay 1." The Hawley essays are available to read by accessing the following website: http://xroads.virginia.edu/~ma02/volpe/canal/hawley_intro.html.
29. Koeppel, *Bond of Union*, 40.
30. Ibid., 64.
31. Bernstein, *Wedding of the Waters*, 197.
32. Ibid., 199.
33. Hawley, "Essay 1."
34. Shaw, *Erie Waters West*, 130.

35. Carolyn Vacca, "The Erie Canal" (article in Monroe County Public Library, n.d.), 1.
36. Merrill, *Towpath*, 147.
37. Hullfish, *Canaller's Songbook*, 57.
38. Pritchard, "On the Erie Canal," 45.
39. Korson, *Pennsylvania Songs*, 287.
40. Harrigan and Hart, *Little Frauds*.
41. Korson, *Pennsylvania Songs*, 287.
42. Hemans, *Poetical Works*, 396.
43. Wittke, *We Who Built America*, 187.
44. Ibid., 101.
45. Ibid., 131.
46. Ibid., 239.
47. Ohio and Erie Canal National Heritage Corridor, "Ethnic Settlements," https://www.nps.gov/nr/travel/ohioeriecanal/ethnicity.htm.

Chapter 3

48. Sandburg, *American Songbag*, 171.
49. Edmonds, *Rome Haul*, 92.
50. Spaeth, *Read 'Em*, 115.
51. *The Farmer Takes a Wife*, Fox Film Corporation, 1935.
52. Interview with George Ward, November 2012. Compare *Oh! That Low Bridge* album and the latest CD of the same name.
53. There is an endless supply of 1905 references on the internet. Wikipedia, "Low Bridge (Song)," https://en.wikipedia.org/wiki/Low_Bridge_(song), "The popular song "Low Bridge, Everybody Down" was written in 1905 by Thomas S. Allen; Erie Canal Song, "Erie Canal Song by Thomas S. Allen," http://www.eriecanalsong.com, "Erie Canal Song: Low Bridge, Everybody Down written by Thomas Allen in 1905"; Erie Canal Village, http://www.eriecanalvillage.com/songs.html, "Low Bridge, Everybody Down (Written by Thomas Allen in 1905)"; "How the Irish Built the Erie Canal," http://www.patflannery.com/IrishHistory/ErieCanal.htm, "The Erie Canal Song (Low Bridge, Everybody Down). It is a Tin Pan Alley song written in 1905 by Thomas S. Allen"; Music for Music Teachers, "The Erie Canal Song," http://www.music-for-music-teachers.com/the-erie-canal-song.html, "'Fifteen Years on the Erie Canal' was written in 1905 by Thomas S. Allen"; "Music from 1900–1923, including

Music from World War I (1914–1918)," http://www.pdmusic.org/1900s. html, "Low Bridge! Everybody Down or Fifteen Miles on the Erie Canal [composed in 1905], Thomas S. Allen"; "Free 1900s Sheet Music," https://www.8notes.com/dates/1900s.asp, "Low Bridge! Everybody Down (or Fifteen Years. Thomas S. Allen. 1905."

54. Spaeth, *Read 'Em*, 115. Spaeth even writes that "this seems to be a real folk-song." The lawyer for Doubleday-Page, in a lawsuit brought by F.B. Haviland in 1928, said, "The Erie Canal number was in circulation long before Mr. Haviland copyrighted it."

55. Lomax and Lomax, *American Ballads*, 467.

56. Merrill, *Towpath*, 49.

57. Ohio State University, Pearl R. Nye Recordings, v. 10, Side B.

58. Bernstein, *Wedding of the Waters*, 332.

Chapter 4

59. Natick, Massachusetts 1880 census lists "Daniel Allen, age 49, Born abt 1831 in Ireland. Home in 1880 Natick. Race-white Head of Household married wife—Joanna Doniher Allen. Both father and mother born in Ireland. Daniel's occupation—works on shoes. Joanna's age, 43. Daniel—19, John—17, Catherine—15, James—14, William—14, George—6, Thomas—3."

60. Silent Film Sound and Music Archive, http://www.sfsma.org.

61. John Stepan Zamecnik, *Wings Musical Score* (Hollywood, CA: Paramount Pictures, 1927), 19.

62. Silent Film Sound and Music Archive, http://www.sfsma.org/?s=Thomas S. Allen.

63. "Obituary," *Jacob's Orchestral Folio*, January 1920.

64. Jacobs' Band Monthly archives, The Online Books Page, onlinebooks. library.upenn.edu/webbin/serial?id=jacobsband.

65. The *Billboard* Charts, known today as the Billboard Hot 100 and the Billboard 200, started all the way back in 1894 with the publication of *Billboard Advertising*. It became a weekly in 1897, publishing lists of the top record and sheet music sales.

66. "Songs from the Year 1903," http://tsort.info/music/yr1903.htm.

67. Discography of American Historical Recordings, University of California, Santa Barbara.

68. Hamberlin, *Tin Pan Opera*, 19.

69. Hill, "Bill 'Bojangles' Robinson (1878–1949)."

70. Hamberlin, *Tin Pan Opera*, 19–23.

71. Ibid.

72. Eliot, *T.S. Eliot*, 125.

73. McKelvey, "From Stagecoach Taverns," 7.

74. Archeophone Archives, Edison Blue Amberol Records, Domestic Popular Series, vol. 8 (1751–1780), https://www.archeophone.com/archives.

75. McKelvey, "Canaltown," 19–20.

Chapter 5

76. The music and words to "Big Chief Battle-Axe" were published in the *East Oregonian* (Pendleton, OR), July 21, 1911.

77. Bleiler, "History of Adventure Magazine," 1–38.

78. Letters to and from Robert Winslow Gordon in the Frothingham Mss, Library of Congress, containing queries and texts sent in to Robert Winslow Gordon, editor of Old Songs that Men Have Sung column in *Adventure Magazine*, 1922–23.

79. Ibid.

80. "Songs from the Years 1903–1913," http://tsort.info/music/yr1903.htm.

81. Ibid.

82. "Obituary," in *Jacob's Orchestral Folio*, January, 1920.

Chapter 6

83. *Golden Book of Favorite Songs*, 9.

84. "Celebration Ode," *Buffalo Emporium and Commercial Advertiser*, October 29, 1825, 3.

85. Janvier, "Evolution of New York," 26–28.

86. *English Poetry II*, 16:485.

87. Hullfish, *Songs*, 8–9.

88. Grant, "Ill-Fated Farmington Canal."

89. Koeppel, *Bond of Union*, 246.

90. Loesberg, *Folksongs & Ballads*, 68.

Chapter 7

91. Thompson, *Body, Boots and Britches*, 247.

92. O'Donnell, "I'm Afloat," 177–78.

93. Hullfish, *Songs of the Horse-Ocean Sailor*, 26–27.

94. Hullfish, *Canaller's Songbook*, 36–37.

95. Ibid., 26–27.

96. Hahn and Kemp, *Canal Terminology*, 65.

97. Ibid., 107.

98. Rideing, "Waterways of New York," 9.

99. Hahn and Kemp, *Canal Terminology*, 107.

100. O'Donnell, "I'm Afloat," 177–78.

101. Nye, "Gay Old Packet Line," in "Captain Pearl R. Nye," Library of Congress American Memory [hereafter LOC]. Nye identifies the tune, "In the Good Old Summertime."

102. Thompson, *Body, Boots and Britches*, 254.

103. Ibid., 242–43.

104. Deoch, *New York to Niagara*.

105. Williamson and Hesler, "Return to Glory."

106. Hullfish, *Canaller's Songbook*, 52.

107. Lee, *Tales the Boatmen Told*, 20.

108. Ibid., 239–40.

109. Ibid., 20.

110. Ibid.

111. Hullfish, *The Canaller's Songbook*, 37.

112. Korson, *Pennsylvania Songs*, 287.

113. Nye, LOC. Nye identifies the tune as "The Irish Washerwoman."

114. Ibid.

115. Ibid.

116. Hullfish, *Canaller's Songbook*, 16–17.

117. "Whoa, Mule," Springfield, Missouri, Missouri State, Max Hunter Folk Song Collection [hereafter MHFSC], Reel 80, Item 8, 1950, as sung by Tom Boyd, Patrick, Missouri, November 3, 1950.

118. "Kickin' Mule," MHFSC, Cat. No. 0231, MFH #337, as sung by Arlie Lynch, Roger, Arkansas, August 13, 1958.

119. "Simon Slick," MHFSC, Cat. No. 1378, MFH #337, as sung by Reba Dearmore, Gathersburg, Maryland, December 31, 1971.

120. Hullfish, *Canaller's Songbook*, 16–17.

121. Allen, *Low Bridge*.

122. Nye "Take a Trip on the Canal," LOC, Disc 13, Side A.

123. Thomas, *Scenes and Songs*, 20–21.

124. Hullfish, *Canaller's Songbook*, 18.

125. Ibid., 16.

126. Nye, "A Canal Dance," LOC, Disc 25, Side A.

127. Harlow, *Old Towpaths*, 359.

128. Ibid., 118.

129. Nye, "Mulie, Keep Your Tail Up," Ohio State University Pearl R. Nye recordings, v. 12, Side A.

130. Nye, "The Old Go-Devil," Ohio State University Pearl R. Nye recordings, v. 10, Side B.

131. Thompson, *Body, Boots and Britches*, 233–34.

132. Merrill, *Towpath*, 49.

133. Hullfish, *Canaller's Songbook*, 33.

134. Totten, "Rhyme of the Old Canal," lines 73–76.

135. Hullfish, *Songs*, 39.

136. *Grand Canal Ballads*, Smithsonian Folkways Archival, FTS 32318.

137. Lee, *Tales the Boatmen Told*, 9.

138. Wyld, *Low Bridge!*, 51.

139. Nye, "We Stick Together," LOC. Nye identifies the tune as "My Horses Ain't Hungry."

140. Lee, *Tales the Boatmen Told*, 8.

141. George Korson, "My Sweetheart's a Mule in the Mine," in *Two Penny Ballads*, ed. Goldstein and Byington.

142. Linscott, *Folk Songs*, 195–96.

143. Thompson, *Pioneer Songster*, 49.

144. Hullfish, *Canaller's Songbook*, 38–39.

145. Nye, "The Clever Skipper," Ohio State University recordings, v.11, Side A.

146. Walton and Grimm, *Windjammers*, 98

147. Thompson, *Body, Boots, and Britches*, 248–49.

148. Hullfish, *Songs*, 44–45.

149. Walton and Grimm, *Windjammers*, 121–22.

150. Nye, "I'm a Little Canaler," Ohio State University recordings, v. 10, Side A.

151. Cliff Haslam, "Shove Around the Jug," *Leaning in the Wind*, 2012.

152. Ibid.

Chapter 8

153. Walton and Grimm, *Windjammers*, 167.

154. Ibid., 168.

155. Program printed in the *Buffalo (NY) Commercial*, September 18, 1843, 2.

156 *(NY) Evening Post*, October 8, 1838; October 24, 1839.

157. Russell, *Life on the Ocean Wave*.

158. Thompson, *Body, Boots and Britches*, 238.

159. "The Raging Canal," Ohio State University Pearl R. Nye recordings, v.10, Side B.

160. Thompson, *Body, Boots and Britches*, 238.

161. Morris, *Raging Canal*.

162. "The Raging Canal," Albany, New York State Library Broadside Ballad Collection, SCO BD1529, [S.L]; [S.N.], 18--?.

163. O'Donnell, "I'm Afloat," 177–80.

164. Hullfish, *Canaller's Songbook*, 28.

165. Thompson, *Body, Boots and Britches*, 238.

166. Hullfish, *Canaller's Songbook*, 29.

167. Brown, *Life of Dan Rice*, 192.

168. McKelvey, "History of Penal and Correctional Institutions," 6.

169. Brown, *Life of Dan Rice*, 192.

170. "Coffee Grows on White Oak Trees (Four in the Middle)," as sung by Mrs. W.B. Apple, August 27, 1962, Batesville, Arkansas, John Quincy Wolf Folklore Collection.

171. Foster, *Song of all Songs*, 287–92.

172. Smith, *Girl from Yewdall's Mill*.

173. Twain, *Roughing It*, 287.

174. Ibid.

175. Seeger, *American Favorite Ballads*, 87.

176. Thompson, *Body, Boots and Britches*, 247.

177. Walton and Grimm, *Windjammers*, 169.

178. Rideing, "Waterways of New York," 8.

179. Morris, *Raging Canal*.

180. Wyld, *Low Bridge!*, 91.

Chapter 9

181. Totten, "Rhyme of the Old Canal," lines 89–92.

182. "Haunted Places in New York," http://www.theshadowlands.net/places/newyork.

183. Hahn, *Towpath Guide*, 36.

184. "Schuylkill Haven Now Boasts of Ghost," *Pottsville (PA) Republican*, June 28, 1887.

185. Smith, *Girl from Yewdall's Mill*.

186. Childs, "Phantom Ships," 146.

187. Palmer, *Oxford Book of Sea Songs*, 21.

188. Korson, *Pennsylvania Songs*, 283.

189. Henry W. Shoemaker Collection 1841–1955, Pennsylvania State Archives, Harrisburg, Pennsylvania.

190. Korson, *Pennsylvania Songs*, 283–84.

191. Walton and Grimm, *Windjammers*, 168–69.

192. Kittredge, *Southwestern Homelands*, 170.

193. Evslin, *Green Hero*, 7.

194. Lomax and Lomax, *American Ballads*, 459.

195. Hullfish, *Canaller's Songbook*, 18–19.

196. Lomax and Lomax, *American Ballads*, 459.

197. Rappoport, *Superstitions of Sailors*, 184.

198. Ibid., 185.

199. Hullfish, *Songs*, 12–13.

200. Hullfish, *Canaller's Songbook*, 10–11.

Chapter 10

201. Korson, *Pennsylvania Songs*, 354.

202. Rideing, "Waterways of New York," 1–17.

203. "De Boatman's Dance," in *Music of the Ethiopian Serenaders*.

204. Hullfish, *Songs*, 26–27.

205. Nye, "Chanty," LOC. Nye gives the tune as "Old Dan Tucker."

206. Lomax and Lomax, *American Ballads*, 459.

207. Nye, "Runaway Mules," LOC. Nye give the tune as "Oh! Susanna."

208. L.V.H. Crosby, "I'm Sailing on de Ole Canal," in *Harmoneons Carolina Melodies*.

209. C.A. White, "I'se Gwine Back to Dixie" (Boston, MA: White, Smith & Company, 1875. Sheet music in the Duke University Sheet Music Collection, Atlanta, Georgia.
210. Nye, "I'm Going Back to the Canal," in "Captain Pearl R. Nye." Nye gives the tune as "I'm Going Back to Dixie."
211. Hullfish, "James A. Bland," 1–33.
212. Nye, "Oilskin Slickers," LOC. Nye gives the tune as "Golden Slippers."
213. Nye, "Chanty: In the Evening in the Summer," LOC. Nye gives the tune as "In the Evening by the Moonlight."
214. Nye, "Chanty: Oh, How I Love My Silver Ribbon," LOC. Nye gives the tune as "Carry Me Back to Old Virginny."

Chapter 11

215. *Democrat and Chronicle*, November 22, 1910.
216. Lomax and Lomax, *American Ballads*, 453.
217. Discography of American Historic Recordings, University of California, Santa Barbara.
218. Lomax and Lomax, *American Ballads*, 453.
219. Totten, "Rhyme of the Old Canal," lines 53–54.
220. Ibid., 89–90.
221. Braham and Harrigan, "Oh! Dat Low Bridge," 2.
222. Ibid.
223. Harrigan and Hart, "Never Take the Hindshoe from a Mule," in *Harrigan & Hart's Mulligan Guard's Surprise Songster*, 8–9.
224. Adams, *Hudson through the Years*, 75.
225. Harrigan and Hart, "Buffalo," in *Harrigan and Hart's "Squatter Sovereignty" Songster*, 52.
226. Braham and Harrigan, "Never Take the Horse-shoe from the Door."
227. "Never Take the Hindshoe from a Mule," in *Harrigan & Hart's Mulligan Guard's Surprise Songster*.
228. George M. Cohan, "Down by the Erie Canal" (1915), *Vocal Popular Sheet Music Collection*, Score 336. https://digitalcommons.library.umaine.edu/mmb-vp/33.

Chapter 12

229. Thompson, *Body, Boots and Britches*, 244.

230. Wyld, *Low Bridge!*.

231. Lomax and Lomax, *American Ballads*, 460.

232. Frank Warner, Guide to the Frank and Anne Warner Papers, 1899–2000 and undated, bulk 1933–1985, WC-36: Frank Warner, "Songs of the Erie Canal," undated.

233. George Ward, "Oh! That Low Bridge: Songs of the Erie Canal," Front Hall Records (FHR-028), 1982.

234. Wyld, *Low Bridge!*, 100; Lomax and Lomax, *American Ballads*, 460–61; Thompson, *Body, Boots and Britches*, 244–45.

235. DeVoto, *Mark Twain's America*, 34.

236. Cazden, Haufrecht and Studer, *Folk Songs*, 41.

237. Bodleian Library, Broadside Ballads Online, Harding B 11(1436), Roud Number, V15522, http://ballads.bodleian.ox.ac.uk/search/roud/V15522.

238. Bradley, *Knickerbocker*, 83.

239. Sam Larner, *Now Is the Time for Fishing*, Washington, D.C., Smithsonian Folkways Records, FW03059, 2007. The liner notes state the following: "This is possibly an English parody of the American song 'Cruise of the Bigler,' and probably is of music hall origin. The reference to the Knickerbocker Line in the last chorus is almost certainly an echo from the very popular music-hall song…known as 'The Knickerbocker Line.'"

240. There is also a British variant, estimated to stem from the 1860s, in which the setting is transferred to the London to Bristol railway line and the tailoress becomes a pickpocket, stealing a watch. This was popularized in music halls and is collected as 2149 in the Roud Index of folk songs.

241. Lomax and Lomax, *Our Singing Country*, 220.

242. Palmer, *Oxford Book of Sea Songs*, 264.

243. Ibid.

244. Sandburg, *American Songbag*, 174.

245. Jürgen Kloss, on his website, "Just Another Tune: Songs and Their History," says, "The collector himself plays an important role, too, especially if he only is able to get fragmentary versions and then tries to collate a more complete text. John Lomax for example was notorious for editing texts before publishing because he was more interested in producing singable songs for public consumption than academic

collections." Kloss goes on to say, "In the case of Lomax, it is not known if and how much he has edited the texts or if he has collated them from different versions."

246. Walton and Grimm, *Windjammers*, 168; Wyld, *Low Bridge!*, 99–100; Lomax and Lomax, *American Ballads*, 464.

Chapter 13

247. Terry K. Woods and Pearl Nye, "Pearl Nye's Akron: Taken from Pearl Nye's Writings in the Archival Department at the University of Akron" (Summit County, Ohio), n.d., n.p.

248. Letter dated "11-25-32," Nye Folder, Ohio State Archaeological and Historical Society Collection.

249. Schroeder, "An Informant," 1.

250. Thomas, *Scenes and Songs*.

251. Schroeder, "An Informant," 1.

252. Ibid., 2.

253. Ibid.

254. Ibid., 3.

255. Lomax, letter.

256. Ibid.

257. Thomas, *Scenes and Songs*.

258. Nye, "Canal Towns," LOC.

259. Nye, "Isabella: A Canal Cook," LOC.

260. *Guide to the Grand Canal*, n.p.

261. "Lockbourne," Ohio State University recording, v. 10, Side B.

262. Ofield, *Adirondack Minstrel*.

263. Hullfish, *Songs*, 18–19.

BIBLIOGRAPHY

Abbott, Jacob. *Marco Paul's Voyages and Travels: Erie Canal.* New York: Harper & Brothers, 1852.

Adams, Arthur G. *The Hudson Through the Years.* New York: Fordham University Press, 1996.

Adams, Samuel Hopkins. *The Erie Canal.* New York: Random House, 1953.

Allen, Thomas S. *Low Bridge, Everybody Down or Fifteen Years on the Erie Canal.* New York: F.B. Haviland, 1913.

Athey, J.A.B. "Jonahs on Modern Whale Factory Ships," *New York Folklore Quarterly* 10, no. 4 (Winter 1954): 295–96.

Barlow, Joel. *The Vision of Columbus: A Poem in Nine Books.* Hartford, CT: Printed by Hudson and Goodwin, for the Author, 1787.

Barry, Phillips. "The Fair Maid by the Sea-Shore." *Bulletin of the Folksong Society of the Northeast* 11, no. 7 (1960): 12–13.

Bassett, Fletcher S. *Legends and Superstitions of the Sea and of Sailors: In All Lands and at All Times.* Chicago: Belford, Clarke and Company, 1885.

Bayard, Samuel, ed. *Hill Country Tunes: Instrumental Folk Music of Southwestern Pennsylvania.* Philadelphia: American Folklore Society, 1944.

Beattie, John, et al, eds. *The Golden Book of Favorite Songs.* Chicago: Hall and McCreary Company, 1946.

Belden Henry. *Ballads and Songs Collected by the Missouri Folk-lore Society.* Columbia: University of Missouri, 1955.

Bernstein, Peter L. *Wedding of the Waters: The Erie Canal and the Making of a Great Nation.* New York: W.W. Norton and Company, 2005.

The Best of American Canals, Number II. York, PA: American Canal and Transportation Center, 1990.

Bleiler, Richard. "A History of Adventure Magazine." In *The Index to Adventure Magazine*, 1–38. N.p.: Borgo Press, 1990.

Blood, Peter and Annie Patterson, eds. *Rise Up Singing*. Bethlehem, PA: Sing Out Corporation, 1992.

Bradley, Elizabeth L. *Knickerbocker: The Myth behind New York*. Piscataway, NJ: Rutgers University Press, 2009.

Braham, David, and Edward Harrigan. "Never Take the Horse-shoe from the Door." Baltimore, Johns Hopkins University, Lester S. Levy Sheet Music Collection.

———. "Oh! Dat Low Bridge." *The Grip*, Baltimore, Johns Hopkins University, Lester S. Levy Sheet Music Collection.

Brown, Maria Ward. *The Life of Dan Rice*. Long Branch, NJ: self-published, n.d.

Browne, Ray. "Superstitions Used as Propaganda in the American Revolution." *New York Folklore Quarterly* 17, no. 3 (Autumn 1961): 202–11.

Buffalo Emporium and Commercial Advertiser. "Celebration Ode." October 29, 1825.

The Canaller's Songbook. Brockport, NY: Bravoproductions, 1984.

Cazden, Norman. *Abelard Folk Song Book*. New York: Abelard-Schumann, 1958.

Cazden, Norman, Herbert Haufrecht and Norman Studer. *Folk Songs of the Catskills*. Albany: State University of New York Press, 1982.

———. *Notes and Sources for Folk Songs of the Catskills*. Albany: State University of New York Press, 1982.

Childs, Ralph. "Phantom Ships of the Northeast Coast of North America." *New York Folklore Quarterly* 5, no. 2 (Summer 1949): 146–65.

Cleveland, Dan, and Don Meixner. *An Evening on the Erie*. n.p., n.d.

Colcord, Joanna C. *Roll and Go, Songs of American Sailormen*. Indianapolis, IN: Bobbs-Merrill, 1924.

———. *Songs of American Sailormen*. New York: Oak Publications, 1964.

Coleridge, Samuel Taylor. *The Rime of the Ancient Mariner*. Dunedin, NZ: University of Otago Press, 2009.

Cooper, John X. *T.S. Eliot's Orchestra: Critical Essays on Poetry and Music*. New York: Routledge, 2000.

Creighton, Helen. *Folksongs from Southern New Brunswick*. Ottawa: National Museum of Canada, 1971.

———. *Songs and Ballads from Nova Scotia*. New York: Dover Publications, 1966.

Deoch, Fulton, ed. *New York to Niagara, 1836: The Journal of Thomas S. Woodcock.* New York: New York Public Library, 1938.

DeVoto, Bernard. *Mark Twain's America.* Lincoln: University of Nebraska Press, 1997.

Discography of American Historical Recordings. http://www.adp.library. ucsb.edu/index.php.

Doerflinger, William. *Shantymen and Shantyboys: Songs of the Sailor and Lumberman.* New York: Macmillan Company, 1951.

Edmonds, Walter. *Rome Haul.* Boston: Little, Brown and Company, 1929.

Eliot, Valerie, ed. *T.S. Eliot, The Waste Land: A Facsimile and Transcript of the Original Drafts Including the Annotations of Ezra Pound.* London: Faber & Faber, 2011.

English Poetry II. Vol. 16 *From Collins to Fitzgerald.* Harvard Classics. New York: P.F. Collier & Son, 2001.

Evslin, Bernard. *The Green Hero: Early Adventures of Finn McCool.* New York: 4 Winds Press, 1975.

Finson, Jon W., ed. *Edward Harrigan and David Braham: Collected Songs, 1883–1896.* Madison, WI: A-R Editions, 1997.

The Folksong Fake Book. Milwaukee, WI: Hal Leonard Corporation, n.d.

Foster, Stephen. *The Song of All Songs.* Brooklyn, NY: D.S. Holmes, 1863.

Fowke, Edith, ed. *Traditional Singers and Song from Ontario.* Hatboro, PA: Burns & MacEachern Limited, 1965.

Gioia, Ted. *Work Songs.* Durham, NC: Duke University Press, 2006.

The Golden Book of Favorite Songs. Chicago: Hall & McCleary Company, 1923.

Golden Eagle String Band. *Body, Boots and Britches: Folksongs of New York State.* Smithsonian Folkways Records, 32317.

Goldstein, Kenneth, and Robert Byington. *Two Penny Ballads and Four Dollar Whiskey.* Hatboro: Pennsylvania Folklore Society, 1966.

Grand Canal Ballads. Washington, D.C.: Smithsonian/Folkways Records, FTS32318, 1981.

Grant, Ellsworth S. "The Ill-Fated Farmington Canal." *Connecticut History* (Spring 2008).

Guide to the Grand Canal: Ireland's Inland Waterways. Dublin: Produced by the Departments of Arts, Heritage, Gaeltacht and the Islands, 1999.

Hahn, Thomas F. *Towpath Guide to the C & O Canal.* Section 2. *Seneca to Harpers Ferry.* York, PA: American Canal and Transportation Center, 1971.

Hahn, Thomas S., and Emory L. Kemp. *Canal Terminology of the United States.* Morgantown: West Virginia University Press, 1999.

Hamberlin, Larry. *Tin Pan Opera: Operatic Novelty Songs in the Ragtime Era.* New York: Oxford University Press, 2011.

Hans, Nathan. *Dan Emmett and the Rise of Early Negro Minstrelsy.* Norman: University of Oklahoma Press, 1962.

Harlow, Alvin. *Old Towpaths.* Port Washington, NY: Kennikat Press Inc., 1964.

Harlow, Frederick. *Chanteying Aboard American Ships.* Barre, MA: Barre Gazette, 1962.

Harmoneons Carolina Melodies. Boston: C. Bradlee & Co., 1845.

Harrigan and Hart. *Harrigan & Hart's Mulligan Guard's Surprise Songster: Containing Another Immense Collection of These Great Champions' Latest Songs… also a Fine Collection of All the Camp-meeting Hymns.* New York: Popular Publishing, 1880.

———. *Harrigan & Hart's "Squatter Sovereignty" Songster.* New York: Popular Publishing, 1882.

———. *The Little Frauds: Harrigan and Hart's Songs and Sketches.* Boston: White & Coullaud, 1874.

Hemans, Felicia Dorothea. *The Poetical Works of Felicia Dorothea Hemans.* London: Oxford University Press, 1914.

Hill, Constance Valis. "Bill "Bojangles" Robinson (1878–1949)." *Dance Heritage Coalition,* 2012.

Hugill, Stan. *Shanties from the Seven Seas.* New York: E.P. Dutton and Co., 1961.

———. *Songs of the Sea: The Tales and Tunes of Sailors and Sailing Ships.* New York: McGraw-Hill Book Co., 1977.

Hullfish, William. *The Canaller's Songbook.* York, PA: American Canal and Transportation Center, 1984.

———. *The Canaller's Songbook (recording).* Brockport, NY: Bravoproductions, 1990.

———. "James A. Bland: Pioneer Black Songwriter." *Black Music Research Journal* 7 (1987).

———. *Songs of the Horse-Ocean Sailor (recording).* Brockport, NY: Bravoproductions, 2000.

Janvier, Thomas A. "The Evolution of New York." *Harper's New Monthly Magazine* 87, no. 517 (June 1893): 26–8.

Jeans, Peter D. *Seafaring Lore and Legend: A Miscellany of Maritime Myth, Superstition, Fable and Fact.* New York: McGraw-Hill, 2007.

Karpeles, Maud. *Folk Songs from Newfoundland.* London: Faber and Faber, 1971.

Kittredge, William. *Southwestern Homelands.* Washington, D.C: National Geographic, 2002.

Kloss, Jürgen. "Just Another Tune: Songs and Their History." www.justanothertune.com/html/about.html.

Koeppel, Gerard. *Bond of Union: Building the Erie Canal and the American Empire.* Cambridge, MA: DaCapo Press, 2009.

Korson, George G., ed. *Pennsylvania Songs and Legends.* Baltimore, MD: Johns Hopkins Press, 1960.

Lamb, Andrew. *A Life on the Ocean Wave: The Story of Henry Russell.* Croydon, UK: Fuller Wood Press, 2007.

Lee, James. *Tales the Boatmen Told.* Exton, PA: Canal Press, 1977.

Lester S. Levy Collection of Sheet Music. Milton S. Eisenhower Library, Johns Hopkins University.

Lewie, Chris L. *Two Generations on the Allegheny Portage Railroad: The First Railroad to Cross the Allegheny Mountains.* Shippensburg, PA: Burd Street Press, 2001.

Linscott, Eloise Hubbard. *Folk Songs of Old New England.* New York: Macmillan, 1939.

Loesberg, John, ed. *Folksongs & Ballads Popular in Ireland.* Cork, IRE: Ossian Publications, 1980.

Lomax, John, and Alan Lomax. *American Ballads and Folk Songs.* New York: Macmillan, 1934.

———. *Our Singing Country.* Mineola, NY: Dover Publications, 2000.

McCombs, Hazel A. "Erie Canawl Lore." *New York Folklore Quarterly* 2, no. 3 (1947).

McKelvey, Blake. "Canaltown." *Rochester History* 32, no. 2 (April 1975): 19–20.

———. "From Stagecoach Taverns to Airport Motels." *Rochester History* 31, no. 4 (October 1969): 7.

———. "A History of Penal and Correctional Institutions in the Rochester Area." *Rochester History* 34, no. 1 (1972).

Manifold, John. *The Penguin Australian Song Book.* Victoria, AUS: Penguin Books, 1964.

Mayer-Arendt, Jurgen. *Introduction to Modern and Classical Optics.* London: Prentice-Hall, 1995.

Meredith, John, and Hugh Anderson. *Folk Songs of Australia.* Sydney: Ure Smith Ltd., 1967.

Merrill, Arch. *Rochester Sketchbook.* Rochester, NY: Creek Books, n.d.

———. *The Towpath.* Rochester, NY: Gannett Company, 1945.

Morris, Pete. *The Raging Canal.* New York: C.G. Christman, 1844.

Murdock, Lee, and Joann Murdock. *Lake Rhymes: Folksongs of the Great Lakes Region.* Kaneville, IL, 2004.

Music of the Ethiopian Serenaders. Philadelphia: E. Ferrett & Co., 1845.

Naval Songs: Original, Selected and Traditional Sea Songs. New York: Wm. A. Pond & Co., 1883.

Nye, Pearl R. "Captain Pearl R. Nye: Life on the Ohio-Erie Canal." The Library of Congress—American Memory. http://memory.loc.gov/memory/collections/nye/title_sound_recording.

———. "Captain Pearl R. Nye Songs" (audio tapes). Columbus: Ohio State University Library.

———. *Songs and Correspondence.* Washington, D.C.: Library of Congress, 1937.

O'Donnell, Thomas F. "I'm Afloat on the Raging Erie." *New York Folklore Quarterly* 13, no. 3 (Autumn 1957): 177–80.

Ofield, Jack. *Adirondack Minstrel.* Bowling Green Films, Inc., 1976.

Ord, John. *Bothy Songs and Ballads of Aberdeen, Banff and Moray, Angus and the Mearns.* Edinburgh, 1930.

Palmer, Roy, ed. *The Oxford Book of Sea Songs.* Oxford, UK: Oxford University Press, 1989.

Peters, Harry. *Folk Music Out of Wisconsin.* Madison: State Historical Society of Wisconsin, 1977.

Potter, Robert K. *The Boston Temperance Songster: A Collection of Songs and Hymns for Temperance Societies, Original and Selected.* Boston: White and Potter, 1849.

Pritchard, Georgiana. "On the Erie Canal." *New York Folklore Quarterly* 10, no. 7 (1954): 45–46.

Randolph, Vance. *Ozark Folksongs.* 4 vols. Columbia: State Historical Society of Missouri, 1946–48.

Rapp, Marvin. *Canal Water and Whiskey: Tall Tales from the Erie Canal Country.* New York: Twayne Publishers Inc., 1965.

Rappoport, Angelo S. *Superstitions of Sailors.* Mineola, NY: Dover Publications, 2007.

Rideing, William H. "The Waterways of New York." *Harper's New Monthly Magazine* 48, no. 283 (December 1873): 1–17.

Roberts, Solomon W. *The Pennsylvania Magazine of History and Biography* 2, no. 4 (1878): 370–93.

Russell, Henry. *A Life on the Ocean Wave.* New York: James L. Hewitt & Co., 1838.

Sandburg, Carl. *The American Songbag.* New York: Harcourt, Brace & Company, 1927.

Sanjek, Russell. *American Popular Music and Its Business: The First Four Hundred Years.* New York: Oxford University Press, 1988.

Schiff, Stephen. "Scurvy Rascal Sees It Through." *New York Times*, May 3, 1986.

Schroeder, Rebecca. "An Informant in Search of a Collector." Paper originally read at the 1973 meeting of the American Folklore Society in Nashville, Tennessee.

Seeger, Pete. *American Favorite Ballads.* New York: Oak Publications, 1961.

Sharp, Cecil. *English Folk Songs from the Southern Appalachians.* London: Oxford University Press, 1960.

Shaw, Ronald E. *Erie Waters West: A History of the Erie Canal, 1792–1854.* Lexington: University of Kentucky Press, 1966.

Sheet Music Consortium. http://www.digital2.library.ucla.edu/sheetmusic.

Shoemaker, Henry W., comp. *Mountain Minstrelsy of Pennsylvania.* Philadelphia: N.F. McGirr, 1931.

Smith, Jimmy. *The Girl from Yewdall's Mill.* Philadelphia: T.M. Scroggy, Publisher, n.d.

Songs of the Horse Ocean Sailor. Brockport, NY: Bravoproductions, 2000.

Songs That Never Grow Old. New York: Syndicate Publishing Co., 1909.

Spaeth, Sigmund. *Read 'Em and Weep.* New York: Doubleday-Page & Company, 1926.

Springer, Ethel M., and Thomas F. Hahn. *Canal Boat Children on the Chesapeake and Ohio, Pennsylvania and New York Canals.* Shepherdstown, WV: American Canal and Transportation Center, 1981.

Stone, John. *Put's Golden Songster: Containing the Largest and Most Popular Collection of California Songs Ever Published.* D.E. Appleton & Co., 1858.

Thomas, Cloea, ed. *Scenes and Songs of the Ohio-Erie Canal.* Columbus: Ohio State Archaeological and Historical Society, 1952.

Thompson, Harold. *Body, Boots and Britches.* Philadelphia: J.B. Lippincott Company, 1940.

Thompson, Harold, ed. *A Pioneer Songster: Texts from the Stevens-Douglass Manuscript of Western New York, 1841–1856.* Ithaca, NY: Fall Creek Books, 1958.

The Thrush: Collection of Songs set to music. London: Thomas Tegg. 1827.

Totten, William DeForest. "The Rhyme of the Old Canal." *Newark (NY) Courier*, March 21, 1912, 1.

Towpath Guide to the C&O Canal. York, PA: American Canal and Transportation Center, 1971.

Twain, Twain. *Roughing It.* New York: Pocket Books, 2003.

Vaughn-Williams, Ralph, and A. Lloyd. *The Penguin Book of English Folk Songs.* Baltimore, MD: Penguin Books, 1959.

Walton, Ivan, and Joe Grimm. *Windjammers: Songs of the Great Lakes Sailors.* Detroit, MI: Wayne State University Press, 2002.

Ward, George. *Oh! That Low Bridge.* Rexford, NY: Mulesong Records, (634479341274).

Warner, Frank. Guide to the Frank and Anne Warner Papers, 1899–2000 and undated. Bulk 1933–1985, WC-36: Frank Warner, "Songs of the Erie Canal," undated.

Williamson, Karen, and Don Hesler. "Return to Glory: The Resurgence of Onondaga Lake." *New York State Conservationist,* June 3 2006.

Wittke, Carl. *We Who Built America: The Saga of the Immigrant.* Cleveland, OH: Western Reserve University, 1939.

Woods, Terry K., and Nye, Pearl. "Pearl Nye's Akron: Taken from Pearl Nye's writings in the Archival Department at the University of Akron." Summit County Historical Society, n.d.

Wyld, Lionel. *Low Bridge! Folklore and the Erie Canal.* Syracuse, NY: Syracuse University Press, 1972.

INDEX

ABOUT THE AUTHOR AND CONTRIBUTOR

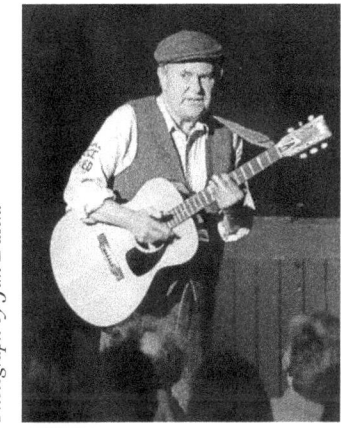

Photograph by Jim Dusen.

DR. WILLIAM HULLFISH is a life member of the American Canal Society and a member of the Canal Society of New York. He has published articles in *American Canals* and is the author of *The Canaller's Songbook* (American Canal and Transportation Center). Bill has toured under a grant from the National Endowment for the Arts with the Golden Eagle String Band and played at the World Canal Conference, Mystic Seaport, Waterloo Village, the Erie Canal Museum, the Great Lakes Symposium (SUNY Oswego), Canal Jam 2015, Allegheny Portage Railroad Historic Site and canal festivals all over New York, Ohio, Pennsylvania, Connecticut and New Jersey.

Bill has canalled in England, Wales and Ireland as well as the Erie Canal and Oswego Canal in New York State. He has canoed, walked and bicycled along the Ohio-Erie, the Chesapeake and Ohio, the Delaware and Hudson, the Chemung, the Delaware, the Delaware & Raritan, the Morris, Rappahannock, Tidewater, Lehigh, Union and the Pennsylvania Main Line Canals. After six years with the United States Air Force Band and Singing Sergeants in Washington, D.C., Bill taught at the University of Mary Washington and the State University of New York College at Brockport and still lives along the Erie Canal in Brockport, New York.

ADDITIONAL RESEARCH

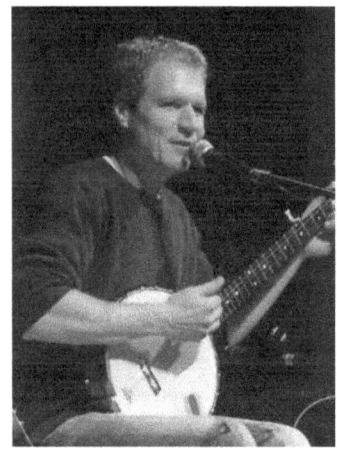

Dave Ruch collection.

DAVE RUCH began playing guitar in 1980. After playing semiprofessionally in Buffalo, New York, and Washington D.C., from 1982 to 1992, Dave became a full-time musician in November 1992, initially teaching music and performing regionally from his home base in Buffalo. In 2010, he founded the Canal Street String Band, which was named to the New York Presenters Network artist roster. Dave has an abiding interest in the traditional and historical music of his home state of New York, having logged thousands of research hours and dozens of recording sessions with older "heritage" musicians. He was appointed to the New York Council for the Humanities' "Speakers in the Humanities" program in 2006 and stayed on through the program's demise in 2015 and is currently a Public Scholar with that organization. He was project director for the Traditional Arts in Upstate New York (TAUNY) award-winning W is for the Woods: Traditional Adirondack Music and Music Making website in 2009, and music director and concert host, producer and musician for TAUNY's 2013 "Songs to Keep" project. Dave was featured in the nationally syndicated 2014 *Songs to Keep* documentary from Mountain Lake PBS, which went on to win a New England Emmy Award.

Visit us at
www.historypress.com